❧ FRONTIER WOMEN ❧

FRONTIER WOMEN

"CIVILIZING" THE WEST?
1840-1880

(REVISED EDITION)

JULIE ROY JEFFREY

HILL AND WANG
A division of Farrar, Straus & Giroux
New York

Hill and Wang
A division of Farrar, Straus and Giroux
19 Union Square West, New York 10003

Copyright © 1979, 1998 by Julie Roy Jeffrey
All rights reserved
Distributed in Canada by Douglas & McIntyre Ltd.
Printed in the United States of America
Designed by Peter Buchanan-Smith
First published in 1979 by Hill and Wang
Paperback edition, 1979
Revised edition, 1998

Library of Congress Cataloging-in-Publication Data
Jeffrey, Julie Roy.
Frontier women : "civilizing" the West? 1840–1880 / Julie Roy
Jeffrey. — Rev. ed.
p.   cm.
Includes bibliographical references and index.
ISBN 0-8090-1601-X (pbk. : alk. paper)
1. Women—West (U.S.)—History.   2. Frontier and pioneer life—
West (U.S.)   I. Title.
HQ1439.W45J43   1997
305.4'0978—dc21   97-36193

For
Chris, Michael, and Sophia

Contents

Acknowledgments

During the years of working on this book, I accumulated more than my fair share of scholarly debts, and it is now time to thank those who so generously helped me. Both David William Cohen and John Walton provided me, at different times, with a quiet place to work; without these hideaways, the book would have taken much longer than it did. Many of my early research questions were answered by Douglas Martin, who also assisted me in planning research trips. I appreciate the help over the early hurdles. Judy and Richard de Neufville, Tom and Dorothy Haskell, and Peg and Bob Peters were hospitable and patient during extended research visits. Without them, doing the research would have been far less enjoyable than it was. Maureen Ursenbach Beecher, historian of the Church of the Latter-day Saints, came forward to help an unknown scholar and assisted me with the chapter on Mormon women. I thank her for her good advice and support. My colleague Jean Baker and my friends Peter Frederick, Bob Peters, and Peter Stearns all read the manuscript and gave helpful and direct criticism. The book is far better than it would have been without their comments. Finally, Ron Walters helped me along at every stage of the project, and as he knows, I owe much to him.

My publisher, Arthur Wang, and my editor, Eric Foner, were patient, critical, and encouraging. It has been a pleasure to work with them. Over the last years, Goucher College both understood my preoccupation with pioneer women and generously supported my work.

My greatest thanks are reserved for my husband, Chris, who coped at home during my many research trips and days at the library, and for my children, Michael and Sophia, who were interested in the project and understanding of the pressures a book can cause. It is because of their understanding and support that I have dedicated my book to them.

FRONTIER WOMEN

Introduction

From the earliest years of this country's history, white Americans turned their backs on their homes and headed for the frontier. The frontier's location crept west toward the Mississippi as pioneers slowly cleared the wilderness and tamed it. By the 1840s, pioneers had pushed their way across the Mississippi to claim areas just west of the river; half the continent still lay before them. In the next four decades, the tempo of the westward movement quickened. Waves of emigration swept over the prairies and plains to the West Coast, then rolled back and began to trickle into the unsettled areas between the Mississippi and the Pacific. Between 1841 and 1867, the years of heaviest traffic on the overland trails, 350,000 traveled by wagon to California and Oregon. Many more went part of the way, to destinations like Utah and Colorado. With the completion of the transcontinental railroad in 1869, the journey west became easier and the frontier ever more alluring. By 1880, the half of the continent that forty years earlier had contained less than 1 percent of the nation's people boasted more than 20 percent of the population. Finally, during the 1880s, eager pioneers pushed out beyond the hundredth meridian into some of the most inhospitable and unpromising of the unclaimed lands that stretched from the Dakotas to Texas. Many of them would retreat, defeated by the hostile and arid plains frontier. By 1893, though uninhabited areas in the trans-Mississippi West remained, most agreed with historian Frederick Jackson Turner that the era of the frontier had finally come to an end.

The frontier fascinated Americans from the beginning with its promise of adventure and the opportunities it held out for land, health, gold, and religious freedom. Historians, sharing the nation's interest in the frontier, tried to explain its importance to American character, culture, and institutions. Frederick Jackson Turner provided the interpretation that shaped the debate over the frontier's significance for decades. Turner argued that "the existence of an area of free land, its continuous recession, and the advance of American settlement westward, explain[ed] American development." As white Americans moved away from early settlements along the eastern seaboard, the new environment gradually weakened inherited culture and forced settlers to create new institutions and new values appropriate for a new country. Democracy, nationalism, and individualism all owed their distinctive form to the frontier process Turner outlined and contributed to the development of a unique American culture.

While much of Turner's work emphasized the frontier as process, he also suggested that the frontier was a place, "the meeting point between savagery and civilization." Although the precise location of the frontier changed over time, the notion that civilization lay on one side of the frontier and barbarism on the other was a powerful one. It legitimated the westward movement by suggesting that white settlers were the bearers of civilization and progress. It tarnished indigenous peoples as savage with no lasting claim to the lands that they occupied. Indeed, in Turner's words, their lands were "free."

Despite the controversy that Turner's hypothesis generated, few historians took him to task for his focus. When Turner wrote of pioneers and speculated on the interaction between them and the wilderness, the pioneers he had in mind were the white men who he believed moved to the frontier in successive waves: first hunters, then fur traders, stock raisers, and finally farmers. While they often attacked or modified his thesis, historians, for the most part, retained Turner's interest in exploring the experience of these white men in the West. They also continued to view the frontier, whether as a process or a place, as the consequence of people moving from east to west.

In the first edition of this book, I challenged this preoccupation with male pioneers. Migration was a family affair, and I pointed out that one could not understand the frontier without considering the experience of the young, married white women who made up the bulk of adult female emigration or of their daughters. While I rejected most of Turner's concerns, I pursued questions raised by his argument that the move to the frontier undermined civilization. A new understanding of gender roles in the first half of the nineteenth century identified culture and morality as female concerns. What, then, did the move to the frontier mean for women, who considered themselves responsible for civilization and morality? Did living on the frontier shatter familiar norms or strengthen them? Did women gain new economic or political opportunities in the West, did they become new women as Turner had suggested their husbands, fathers, and brothers became new men? What part did women play in the process of mediating between culture and environment and in building new communities on the frontier?

Because the definition of a woman's place was such an important aspect of nineteenth-century culture, I organized the book around the ways in which new standards for middle-class female behavior affected white women's experiences in the West. I saw the West as a test of the power of nineteenth-century understanding of gender roles. Most of the primary sources I used were letters and diaries written by women, most recently from the Midwest and upper South and often from rural or small-town backgrounds. Despite the ways in which gender ideology and norms seemed ill suited to the realities of frontier life, I found that these women did not abandon familiar notions of woman's place. Even if it was impossible initially to live up to domestic and cultural ideals, these ideals helped women retain their sense of self and offered them hope of an ever-improving life. Over time, as the frontier period came to an end, the lives of the pioneer generation came more and more to resemble those of relatives and friends in the East. Some historians have suggested that children who grew up on the frontier freed themselves from many of the gender constraints of eastern society. Until more comparative studies are done and until historians recognize how the character of society and culture in both the East and West was changing as the nineteenth century drew to a close, I believe we must be cautious about accepting such assertions.

Since writing this book, my own research and that of many other historians have highlighted the elastic character of gender ideology during the nineteenth century. My conclusions about its survival in the West seem less surprising than they once did to me. In addition, debate over the validity of the concept of frontier has raised new concerns reflected in this edition. Historians have rightly pointed out the limitations of seeing the frontier, whether understood as a place or a process, as the creation of the movement of white Americans from east to west. While whites (and many Native Americans) emigrated west, Hispanics from Mexico for hundreds of years headed north. Indian tribes, over centuries, left tribal lands for new locations—some moving south, others east, still others north or west. The vision of a West with groups in perpetual motion has led some historians to abandon the term "frontier" altogether. I have chosen to keep the term but to redefine the frontier as a place of cultural contact and interaction between groups. This view underlines an important and recurring process in American history. Time and again, different peoples have encountered one another as settlers entered new territories, took up lands, exploited resources, and faced resistance from those with prior claims and different values and lifestyles.

With this understanding of the frontier, I have considered what the emigration of white women might have meant for the other women—Native American, Hispanic, Chinese, and African-American (in small numbers)—who were also participants in western life. Because middle-class white women and men relied on their own cultural standards to judge others, they found many groups deficient and unworthy of social inclusion when they did not adopt white values and standards of behavior. For Native American, Hispanic, and even working-class white women, the presence of middle-class white women meant displacement, being shoved to the margins of what became the dominant society. Violence and the appropriation of land and resources could be and often were justified as necessary for the protection and livelihood of white women and their children. Women of color or of working-class background often struggled to maintain themselves and their families in a hostile environment. Whether or not individual white women were aware of the far-ranging impact of their arrival, few of them sympathized with westerners who rejected their middle-class notions of the community and its future.

This harsh view of the frontier is a mark of the "new western history." As Patricia Limerick states simply, "The history of the west is a study of a place undergoing conquest and never fully escaping its consequences." While here I have suggested only some of the possible experiences of these other western women, partly because primary sources are so scarce, I have been persuaded of the necessity of seeing the frontier period from a more complex perspective than the one I adopted in the first edition. Certainly, understanding that emigrant white women struggled for control of resources and culture not only with white men but with women and men of other backgrounds casts a different light on the outcome of their civilizing mission. Although white men and women appeared to triumph, their victory was not as sweeping as it seemed to them and many later observers. Native American, Hispanic, and Chinese peoples and their cultures, for the most part, did not disappear. While they adopted and adapted aspects of white culture, and suffered from poverty and discrimination, most did not abandon their own identity. The persistence of other values and ways of life signifies the limits of white women's cultural mission.

The evidence for this study comes primarily from literate white women who left journals, reminiscences, and collections of letters. Some transcripts of interviews with pioneer women also provide a picture of their lives. While many more primary sources are available in published form now than when I first wrote the book, many still must be consulted in the collections of major western libraries and in state historical societies. These repositories are listed in the bibliography. Yet even these new sources represent materials from only a few of the women going west. Most emigrant women were too busy to write much, while others probably agreed with Rachel Haskell, who thought the events of her life "so slight it is hard to keep the sum." It is, of course, the slight events that interest the historian who wishes to examine the experiences and feelings of ordinary women living ordinary lives in the West. Although the number of sources is limited, they are varied in content and style. Together, they give a good picture of the diverse frontier experiences of white women. In addition to women's records, I have consulted men's accounts, legal records, scattered educational and church records, and some material on women's organizations. Most quotations in the book retain the spelling and punctuation of the originals; in some cases, editors have made corrections in sources before publication, and I have had no choice but to reproduce these quotations as I found them in their published versions. A wide range of secondary sources, especially recent studies of Native American, Hispanic, Chinese, and working-class white women, and the meager material on black women, also proved valuable in the revision of this book. In my discussions of Native American women, I have used tribal names and the terms "Native American" and "Indian" interchangeably.

While I have a more complex picture of the West during the decades of white emigration and settlement and recognize the more violent side of frontier history than I did when I first wrote this book, I do not believe we need to reject or demonize white frontier women. They showed admirable spirit and energy in often trying circumstances and worked hard to establish family life and prosperity in the West. That they were unable to see beyond the boundaries of their culture should remind us of the difficulty of that task—in the past and in our own day.

⁕ 1 ⁕

"Glimpses of Western Life"

In March 1835, the popular *Western Monthly Magazine* published a poem titled "The Emigrant Bride." Although it was hardly a literary masterpiece, the awkward verses' depiction of westward emigration must have captured the attention of many of the magazine's female readers. The opening lines encourage readers to visualize a bride, joyously poised to accompany her new husband to the "far-off west." Eager enthusiasm and willingness to head for the frontier, however, give way to grief as the bride realizes that she is abandoning her mother's grave, perhaps forever. Going west, even with an affectionate husband, means leaving female friends, relatives, and the familiar domestic sphere. Such thoughts rush over the young woman "in a heavy, whelming tide." When her dear friend and bridesmaid takes on a daughter's duty and promises to care for the sacred grave site, the bride's anguish passes. In the final verse, the bride follows her husband with a clear conscience.

Although the poem neatly resolves the conflicts between duty to mother and duty to husband, love for the old home with its well-known rhythms and norms and desire for the new (mother is, after all, dead and not weeping inconsolably on the threshold of the family homestead), it captures the contrary feelings of anguish and joy that many white women felt as they participated in the national adventure of moving west. The emotional moment of departure that the poem so vividly expresses was only one of the many experiences emigration would bring to women who settled the trans-Mississippi frontier. Primitive living conditions, unaccustomed duties in an unfamiliar environment, encounters with peoples very different from themselves—all would influence women's response to frontier life. But "The Emigrant Bride" suggests that cultural values and norms, particularly those concerning gender and domestic life, would also color women's expectations of and adjustments to the West. They would make her life very different from that of her mother and grandmother.

By the 1840s, many middle-class women had internalized cultural ideals and norms of female behavior that were ill suited to the realities of frontier life. As scholars have often pointed out in their analyses of the male pioneering experience, the frontier brought culture into conflict with environment. White women faced a similar struggle as they balanced the demands of everyday life on the frontier with the proscriptions about woman's place that were so aggressively trumpeted in mid-nineteenth-century America.

Any analysis of women's pioneering experiences in the trans-Mississippi West, then, must begin with the ideas of womanhood formulated in the early decades of the century. Economic changes triggered a reconsideration of woman's place. The development of a market economy and the beginning of industrialization in the Northeast initiated a separation of the sexes by transforming the place and nature of work. Put more simply, economic changes ended a home system of production involving the whole family and began one involving men and a few single

women working away from home. The new workplace of factories, shops, and businesses increasingly emphasized disciplined
work styles and valued production, rationality, time, and money.
At home, however, women continued to labor in an unstructured
and sociable manner. Home became more and more distinct
from the male workplace.

As approaches to work changed, and as the places where
men and women labored diverged, the value and significance
of women's traditional work decreased. Though often toiling
long and hard, middle-class white women no longer performed
tasks that were economically central to their families; they
rarely produced vital goods or earned much money. As women's
activities became less important to their family's economic circumstances, female prestige suffered. The initial impact of a
market economy and industrialization, then, was to marginalize
the position of women.

Although these changes had the greatest impact on the urban
middle classes in the industrializing Northeast in the early decades of the century, they more and more affected the majority
of American women who still lived in rural areas. There, the
increasing availability of manufactured goods after 1810 reduced the importance of female home manufacturing. When
farmers began to produce cash crops for regional markets, the
proportional value of their wives' labor declined. Finally, although men and women both worked on family farms, the responsibility of men for outdoor labor and of women for home,
children, and garden suggested that the basic idea that men
and women occupied separate spheres could apply to farm families as well as urban ones. By the 1820s, language recognized
the distinction between the domestic and private world of
women and the public world of men.

To compensate for women's shrinking economic importance,
Sarah Hale, editor of *Godey's Lady's Book*; Catharine Beecher,
the popular writer and lecturer; and numerous others argued
that women had significant cultural and social responsibili-

ties. Accepting the gender polarization triggered by economic changes, those who were redefining understandings of gender asserted that the competitive public world of men was dangerous and destructive. Home, woman's sphere, was described as a place of "retirement" and "retreat," as a private spot where women provided men with the peace and quiet missing in the public world.

But women did more than provide domestic tranquillity for harassed men. Advocates for new gender norms claimed women were responsible for communicating moral and cultural values, too often forgotten in the workplace, to their families. Husbands, exposed as they were to the hazards of the public world, were, of course, a major focus of feminine concern. "Who, like a guardian angel, watches over his interests, warns him against dangers, comforts him under trial; and by . . . pious, assiduous, and attractive deportment, constantly endeavors to render him more virtuous, more useful, more honourable, and more happy?" asked one popular preacher. Who else but a woman? And who else but women were to shape and mold the young, who would, in turn, determine the ultimate nature of society? A mother's failure to train her children to value restraint and honor moral virtues was the Republic's loss. The proponents of domesticity insisted that women had the responsibility to maintain values and ensure social stability in a time of rapid change; women were ultimately the guardians of the national welfare.

Characteristics unique to women helped them carry out their social mission. Unlike acquisitive and materialistic men, women were said to be "disinterested." Sheltered from the business world, possessing few material goods (the earnings and property of married women belonged to their husbands), women lacked the resources and reasons for pursuing selfish goals. They naturally devoted themselves to others. As feeling rather than thinking creatures, lacking egotism and pride, women were uniquely able to perceive and act upon moral truth. Their physical charms and affectionate nature provided them with useful advantages in their encounters with husbands and children.

Economic changes suggested that women were socially marginal, but advocates for a new understanding of women's role insisted that women were responsible for the nation's moral health. How could the claim of women's moral superiority be reconciled with their subordination in American society? Acknowledging the legal and social reality of male power, those who were reworking American gender relations argued that female submission symbolized female superiority and moral leadership. Women, like Christ, humbled themselves so they could be exalted. In any case, moral superiority depended on innocence, not knowledge; women had to be shielded from the corruptions of the world. Husbands were entitled, if not obliged, to guard women's purity so they could fulfill their moral obligations to society.

Although the cult of domesticity evolved in the East and applied specifically to urban middle-class women there, its influence ranged beyond the confines of New England and the urban middle class. In all regions, members of the middle and upper classes worried about the transformations stemming from industrialization and the growth of a market economy. They also feared the dislocations caused by the westward movement, geographic mobility, and eventually emigration. The support they gave to the idea that woman had her own sphere suited to her female nature derived from their hope that this domestic sphere would provide the necessary social and cultural stability in a changing world.

Between 1830 and 1860, the new ideology became embedded in American culture. Although the depictions of woman's sphere and her nature might bear only the slightest resemblance to the reality of individual women's lives, they proved elastic enough to flourish in different regional settings and appealing enough for many women to take them to heart despite the awkward fit.

In the rural South, for example, journals, sermons, novels, and speeches all promoted new ideas of woman's sphere. That wellborn southern women, at least, attempted to live up to the new cultural norms is evident in their diaries and other writings. "To repress a harsh answer, to confess a fault, and to stop (right or wrong) in the midst of self-defence, in gentle submission, sometimes requires a struggle—like life and death; but these *three* efforts are the golden threads with which domestic happiness is woven; once begin the fabric with this woof, and trials shall not break or sorrow tarnish it," testified one woman.

In the South, it was not the new industrial order that undergirded domestic ideals but slavery. The clear demarcation of woman's sphere as separate and subsidiary was a necessary part of a social structure that gave white males total authority over all others, especially slaves. Not surprisingly, some of the most avid proponents of slavery were also staunch publicists for the cult of domesticity. George Fitzhugh, defender of the peculiar institution, explained: "Woman naturally shrinks from public gaze, and from the struggle and competition of life." Thus, each woman should have "a husband, a lord and master, whom she should love, honor and obey." "In truth," Fitzhugh concluded, "woman, like children, has but one right and that is the right to protection. The right to protection involves the obligation to obey."

Although southern women were thought to be "most deeply interested in the success of every scheme which curbs the passion and enforces a true morality," and although their task included restraining "man's natural vice and immorality," the emphasis on obedience suggests that the presence of slavery and the need for conformity severely restricted women's social role. The southern version of domesticity ran the risk of becoming nothing more than a glorification of female charm and gentility, leaving woman as merely "the most fascinating being in creation . . . the delight and charm of every circle she moves in." Many southern novels of the pre–Civil War period portrayed women as marginal ornaments, suggesting that elite southerners, at least, interpreted domesticity in this way.

A similar version of womanhood existed in the North. Even

though domestic propagandists stressed the significance of the female sphere and described women's duties as essential to society's moral well-being, the catalogue of supposedly innate female characteristics pointed to a model of female behavior. Genteel conduct could easily become a goal in itself for those women who, in truth, found little productive work to do in their homes or opportunity for transforming either their families or society. An examination of the popular *Godey's Lady's Book* shows that, despite editor Sarah Hale's dedication to the goal of carrying "onward and upward the spirit of moral and intellectual excellence in our own sex, till their influence shall bless as well as beautify civilized society," there was a growing emphasis on fashion, manners, and romanticism. Gentility, which many of the women's magazines espoused, could become a mask for fashionable idleness and superficiality.

The development of inexpensive printing techniques during the early nineteenth century had made magazines an important medium of cultural communication. By the 1830s and 1840s, women's magazines had become prime vehicles through which the ideology of domesticity spread. Cheap and accessible magazines carried new female norms even to readers in rural and frontier areas. Journals and newspapers for the general public, speeches, and printed sermons echoed the ideas contained in women's magazines. Those who missed these messages found woman's sphere clearly described in their schoolbooks.

After the Bible, more Americans read textbooks than any other kind of printed material. As they studied their school texts, students encountered the self-sacrificing woman whose demeanor embodied acceptable female behavior. Her "voice is gentle; her pronunciation is delicate; her passions are never suffered to be boisterous . . . she never foams with anger; she is seldom seen in any *masculine* amusement." Girls discovered that a woman's destiny was to care for her husband "with tenderness . . . [and] to recompense his care with soft endearments." For those who could read (and by 1860 the white literacy rate was 90 percent), the pictures of women were consistent, clear, and available in many forms.

Geographic mobility, aided by improved transportation in the first decades of the century, also facilitated the spread of ideas. Pioneer families, often moving three or four times, were, in fact, carriers of domestic ideology. Existing diaries, letters, and reminiscences of women who emigrated to the Far West reflect the influence of domestic ideals. These women were generally married, from differing economic strata, and most recently from small-town and rural areas in the Midwest.

Of course, domesticity described norms, not the actual conduct of American women. There was considerably more variety in the behavior of women than ideology would suggest. Still, norms were important because they established the behavioral context for those who tried to reject them as much as for those who attempted to realize them. They existed as goals for women who saw gentility as a mark of respectability and middle-class status. They shaped personality, colored expectations, and provided a source for identity and self-esteem. For many women, domestic ideals furnished a psychologically compelling meaning for their lives.

Some of the psychological gratification stemmed from the insistence on woman's moral superiority. But other satisfactions existed as well. As women were increasingly seen to have duties and qualities different from men's, and as woman's sphere was portrayed as equal if not, perhaps, superior to man's, female friendships took on a special meaning. The characterization of men as being driven by base carnal passions suggested that they were unsuitable companions for women. Women were the best companions for one another. The reality of many women's lives undergirded female friendship. The separation of the male and female worlds and the shift in women's status often gave women more in common with one another than with men. Shared experiences and perspectives may have made female friendships more central for many women than their relationships with their husbands, even though domesticity suggested that women were to devote their lives to their husbands and children. Evidence suggests that many women found security and well-being through their relationships with other women.

As female companionship took on added importance in women's lives, so, too, did female association on a wider scale. The conception of women as different from men that facilitated female friendship also brought them together in voluntary female associations, which mushroomed between 1800 and 1830. Within the female benevolent society, women found a congenial peer group and tasks especially suited to their moral nature. Protestant clergymen supported female associations, with their religious and charitable goals, and fostered women's special ties with Protestantism. Although voluntary associations were, in one sense, a natural outgrowth of domesticity and American religious life, they nevertheless emphasized that women had some public and religious responsibilities outside the family circle. Moreover, no matter what an organization's purpose was, the mutual association of women helped to establish a sense of collectivity and the belief that women as a group had distinct interests that men might not share. When women in the 1830s added specific moral concerns, such as the abolition of slavery and prostitution, to their missionary and benevolent work, their activism increased the possibility of conflict with the male world and promoted a sharpened sense of gender identification.

Regardless of how individual women interpreted new ideals in the context of their own lives, the ideology provided them with a comprehensible place in a changing world. But emigration to the West could pose a threat to the ways in which both men and women perceived themselves. As families moved into the wilderness, they entered a world bearing little resemblance to the one they had left. Far from the city marketplaces and factories, far from the country peddler with his pack of manufactured goods, frontier families resumed the subsistence ways of an earlier time. Pioneer women gained economic importance at the expense of new norms for female behavior and clear boundaries between male and female spheres. The hard work frontier women routinely performed highlighted the absurdity of the view of women as weak and suggested a more robust vision of women. But without that "delicacy in woman" that was "the most powerful enemy to the barbarism of man," what would happen to progress?

On the one hand, the rhythms of frontier life suggested that the cult of domesticity was irrelevant to women's real concerns. A more flexible definition of woman's place, however, threatened to rob women of their claim to moral superiority. On the other hand, the cult of domesticity, with its insistence on female service, could be stretched to expand women's moral and cultural responsibilities, as some women who labored in the anti-slavery movement discovered. If women served families and society by maintaining social values, molding behavior, and preserving culture (tasks men had abandoned by entering the marketplace), the necessity of creating a new society in the West could be seen logically as theirs, not men's. Rather than being guardians of culture and morality, women might become creators.

Some women anticipated that the West would provide just such an opportunity for maximizing their social and cultural responsibilities. As emigration was recognized as one of the nation's greatest challenges, the schoolroom presided over by a female teacher was offered as the means of civilizing the West. Catharine Beecher, one of the most prominent women of the antebellum period, propagandized tirelessly both for increasing support for western education and for restructuring the teaching profession to favor women. Backed by the American Lyceum, a New York lecture organization, Beecher began in 1835 to send groups of women teachers to the West. In the following years, she made a convincing case, warning that western children were growing up without the benefit of either a practical or a moral education. As many as ninety thousand teachers were needed, she suggested, to push back the tides of barbarism. From a practical point of view, few would be men. "It is chimerical to hope," Beecher pointed out, that men would respond to the call "when there are multitudes of other employments that will . . . lead to wealth." Teaching did not pay enough for men, but it did for "disinterested" women. Thus, Beecher concluded, "it is woman who is fitted by disposition and habits and circumstances for such duties, who to a very wide extent must aid in educating the childhood and youth of this nation."

Beecher's proposal represented a logical, economical extension of the cult of domesticity. The teacher was a kind of mother; teaching represented "the road to honourable independence and extensive usefulness," because a woman would never find it necessary to "outstep the prescribed boundaries of feminine modesty." Dealing as she would with the world of children, not the world of men, retaining all her natural graces and virtues, the female teacher would threaten neither the position of women in general nor society at large.

Yet Beecher's proposal had radical overtones. She urged women to capture the profession and, once ensconced in the schoolroom, to reach out to influence their frontier communities. Teachers would, in fact, play the crucial role in community building. "Soon, in all parts of our country," prophesied Beecher, "in each neglected village, or new settlement, the Christian female teacher will quietly take her station, collecting the ignorant children around her, teaching them the habits of neatness, order and thrift; opening the book of knowledge, inspiring the principles of morality . . . Soon her influence in the village will create a demand for new laborers, and then she will summon from among her friends at home, the nurse . . . the seamstress, and the mantuamaker; and these will prove her auxiliaries in good moral influence, and in sabbath school training. And often as a result of these labors, the Church will arise, and the minister of Christ be summoned to fill up the complement of domestic, moral and religious blessing." Other women were even more explicit about the central cultural role women could play in fledgling western communities. "No clergyman, however well qualified, could have wrought such favorable changes in so short a time," one writer maintained, as a "young lady from New England," who taught school and had an "unbounded, and almost transforming" influence in her community. Female voluntary associations, if carried to the frontier, had similarly radical possibilities of capturing cultural and moral leadership. Emigration thus signified cultural and social opportunities for women.

Beecher's was not the only voice suggesting how frontier life might affect woman's sphere. By the 1820s and 1830s, abundant written materials joined a rich oral tradition about the West. Though the focus was on the northwestern frontier of Ohio, Indiana, and Michigan, still in the process of settlement, rather than on the unoccupied trans-Mississippi West, the meaning was less about place than about the significance of the frontier for American culture and society. To the optimists, the West symbolized American growth and progress, to the pessimists the collapse of social stability and civilized values. Implicitly, the literature raised questions about woman's place and mission on the frontier. Some accounts suggested that the pioneer experience destroyed woman's sphere, others that it posed no threat to it or even inflated it. Conflicting as these views are, the literature helps us recover the mental world and expectations of women who emigrated to the West.

Emigrants' guidebooks provided important information for those planning to take overland routes west between 1845 and 1865. Guides instructed emigrants how to take the long trip safely and efficiently. Prosaic in nature and form, they advised emigrants about equipment and average costs and evaluated the different trails. Often they also included recent information drawn from letters and private journals. Although primary sources usually do not reveal whether women read the guides as avidly as their husbands, Lodisa Frizzell recalled that she had perused several of "the various guides of the rout to California." Although Frizzell may well have been unusual in the number of volumes she read, that a popular magazine like *Godey's Lady's Book* brought guidebooks to the attention of its readers suggests female interest. As one reviewer pointed out, "This is one of the most useful [guide]books we have seen for a long time. The amount of practical information it embodies is immense, and possesses what we Americans call a *cash value* . . . This volume is really worth its weight in gold." Another guide, the reviewer noted, was of particular interest "to the ladies." Even women who did not read the guides for themselves must have understood some of their general points as they talked to their husbands about the trip and aided in preparations.

As they conveyed a wealth of practical information to the men in charge of the undertaking, however, the guides all but ignored women. This neglect suggests that, during the trip at least, women were at best irrelevant and at worst in the way. Certainly, the descriptions of the journey indicated that women, who were so closely linked with civilization and its values, were out of place, for emigrants would enter "a state of nature, amid the confused, revolving fragments of elementary society," where they would be "surrounded only by . . . herds of wild beasts of prey, and danger and death." In this primitive and hazardous world also roamed Indians, characteristically portrayed as crafty and vicious. "They use every conceivable artifice at times, to elude the vigilance of the sentinels," warned a popular guidebook. On the journey west, then, civilized restraints were unknown. Obviously, an aggressive man with "a good gun; at least, five pounds of powder, and twenty pounds of lead . . . prepared for any warlike emergency . . . [and] with the requisite energy and courage" was the model emigrant. The guides' advice on traveling light ("Do not encumber yourself with anything not absolutely essential to your comfort") reinforced the notion that women and their domestic world were burdens. Too many belongings threatened the success of the trip by slowing down the pace. The significance of home and things from home that nineteenth-century culture believed helped to shape and civilize the family was rejected under the pressure of "long and arduous expeditions."

Yet if guidebooks generally saw women as burdens, there was an occasional hint that the "gentle" sex would take on a vital role. Although these books rarely discussed women specifically, they were expansive about provisions, appetites, and health. Each guidebook specified what food emigrants should buy for the six-month journey, analyzed the size of appetites, and discussed the planning and cooking of meals. As for health, the guides warned that many would come "down with sickness, mostly bilious complaints," during the trip. Recovery was essential, since "in many places the wagons will have to be forced up the ascent or ravines by manual force." Here were tasks for women, but hardly for those who were soft and genteel. The trip entailed strenuous work for women—cooking, caring for the sick, perhaps even carrying baggage up and down mountains. Women had to be ingenious (a "good pickle" could be made of a "prairie pea"; the limited number of cooking utensils presented culinary challenges), healthy, and strong. They could expect to eat twice as much as they did at home and anticipate "being subjected to continued and regular exercise, in the open air, which gives additional vigor and strength." The trip west was no place for a fragile lady.

The wild world into which emigrant wagon trains ventured would physically transform women into robust, hardy creatures and give them tough, crucial duties. Yet in the course of the trip, several guides suggested, conventional female attributes might come in handy. As *The Prairie Traveler* pointed out, "On long and arduous expeditions *men* are apt to be *irritable* and *ill-natured*, and oftentimes fancy they have more labor imposed upon them than upon their comrades." Contentious behavior threatened the success of the entire venture, and those possessing "the greatest forbearance under such circumstances" deserved "all praise." "Cultivate a spirit of civility and accommodation," *The Emigrants' Guide to California* advised. "Let there be no contention or intrigues in your camp. If dissensions break out . . . separate peaceably." Although men could be peacemakers, nineteenth-century society saw it as woman's task to restrain men, to "lead and guide" them. Women perusing guidebooks would realize they needed male qualities—strength, resilience, and resourcefulness—to survive the trip and female qualities to soothe and socialize men and to ensure social stability on the way west.

Women might sense that they were to be all things to all people. Though such expectations might well be disconcerting, the guides always promised that any adjustments women made would be short-lived, for the books all presented a rosy picture of a West fast civilized. It took only a little foresight and imagination to see the frontier to which the emigrants traveled transformed. Wilderness would soon exhibit "all the enjoyments and luxuries of civilized life . . . numerous churches, magnificent edifices, spacious colleges and stupendous monuments." The West would boast of all the East had, and more. The "ignorance, superstition and despotism" that characterized the parts of the West controlled by Mexico would inevitably disappear forever "before the march of civilization." "Be firm," counseled one guide, to emigrants headed for California, "and soon the destiny of California will be governed by yourselves."

Guidebooks represented only one source of information about the West. Although they certainly must have created expectations about the pioneering experience, few women read more than one or two. But many must have been acquainted with popular adventure stories that highlighted the character of the frontier and suggested how women might fit into western life.

Several regional versions of the life of Daniel Boone, the frontier fighter and hunter, were in circulation by 1830. Although the tales of Boone's wilderness adventures, like the

guidebooks, placed women in the background, they used depictions of Boone's wife to convey the significance of the
western experience for the female sphere and its values.

Eastern versions of the Boone story reflected regional chau-
vinism. Early stories suggested that emigration lured the young
to leave home and threatened values (including female values)
considered fundamental to civilized society. C. Wilder's 1823
edition of the tale, for example, represented Boone (and the
move west that he symbolized) as the negative force of the wilderness that inevitably led to societal breakdown. Boone, Wilder pointed out disapprovingly, was "greatly prejudiced . . . in
favor of the tawny inhabitants of the Western wilderness, whose
manners and habits he did not hesitate to declare to the day of
his death were far more agreeable to him than those of a more
civilized and refined race." In later versions of the story, eastern
values triumphed as Boone became a symbol of civilization and
a protector of "peaceable habitation[s]"—thus offering the possibility that emigrants could realize traditional values in a new
environment. In his 1847 *Life of Daniel Boone*, John Peck transformed the frontiersman into a model husband for his paragon
of a wife. The "affectionate" Rebecca "was an excellent household manager," Peck wrote admiringly, and a great support to
her husband. Faced with one of her husband's departures, she
"kindly and quietly consented to this separation, and called into
requisition her skill as a housewife in assisting to provide the
necessary outfit."

Southern writers made the West a backdrop for stilted romantic plots. Boone became the aristocrat, his wife the genteel
and powerless southern lady. As William Gilmore Simms, a
novelist of the 1830s, 1840s and 1850s, pointed out, Boone,
"in an age of chivalry—during the Crusades . . . could have
been a knight-errant, equally fearless and gentle. That he would
have been a Squire of Dames is very uncertain—but he loved
his wife, and risked his scalp more than once to rescue beauty
from the clutches of the savage." From this perspective, the

West represented an extension of the prevailing southern system with women occupying an ornamental and restricted place. ⟶ From the West came versions of the hunter story both more realistic and more reflective of oral culture. Neither a natural aristocrat nor a docile family man, Boone became the man of action, the wilderness hero. Judge James Hall of Illinois, whose popular *Letters from the West* was published in 1828, described Boone as "the very prince of hunters." Explaining that the hero's migration was driven not by antisocial feelings (as early eastern writers would have it) but by love of the wilderness, Hall made it clear that Boone recognized society's value. It was Boone's understanding of civilization that led him to bring his wife, Rebecca, and their family into the wilderness. In this rendition of the story, Rebecca both shared her husband's love of the wilderness and helped to domesticate it. Self-sufficient and hardy, she exhibited characteristics that went beyond the usual domestic virtues. Above all, she was tough, resourceful, and intrepid. When her husband was held in captivity, she courageously "returned with her family to her father's house in North Carolina, braving the toils and perils of a journey through a wilderness of immeasurable extent and gloom."

The depiction of the frontier woman as spirited and resolute was repeated in other literature about the West. In 1835 the *Western Literary Journal and Monthly Review* published an article titled "The Pioneer Mothers." The women going forth "as volunteers to act as hand-maids in rearing a nation in the wilds of the West" were at once heroic and noble. Although "they were not so refined, so deeply schooled in that which is delicate and beautiful," these women, the author insisted, "had those [qualities] which were the developments of their nature's purity, uninfluenced by the fashion and artifice of society. We admit they were masculine, if you term that masculine, which prompted them to defend, aye die, for their husbands, their children."

That a woman could be both masculine and feminine was

confusing to any nineteenth-century female reader who had absorbed cultural messages about the differences between men and women. At the very least, it appeared that the frontier could blur distinctions. If some women were troubled by this possibility, they must have found the tales of Boone's alter ego, Davy Crockett, even more disturbing. *A Narrative of the Life of David Crockett*, appearing in 1834, claimed to give Crockett's own account of his rise from poor frontier farmer to successful politician, land speculator, and hunter of wild beasts. Avidly interested in proving his prowess to the world, Crockett viewed women as merely another prize in the race for reputation and notoriety. Not surprisingly, he had three wives, who, far from being shapers of values, were insignificant in the story of his life and certainly far less important than the other symbols of his vaunted achievements—pelts, votes, and admiration. The vulgarity of the swaggerer annihilated woman's sphere, while his sexuality threatened woman's purity and innocence.

Captivity stories also made it clear that the frontier was associated with violence that threatened a woman's virtue, her place, even her life. Unlike other literature about the West, captivity narratives, popular from the seventeenth century on, often focused on women. In these accounts, fiendish Indians imposed cruel torments on their female captives. Some women, however, proved the match of their captors in courage or fierceness. Hannah Dustan reportedly killed at least ten Indians with a hatchet and then scalped them. A picture in an 1846 anthology of a decidedly ungenteel Mrs. Merril shows her gloating over dead Indians at her feet and ready to dispose of another "savage" coming through the door to her house.

Readers were given their fill of sensationalism, but much of the dramatic impact of the tales stemmed from the uncertain fate of the women captives. Would they lose their lives because they were white women and too frail to resist their tormentors? Jane McCrea, whose tale appeared in many versions, often accompanied by illustrations, suffered mutilation and death at the hands of her native captors. Would these women survive their experiences by losing their femininity altogether, like Mrs. Dustan and Mrs. Merril? Would they lose their purity through rape or rape disguised as marriage to an Indian? While Elizabeth Hanson, a former captive, noted that "the Indians are seldom guilty of any indecent carriage towards their captive women, unless much in liquor," who could count on Indians' sobriety?

No matter what readers took away from published or oral versions of captivity narratives, they must have been influenced by the depiction of the Native American as the threatening and savage "other." Accounts of the "fearful deeds of the savages" who had carried her grandmother and aunt into captivity colored Virginia Reed Murphy's attitudes when she started on her journey. Doubtless many other emigrant women also set out from their homes with negative images of the Indians drawn from captivity tales. Few would learn from the captivity tradition anything about the actual motivations behind raids and the taking of hostages or understand that Indian actions were part of an effort to prevent white settlement and resist white culture.

Finally, the plot of some captivity tales raised the possibility that women might abandon white culture altogether and remain with their adoptive tribes and families. Mary Jemison stayed with her Iroquois captors, married, and raised mixed-blood children. The experiences and choices of captives like Mary Jemison suggested that Indian culture might not be inferior, as most white women firmly believed. These narratives made the point that the frontier was not empty of culture or people; white women would not be bringing their culture into a vacuum. The West was a place where other peoples, not just the "wilderness," might contest the values and way of life that white women hoped to establish.

With such a plethora of views of the frontier, it is intriguing to speculate about what women made of them. Although the women who read stories, broadsides, poems, pamphlets, and novels about the West, who saw pictures or heard songs or tall tales, left little record of their thoughts, one clue to female preferences is available. Numerous articles, stories, novels, and poems written specifically by and for women treated the western experience. Unlike stories about Daniel Boone or Davy Crockett, these devoted full attention to the meaning of the frontier for women.

Women's literature often acknowledged the emotional impact of emigration. On the frontier, women could expect to "struggle with that feeling of isolation and loneliness which presses heavily on those who have severed all the endearing ties of home, where cluster those fond attachments only formed in youth." Each woman faced "many a sad hour" without her fond circle of friends, though a husband might become a "sympathizing friend." But women were hardly passive victims of fate. The song "To the Prairie I'll Fly Not," published in *Godey's Lady's Book*, pointed out that single women, at least, had options. They could refuse to go. "What, fly to the prairie? I could not live there, / With the Indian and panther, and bison, and bear." The second stanza emphatically stated, "I'll not give my hand, / To one, whose abode's in so savage a land," while the third disposed of the emigrant suitor with a curt farewell: "Then tarry no longer."

Women's literature, whether fictional or "true," pictured the West as offering women the opportunity for influence and power. A favorite character, the pioneer mother and wife, was a heroic and domestic figure. Danger, privations, and trials, duly acknowledged, became a means of realizing the female sphere. Mrs. Harper, an Ohio pioneer, for example, "was never known to yield to despondency, but with untiring energy exerted herself to encourage all within the sphere of her influence, teaching them to bear up against misfortune, and make the best of their home where their lot was cast. Her own family knew not, until the hardships of pioneer life had been overcome, how much she had endured." Truly, she was a "benevolent heroine." Nor did hardships force women to abandon the female sphere, for they were shown to have "a delicate sense of propriety" in both deportment and conversation. Though untutored, pioneer women learned delightful manners and gentle ways from the Bible, wild birds, and even Indian powwows. With the necessary addition of courage and heroism, each pioneer woman could be a perfect lady, "never [to] be looked upon as . . . [an] ordinary country-woman."

These supposedly realistic characterizations described pioneer women of the generation just passing away. Accounts of contemporary pioneering acknowledged the challenges to domestic ideology. Caroline Kirkland's series of books on the West, which appeared in the 1830s, 1840s, and 1850s, featured vignettes of "common-place people" and described incidents "in which the fastidiousness, the taste, the pride, the self-esteem of the refined child of civilization" might be "wounded by a familiar intercourse with the persons among whom he will find himself thrown." Yet despite customs that might appear at worst offensive and at best picturesque, Kirkland assured her readers that "familiar intercourse" with rough-mannered frontier men and women had its compensating features. Women could expect, in time, to shape the lives and habits of their new companions. The "silent influence of example," she wrote, "is daily effecting much towards reformation in many particulars." Moreover, those who missed the comforts and niceties of civilized life could be "the first to attempt the refining process, the introduction of those important nothings on which so much depends." Finally, there was merit in being free "from the restraints of pride and ceremony." Too often women ensnared in genteel conventions lost sight of their true sphere and obligations. The West was a challenge for which true women were well equipped.

Moreover, the freedom of western life meant that men would help women with their tasks. This did not, however, imply a permanent confusion of spheres. Generous male assistance would help realize the ideal of a harmonious home, for "if he is too proud or indolent to submit to such infringements upon his dignity and ease," Kirkland warned, "most essential deductions from the daily comfort of his family will be the mortifying and vexatious result of his obstinate adherences to early habits." If the conventional division of labor might collapse in the first stages of pioneer life, women need not fear they would become masculine, for men and women had different natures and, thus, different obligations. As one writer pointed out, "To bring them into the same field of employment would be as absurd as to make the value of porcelain consist in its power to do the work of iron." Were women, for example, to do outside work, as they did in European countries, they would lose their looks and their value in the eyes of society. "Their skin becomes shriveled, their complexions like coal, their features coarse and homely, and they fall into a premature decrepitude, more hideous than that of old age." Even worse, men finding little comfort and no refinement became barbarous overlords. Only by holding to "appropriate tasks" could women retain their beauty and exercise "just influence and power."

Those women who crossed the boundaries of their sphere could expect disaster. And the West, female writers insisted, did not demand this of women. Stories in *Godey's Lady's Book*, such as "Beauty Out West: or How Three Fashionable Ladies Spent a Year in the Wilderness" and "May: The Squatter's Daughter," pictured genteel life not only flourishing on the frontier but even improving far from "the city with its vanities and false glare." The frontier offered a healthy and useful domesticity purged of the threat of vacuity. It provided "the truest and noblest life," with well-bred and marriageable youths, snug homes, and happy children, and the likelihood of a prosperous future.

If the frontier offered women benefits, one of them was appreciation, especially from their husbands. Without wives and lovers, men suffered deep depression. The fair sex, as a poem in *Ladies' Repository* pointed out, dispelled "the cloud of sadness . . . from [men's] soul[s]." It was women, poet Lydia Sigourney insisted in her 1854 volume *The Western Home*, who "strove, with still advancing skill, / To make her home secluded bound / An Eden refuge, sweet and blest, / When, weary, he return'd for rest."

Women's literature was definite about the order of priorities in the West. If men gathered gold, one editorial observed, who was "to diffuse the wisdom which is more valuable than fine gold" and to instill the principles "of moral rectitude and social refinement" that could make the metal a blessing rather than a curse? Who else but women in their roles as mothers and teachers? Viewed from the female perspective, the moral and cultural success or failure of the venture west lay with women.

The suggestions of female irrelevance, the loss of femininity, the threat of male sexuality are therefore diminished. Much of the literature by and for women consciously attempted to fit the western experience into a framework that promised them the opportunity of fulfilling their social role. It shows an acceptance of social norms of domesticity and an expectation, or hope, that the norms could function on the frontier.

The consistent picture these works presented of female experience on the frontier does not mean that readers believed this interpretation corresponded to reality. They were familiar with the Boone and Crockett accounts and others. Many knew or heard folk songs about emigration that contained conflicting messages about the West. Where women's literature was reticent about sex, for example, songs portrayed a frontier brimming with sexual vitality, illicit as well as licit, and indicated possible confusion of gender roles. Despite what some women chose to believe, then, there were many cultural indicators during the decades of emigration to the Far West that suggested the frontier might undermine the cultural and social framework established for women during the early decades of the nineteenth century. But, as the literature by and for women made clear, many women hoped to resist the disintegrating forces of frontier life and to realize and even extend their social role. The goal was to shape the frontier into an image to their liking. Thus, a conflict between culture and environment was established even before emigration began. The tension would not work itself out before they left home, but the process would begin as families bade friends and relatives farewell and set out for the West.

2

"Ladies Have the Hardest Time, That Emigrate by Land"

Many years after her overland journey to California in 1860 southern-born Lavinia Porter found the experience as vivid in her mind "as . . . yesterday's events." The trip, she observed, had been so difficult that it was still "a constant source of wonder to me how we [women] were able to endure it." Upon reflection, Porter attributed female survival to shared characteristics. "An American woman well born and bred," she explained, "is endowed with the courage of her brave pioneer ancestors, and no matter what the environment she can adapt herself to all situations, even to the perilous trip across the western half of this great continent, ever ready to wander over paths which women reared in other countries would fear to follow."

Porter's emphasis on the courage and adaptability of women emigrants suggests that overland travel forced women to modify normal behavioral patterns. As she realized, the frontier, which for most women began as soon as they left home and friends, challenged conventional gender roles and accepted modes of behavior. During the five- or six-month ordeal on the Overland Trail to California and Oregon, thousands of white women overcame domestic stereotypes by assuming male responsibilities and undertaking men's work. In extreme cases, when husbands became ill or died, women took charge of the whole venture of moving west. Just as women performed men's work, so too, at least occasionally, did men find themselves doing tasks that society defined as women's. Gender distinctions, theoretically and often actually so clear in a culturally established setting, blurred. The months on the trail offered women an opportunity to question and modify conventional stereotypes. Yet few women did so; most did not find it easy to throw off accustomed ways of thinking even when forced into new ways of behaving. The trail experience suggests that women found comfort and personal reinforcement in their own sphere and were reluctant to abandon it altogether, no matter what stresses and tensions existed within it, no matter how far short of its standards women's conduct was.

Porter's insistence on the perils of the journey highlights another aspect of overland emigration. The notion of peril not only included the travail and dislocations encountered on the trail but also the danger and threat women believed the inhabitants of the wilderness posed to their safety and well-being.

Like their husbands, fathers, and brothers, few women revealed an awareness that they represented more of a peril to the Native American way of life than the Indians posed to white travelers. Overland emigration contributed to a disastrous cycle of change already under way in many parts of the trans-Mississippi West. On the central plains, tribes like the Sioux and Comanche, on the move because of the pressure of white settlement, vied for bison, trade, and horses. The population on the increasingly crowded plains roughly doubled between 1820 and 1840. Even before the first wagons rolled across the plains, the pressure on the natural resources of the region had increased to a dangerous level.

White emigration helped to upset the ecological balance, while white diseases hastened the disorganization of Indian life. For the Lakota, the measles epidemic of 1844 marked that year as "The Rash Breaks Out on Babies Winter," while the southern Cheyenne called 1849 "The Winter When the Big Cramps Take Place." Almost half the Cheyenne tribe died from cholera that year, and it is not hard to imagine the impact of disease and death on those who survived.

Although from a modern vantage point it is possible to see the far-reaching implications of the overland migration for Native American life, few sources reveal the thoughts and perspectives of the Indians themselves. Their actions, their words, usually reported by white observers, can only hint at what might have been passing through their minds. Of Native American women, we know very little.

Even for white women, generalizations are difficult, since so few left any evidence of their passage. As one emigrant pointed out, "Pioneer women were quite too busy in making history to write it." The majority of women as well as men lacked the time and perhaps the skills to keep a diary or journal. Those who did keep accounts of their trip probably agreed with Elizabeth Geer, an Indiana woman, who observed, "I could have written a great deal more if I had had the opportunity. Sometimes I would not get the chance to write for two or three days, and then would have to rise in the night when my babe and all hands were asleep, light a candle and write." Reminiscences written years after the trip supplement travel journals, but these must be used cautiously, since time often cast a rosy glow over events on the trail. Still, we know more about white women taking the overland routes west than we know about them before or after. Since the long journey was a major event, quite different from the three or four shorter moves many had made to other frontiers, women kept diaries or reminisced about it.

Then, too, men kept diaries, which also reveal information about women during the months of enforced and intimate interaction. For many men and women, the trail saga constituted their only contribution to the historical record of the westward movement and, in fact, the only record of their own lives.

Their journals, which focused on the five to six months of travel, first along the valley of the Platte River, then through the South Pass to destinations in California or Oregon, described the most popular but not the only means of reaching the Far West. It was possible, if costly, to sail from East Coast or Gulf ports to Central America, cross by land, and then continue by ship to final destinations in the West, or to go by sea around Cape Horn. During the first year of the gold rush, about 40,000 of the 100,000 fortune seekers chose ships. But the majority always went by land. Between 1841 and 1867, the years of heaviest traffic on the trails, 350,000 took the overland route to California and Oregon; others traveled part of the way by trail. So heavy was the traffic that eventually parts of the trail resembled a highway several miles wide. Although the priest who reported that his Indian companions were "filled with admiration" when they saw the trail in 1851, "this noble highway . . . as smooth as a barn floor . . . [with] not a blade of grass," might have been mistaken about the Indians' response, he captured the ways in which the crowds modified the landscape as they wended their way west. With the completion of the transcontinental railroad in 1869, traffic on the trail gradually declined, although wagons crossing the South Pass were reported as late as 1895.

During the 1840s, 1850s, and 1860s, the basic pioneer pattern diverged from the familiar one. Instead of moving from one area to an adjoining frontier, people began to emigrate across half a continent to the Far West. Land directly adjacent to the Midwestern frontier was Indian country, closed to white settlement, and, in any case, considered unsuitable for farming. Propaganda painted California and Oregon territory in glowing terms. Emigrants in the early 1840s demonstrated that it was possible to make the two-thousand-mile journey, and in 1843 the first mass migration set out for Oregon. Each year thereafter more emigrants sold out and started on their way to the coast. In 1847 the Mormons opened their own trail across the prairies. Eventually Salt Lake City would become a resting point for many emigrants headed for California.

Only in the 1870s did settlers push eagerly out onto the prairies of Minnesota, the Dakotas, Nebraska, and Kansas. A decade later, they moved to the chancy, arid frontier that swept from the Dakotas and Montana in the north to Texas in the south.

Most of those who passed over the trail were young. With the exception of the emigration of 1841 and the years during the height of the gold rush (1849–1851), families rather than single people dominated the trail. Geographically, emigrants tended to come from rural and small-town backgrounds in the Midwest and upper South, although some hailed from the urban East or the newer cities of the Midwest. Many had moved several times before, often as children.

Economically, emigrants came from the middle ranks of society. Though family situations differed, they all needed a substantial amount of cash for the trip. Guidebooks estimated that emigration for four would cost more than $600, although the sale of wagons and cattle at the trip's end might reduce final costs to $220. (A trip around the Horn was estimated at $600 per person.) As travel over the trails increased, the journey became more expensive, with ferry tolls and other charges becoming commonplace. Even those pushing out to adjacent frontier land in the 1870s and 1880s required capital. Thousands began farming on the plains with less than $500, but the risks of doing so were high. Obviously, emigration was not an option for the poor.

Women diarists, few when compared to the total number of women going west, are representative of the overland migration. Most had recently lived on farms or in small towns in the Midwest, though a few came directly from the East. Despite earlier moves to frontier settings (from Vermont to Indiana to Iowa, for example), they were middle class in attitude and well acquainted with ideas of woman's sphere.

It is true that there were other kinds of women on the trail. Lavinia Porter, a southern emigrant, betrayed her standards and class position when she described the rough and uncouth pioneers from Texas, Arkansas, and southwestern Missouri. The men were blasphemers, the women "fitting mates for the men." She was not the only one who found such emigrants distasteful, a "ruff set" lacking the manners and behavior so central to the new middle-class lifestyle. Perhaps these travelers were southern subsistence farmers who somehow scraped the money together for the trip. Because they left little in the way of written records, we cannot know the ways in which their trail experience may have differed from that of individuals of different classes or regional backgrounds. We do know, however, what literate women thought and felt on the weary road west.

Their thoughts and emotions in the months preceding departure are, however, usually hidden. Most often their diaries start when the journey does. Yet all had been helping with family preparations for months and must have been contemplating what the journey described in guides and newspaper accounts would mean for them. Perhaps they remembered the folk tune that highlighted the theme of hardship: "The ladies have the hardest time, that emigrate by land, / For when they cook with buffalo wood, they often burn a hand; / And then they jaw their husbands round, get mad and spill the tea, / And wish the Lord, they'd be taken down with a turn of the di-a-ree."

Since emigration meant months of hard living, one wonders what motivated women to go west at all. Were they dragged unwillingly by their men, or did they participate in the decision? If they contributed to the decision, what were their reasons for doing so? Though the sources are meager, they suggest some answers to these questions.

The major impulse behind emigrating appears to have been economic. To one Ohio woman, "going to the far west seemed like the entrance to a new world, one of freedom, happiness and prosperity," while a southern woman candidly admitted that "imprudent financial speculations" and embarrassments led to her family's decision. The West was a land of promise, though whether the promise was land, gold, or professional opportunity partly depended on the destination. An important secondary factor involved health and climate. "We were bound to search for a healthier and milder clime than Illinois to spend the remainder of our days," one emigrant woman explained. "I do not in the least regret leaving the sickness and cold, sand piles and lakes . . . behind and am looking forward for the time to arrive when we may all get settled safely at the place of our destination." Other women focused specifically on their own health and their hopes for its improvement.

Men were, of course, expected to make decisions, especially about economic matters, and the evidence suggests a pattern in which men brought up the subject of emigrating. Some women were taken by surprise, for, as one said, "the thought of becoming a pioneer's wife had never entered my mind." But this did not mean that women were passive spectators. Their style was to respond, to influence, even to argue. One woman questioned her husband's proposal because it did not seem "a wise business move." Enough women participated in the decision-making process to pass into western folklore. A popular folk song, variously titled the "Wisconsin Emigrant," the "Kentucky Song," or the "California Emigrant," suggests the power of female influence. In it, a farmer suffering hard times at home decides to go west. His wife, reluctant to emigrate, offers one reason after another for him to change his mind. All fails until she points out, "Remember, that land of delight / Is surrounded by Indians who murder by night. / Your house they will plunder and burn to the ground, / While your wife and your children lie murdered around." Her appeal succeeds, and her husband gives up his scheme, confessing, "I never had thought of your dying before . . . you, my dear wife, are more precious than all."

Other evidence corroborates female power to affect decision making. Since the trip's success usually hinged on the participation of all family members, a wife's stubbornness could block her husband's plans. "All my father could do," wrote one woman, "was to read every item of California news he could get and talk . . . for my mother would not be persuaded to undertake such a journey." Only when her daughters and their husbands decided to emigrate for health reasons did this reluctant pioneer change her mind. Even then, she insisted that their home be kept "unencumbered to return to in case we should not like California." In another family group, a young woman refused to go west with her husband's relatives, for she was "unwilling to leave her parents." Whatever ideology had to say about the necessity of female submission, women felt free to disrupt male emigration projects and, because of the cooperative nature of pioneering or their single state, had bargaining powers. Of course, opposition to male schemes did not necessarily constitute a departure from female norms. Women, blessed with superior insight, had been told to direct and influence their less sensitive husbands. The line between obstinacy and duty might well become indistinct.

Those who shuddered at the idea of undertaking a "long and perilous journey" did not openly oppose their husbands. Their timid behavior reflected how well they had internalized norms. Many women apparently forced themselves to acquiesce to the "dictates of duty." "My dear mother" did not oppose my father, recalled one daughter. "She tried to put down her fears for the perilous undertaking." Striving to act as a good wife, Abbey Fulkerath began her journal with these telling words: "Agreeable to the wish of my husband I left all my relatives . . . although it proved a hard task to leave them but still harder to leave my children buried in Milton graveyard but such is our lot on earth we are divided." There is no hint of resistance to her husband's plans.

But not all women were reluctant emigrants. "I was possessed with a spirit of adventure and a desire to see what was new and strange," Miriam Thompson Tuller remembered when she thought back to her 1845 trip as a new bride. Women who considered emigration "a romantic wedding trip," or who shared the perspective of Lydia Rudd—who wrote in her journal one day in May 1852, "With good courage and not one sigh of regret I mounted my pony"—were positive about the move west. They felt involved in the decision to move and shared men's opportunism. "We had nothing to gain but a fortune," one woman wrote, hardly sounding the disinterested female. The dream of easy circumstances often attracted women as strongly as it did men, even leading one woman to conceal her pregnancy and suppress her fears about her health so that she could go west.

Women's interest in the economics of emigration betrayed contradictions in the concept of domesticity. Women, unsullied by material concerns, were supposed to find fulfillment at home. Yet, their ability to do so depended in some measure on their husband's economic success. Though ideology might proclaim that home was home, no matter how humble, most women knew better. They wanted to live in easy circumstances in their own homes, which required money. "Disinterested" women, therefore, were necessarily interested in economic questions, and in emigration if it seemed to offer a way of acquiring the resources needed for comfortable domesticity.

The vision of family life so central to domestic ideals also encouraged a positive female response to emigration. Mary Jane Hayden's explanation of the family decision to emigrate is revealing. When she learned her husband was contemplating a journey to California alone, Mary Jane told him she had resolved to go, too. "We were married to *live together*," she said, "and I am willing to go with you . . . and under these circumstances *you have no right* to go where I cannot, and if you do, you need never return for I shall look upon you as dead." By insisting on accompanying their husbands, women like Mary Jane showed how firmly they believed in the family and how

determined they were that their husbands accept familial responsibilities. Letting a man go west alone, unless it were to
prepare a homesite, was a risky venture at best, even if the
rationale was that of improving family finances. Women's magazines condemned gold fever because it unhinged men, making
them feel "free as a bird" as they flew from "many a cheerful
fireside . . . many a happy home." This "fearful curse" destroyed
families and, in the end, the gold seekers themselves. Abandoning wives, children, and home meant "no fond arms wherein
to rest . . . [a] cold brow as life fled!" So it was hardly surprising
women willingly accompanied their husbands. "Where he could
go I could," remarked one Missouri woman, while another
pointed out, "It is the females that can improve your condition
and make a home, and them alone."

Since the family provided meaning for women's lives and the
basis for self-esteem, women might well wish to cooperate with
emigration plans. How many were enthusiastic, how many reluctant, is unclear, since sources so rarely discuss the pre-trip
scene. But those that do show a range of responses and suggest
the need to avoid characterizing all women as reluctant emigrants. Of course, other factors also led to positive attitudes.
The adventure and romance of emigration were appealing for
some; a few mentioned their affection for their husbands. "I was
very fond of my husband," recalled one, "and was nearly bro-
kenhearted at the thought of the separation."

Missionary wives were a decidedly eager group of pioneers.
Most had had early conversion experiences and fixed on foreign
mission work as a means of realizing their religious vocation.
In the early 1830s, there was great excitement about the possibility of carrying salvation to the Indians of the Far West,
who, it was said, were eager to learn about the white man's
God. Missionary societies generally frowned on sending single
women into the mission field, however, so no matter how fer-
vently an unmarried woman might wish to go, she found herself
confined to teaching and good works at home. Only marriage to

a male missionary could remedy the situation. More often than one might expect, men who needed wives as assistant missionaries turned up. Hasty proposals and marriages on the eve of leaving for the West resulted.

Although women might view such a marriage as part of a divine plan, the appearance of potential husbands was not entirely due to chance or God. Women like Almira David did pray "earnestly for some person who it appeared I was dependent on for going," but a network of friends and acquaintants often helped prayers come true. An Ithaca, New York, minister's letter to the mission board reveals the process of matchmaking at work. "A word in reference to their engagement and marriage," the pastor wrote. " 'Tis true their acquaintance had been very short—of but two or three weeks . . . But Mr. Gray came well recommended to the Rev. Samuel Parker, thro' whom he became acquainted with Miss Dix." Nor were the women themselves unresourceful. One young woman, who at twenty-six was considered an old maid, albeit one with a missionary enthusiasm, attended the General Conference of Congregationalists in Bangor, Maine. There she met a young man sharing her devotion to missionary work who, in turn, wondered whether "possibly his prayers were being answered in the person of this lady." After corresponding, the two married and set out for Oregon in 1856. Since eastern missionary societies sent more than twenty-six hundred men to the West by mid-century, the number of enthusiastic wives was substantial.

In an April entry of his 1853 trail journal, Henry Allyn observed, "Miss Martha Wood wishes to go with us and we conclude to take her." Allyn's entry noted an unusual event on the trail, the single woman moving west without the protection of family or friends. Their motives are usually hidden. There are tantalizing references such as the one in the Bradley diary to "four lewd females" on the trail and occasional comments about young women moving west to join bachelor brothers. But certainly, whether they hoped to support themselves, find husbands, or just have adventures in the West, these women decided for themselves.

The motives of one group of single women—teachers—for going west are clearer. Like female missionaries, these women saw themselves as part of a national effort to save the West for Protestantism and civilization. Catharine Beecher's educational campaign, initiated in 1845 with her book *The Duty of American Women to Their Country*, encouraged hundreds of these women to go west to teach. A group, formed at the Mt. Vernon Congregational Church in Boston in 1846, defined its goal as sending "competent female teachers, of unquestioned piety, belonging to the Congregational Churches in New England," to the West. Although sectarian aims were apparent, the group also recognized that it could offer "a merciful provision for hundreds of well-educated Christian young women, whose sex forbids their adventuring as their brothers do, and yet who, if such a Society will encourage them, and send them forth, may go cheerfully and understandingly right to the best spot for them in all that wide region." Acting as an agency for single teachers, the group sent 109 women west before merging in 1854 with the Board of National Popular Education, founded by Beecher in 1847. The board not only acted as an agency but also gave prospective teachers some job training. Although the religious mission was strong, the organization was nonsectarian. By 1858, it had sent across the Mississippi more than a hundred women, who, in turn, often found positions for friends. The organization's work, publicized through magazines like *Godey's Lady's Book*, inspired other women to leave home for western schoolrooms.

Applications from prospective teachers to the Board of National Popular Education offer a window into these women's motives. Of course, no application was entirely straightforward; candidates had to prove their religious zeal to acquire a position. So Augusta Allan described her conversion and explained that "my motives in going West, are a desire to benefit others, and to be benefited myself." Most women emphasized their desire to be useful in a region they described as religiously and culturally destitute. But the women offered a variety of other reasons for wishing to go west that reveal not only their own situation but their expectations. Many of them were already teaching and thought the frontier might provide more opportunity and even more money, which, frankly, they needed. "Being dependent upon my own exertions," wrote Betsey Brownell, "I feel it necessary also to look at the subject, in another light, which I think is not inconsistent with the spirit of doing good." These applications reveal the impact of economic change on single women in the East. No longer economically essential within their families, unmarried women found themselves in a hazardous world offering them few means of support beyond factory work, domestic service, and teaching. Teaching was the most respectable and available means for independence; teaching in the West might be an improvement.

Women also spoke of their desire for a better climate and hinted at health problems. Some told the board of a longtime interest in emigration, for the prospect of adventure could attract women just as it did men. As one candidate explained, she was interested in the welfare of others, but she was also driven by the "love of adventure and desire to be acquainted with the manners and customs of the inhabitants of more distant parts."

Evidence of women's motivation and involvement in planning the trip west, then, suggests the danger of viewing them solely as unwilling emigrants. Agreement did not mean that women would not experience a sense of loss at leaving family and friends behind. They were, however, not merely passive victims of men's choices but at times active participants in the process of emigration.

No matter how the decision to go west was reached, no matter how great or small a part women played in it, leave-taking was traumatic. Weeks of activity preceded the day of departure and, for some perhaps, concealed the reality of leaving itself. Women were busy sewing—making dresses, sunbonnets, tents, wagon covers—and seeing their friends. While women attended to these chores, men sold or rented the homestead and acquired the stock, wagons, and supplies the guides recommended. Finally, the moment came for farewells. Leave-taking occurred at home, or friends and relatives accompanied the emigrants for a day's journey. The occasion was usually a solemn and sad one as both the emigrants and the stay-at-homes contemplated the implications of the departure. "On the evening before [starting], the whole family, including my mother, were gathered together in the parlor, looking as if we were all going to our graves the next morning," one woman wrote. "There we sat in such gloom, that I could not endure it any longer, and I arose and announced that we would retire for the night, and that we would not start tomorrow morning, not until everybody could feel more cheerful."

Some diaries poignantly describe the tears shed by men and women alike as they set out. Others have terse, yet equally revealing, entries, like the one written by Amelia Knight, "STARTED FROM HOME." The very brevity conveys the emotion of the scene. Men and women both experienced a sense of loss. For the women, however, though emigration might symbolize a means of achieving domestic comfort and, in the future, tranquillity, it also ripped away some of its present framework. True, the immediate and sometimes not so immediate family might remain intact when groups of relations and friends traveled west together. Equally true, women were socialized to expect losing family and friends when they married and moved away from their parents' home. But this did not make it any easier to leave the current home with its familiar objects and rituals, with its groups of female companions and relatives who had contributed so much to one another's emotional life. And this move, unlike earlier moves to nearby frontiers, would separate friends by vast distances. It represented what might well be a permanent break. No wonder a deep sense of loss pervades the records. In her journal, Lodisa Frizzell asked herself, "Who is there that does not recollect their first night when started on a long journey, the wellknown voices of our friends still ring in our ears, the parting kiss feels still warm upon our lips, and that last separating word *Farewell!* sinks deeply into the heart. It may be the last we ever hear from some or all of them, and to those who start . . . there can be no more solemn scene of parting only at death." That women so often compared leave-taking to death was at once a realistic assessment that it was "not at all probable that we ever will meet again on this side of the dark river" and a symbolic recognition that the emotional void was like death itself. As for what lay ahead, it was "so far away and vague, that it seemed very unreal" to many of the women at the outset of the journey. What was real was what was left behind.

Women's diaries, more than men's, tended to focus on friends at home. An early entry in Anne Booth's journal is representative of many others': "Nothing can atone for the loss of society of friends." The trip was hard enough, women wrote, without having "our hearts torn by the loss of dear ones." Although their marriage might be affectionate, a husband did not usually compensate for the loss of female friends. Men, of course, missed old companions, but Asahel Munger's reaction to his wife's grief typifies the male point of view. "This day has been rather long and lonesome to E," he wrote. "She thought much of home— friends—prospects—& present condition. I tried to have her get above these things." Men did not dwell on absent friends in their journals; women did. Perhaps the long hours women spent sitting in wagons while men herded cattle, forded rivers, and drove wagons encouraged them to reminisce about absent friends.

Most women did try to "get above these things." As they catalogued each sign of the passing of civilization, women coped with their sense of desolation by reproducing aspects of the world they had left behind. Thus, women arranged their wagons, writing in their journals of the little conveniences they had fixed, the pockets in the wagon's green cloth lining that held "looking glasses, combs, brushes, and so on," the rag carpet to keep the floor of the tent snug at night, the bedding, sleeping, and dressing arrangements. As one woman explained, she was busy making "our home" comfortable so that there would be little time "for that dreaded disease, 'home-sickness.' " Another hoped to maintain some continuity by dressing as neatly on the trip as she might at home, in a blue traveling dress with white collar and cuffs rather than in homespun, linsey-woolsey, or calico.

These attempts to reproduce the rudiments of a home setting and to perpetuate a sense of the familiar were hardly trivial. Advocates of new domestic norms had encouraged women to believe that the physical arrangements of their homes exerted a powerful influence over their families. The makeshifts of the journey were an unconscious way of asserting female power and reassuring women of their identity. And, of course, the objects symbolized an entire way of life temporarily in abeyance. When her husband grumbled about the quantity of her baggage, Lucy Cooke revealed how vital her knickknacks were. Fearing that she would have to discard some of her luggage, she confessed, "I had a cry about it . . . as I seemed to have parted with near everything I valued."

Although Cooke's husband promised to stop complaining about the possessions that provided so much comfort for her, other women would find it difficult to maintain symbolic ties with home life and the female world. The woman who started out in a traveling dress with clean collar and cuffs soon found she had to abandon it for clothes she originally had refused to wear. Indeed, changes in clothing hinted at the social disruption the frontier could wreak. By 1852, some women on the trail were wearing the bloomer costume, finding the "short skirt and pantletts" a "very appropriate dress for a trip like this." Although bloomers were practical, the costume, espoused by advocates of women's rights as dress for liberated women, carried a radical meaning and was, in the words of one magazine, "ridiculous and indecent." So one woman who had brought bloomers with her found she lacked the "courage" to wear them and vowed, "I would never wear them as long as my other two dresses last." Women bickered over the pros and cons of the costume. Supporters accused women in dresses of being vain and preoccupied with appearance, while opponents, in turn, replied that bloomers led to male gossip. As one opponent stated, "She had never found her dress to be the least inconvenient . . . She could walk as much in her long dress as she *wanted to, or was proper for a woman* among so many men."

At the beginning of the trip, however, there were only hints of a disruption of propriety as both men and women attempted to maintain the comforting division of labor based on the concept of separate spheres. Generally, men drove the wagons, repaired them, hunted, ferried the cattle and wagons across rivers, and stood guard at night, while women were responsible for the children, meals, and family washing.

"Felt very tired indeed—went to bed early," wrote Ellen Tompkins Adams in a typical journal entry. The refrain of constant fatigue occurs over and over again in women's diaries. On the trail, women's work was difficult and exhausting. Maternal duties were taxing. As many as 20 percent of women were pregnant, and, although few mentioned their condition in their diaries, some were in the last stages of pregnancy. Apparently pregnancy was a subject discussed among friends but not on paper until the baby had been safely delivered. (Even in letters to female relatives, women approached the subject indirectly by talking about making baby clothes.) Once the baby was born there was little time to regain strength. A day or so of rest before the trip resumed was about the most any new mother could expect. Some recovered quickly and resumed their chores, but for others childbirth proved a nightmare. "Her sufferings were so great," wrote one woman of her sister, "that she does not remember anything for quite a space along there. It all seems like a jumble of jolting wagon, crying baby, dust, sagebrush and the never ceasing pain."

Traveling complicated child care. Although older children often walked and herded loose cattle, mothers had to supervise small children in the wagon all day. It must have been almost impossible to keep children good-tempered in cramped quarters; accidents were an ever-present possibility. Diaries refer to children falling out of wagons, under wagons, miraculously escaping harm, breaking limbs, or even being killed. Their more careful older brothers and sisters caused concern by wandering or riding off or lagging behind and disappearing. Children of all ages came down with fevers, diarrhea, even cholera and became fretful in a lurching, hot, and uncomfortable wagon. It is not surprising that journals often mentioned children as frightened, weeping, or disagreeable. Mothers who characterized their children in this way were not unfeeling or even unsentimental. Hovering behind many of their comments lay the very real fear of a child's death, of leaving a "little body in that strange country for the Indians to dig up or wild beasts to devour." Part of women's exhaustion was psychological.

Preparing meals was also a challenge. Morning and evening cooking took place over campfires or camp stoves in all weather. "Unpleasant as it is, I have been cooking beans and stewing fruit and baking bread," noted one woman on a blowy, rainy day. Clothes were reduced to tatters "from coming into frequent contact with the camp fire," and occasionally serious accidents occurred. "Her dress caught fire from the stove," Mary Fisher observed, "and before it could be extinguished it was nearly burned off her." This she passed off as *almost* a bad accident.

Despite these trying conditions, women were gratified when they succeeded in accomplishing their traditional tasks. One woman suspected that the other women "engaged in helping to cook supper . . . all enjoyed it heartily, as I did." In some trains, men had been hired to do the cooking. But rather than enjoying their freedom, privileged women in those trains often reported that they wished to take over, either because "the boys keep everything so dirty" or "because we liked it." When women did the cooking, one explained, the meals were tasty, more regular, and less wasteful. She could also have added that when women cooked it was more like home.

In numerous other ways, women sought to continue their familiar round of activities during the early and relatively easy months of travel through the Platte River Valley. Their journals noted when they cared for the sick and dying of their own company and when they visited other trains to help out. As at home, they sustained one another in the familiar rituals of birth and death. "Late in the afternoon a group of women stood watching Mrs. Wilson's little babe as it breathed its last," wrote one woman. And women made efforts to maintain their network on a daily rather than just an emergency basis. They reached out to construct new emotional support for the journey. "During the day," Catherine Haun, an emigrant from Iowa, explained, "we womenfolk visited from wagon to wagon or congenial friends spent an hour walking, ever westward, and talking over our home life back in 'the states'; telling of the loved ones left behind; voicing our hopes for the future . . . and even whispering a little friendly gossip of emigrant life." As women exchanged recipes, as they knitted and crocheted, they were keeping themselves "in the practice of female occupations and diversions." The journals indicate the feelings of satisfaction women felt when they visited, cooked together, or went swimming and their frustration when "the plain fact of the matter is, *we have no time for sociability*."

But as the trip wore on and the rolling prairies gave way to harsh deserts and mountains, it became clear that women would be unable to keep the world they valued intact. Treasured belongings were cast aside in an effort to lighten the wagons and quicken the pace so that provisions and animals would survive until the journey's end. Female friendships were broken off as companies separated. When friends parted, women wept. "We had become so attached to each other having travelled so far together, and being dependent on each other in times of danger and accidents," explained one woman, while another, facing separation from her sister because of their husbands' "first class row," confessed that her sister "did not feel that she would ever be happy again." Troubling, too, was the prospect of being without the comforting company of other women. Ellen Adams, who nursed a sick woman in her train, finally had to leave the invalid and her husband behind at an army barracks. "I felt very badly to come away as there are no women at the Fort," she reported, evidently thinking the presence of soldiers and husband hardly compensated for the loss of female companionship.

Ultimately, even standard chores became unfamiliar and unfeminine. Meal preparation often included gathering buffalo dung ("chips") for fuel. Since firewood was scarce, some women saw the dung as a practical solution to the fuel problem. Others found gathering the chips demeaning and indelicate. "This caused many ladies to act very cross and many were the rude phrases uttered, far more humiliating to refined ears than any mention of the material used for fuel could have been," observed one of the pragmatists from Missouri. Some of the women wore gloves to avoid touching the dung, although eventually "most of them . . . discarded their gloves" and accepted unpleasant reality. Using the chips to cook was another problem. "Mother thought at first she could not do that," recalled one daughter, and though, as always, her mother compromised, "she was never reconciled to that kind of fire, and never liked to think of those experiences afterwards."

Familiar patterns disintegrated under the trip's strain, and even the comforting sense of the flow of time vanished. Most striking was the disappearance of the Sabbath, which had become by mid-century a symbol of women's religious and moral authority. Initially, many women hoped to use the day for worship and rest. Parties lucky enough to have both a preacher and leaders who considered layovers no threat to the train's pace observed the Sabbath. But often the need to find water and food for the cattle, and the need to make mileage, made traveling on the Sabbath necessary, especially as the months passed. Women had to agree but confided in their journals that they were unhappy with the situation. Traveling "does not seem pleasant" on the Sabbath, wrote one, while another felt that the waters of the river her company had forded "seemed to reproach us."

Even when the caravan broke the journey to observe a day of rest, women found they had few moments for meditation or relaxation. "I was obliged to do many things I was very loth to do on the Sabbath," Esther Hanna revealed in her diary. Her life in Pennsylvania had been different. On the trail, baking, washing, mending, sewing all continued, Sabbath or no, while men had a break from their activities. Men, one sympathetic woman explained, needed "physical rest, so they lolled around in the tents and on their blankets spread on the grass, or under the wagons out of the sunshine, seeming to realize that the 'Sabbath was made for men' . . . [Yet] women, who had only been anxious spectators of their arduous work [during the week], and not being weary in body, could not fully appreciate physical rest." Whether men deserved the rest or not, "Does not seem like Sunday at all today—have been obliged to work nearly all day" was a refrain echoed by many women. One reflected sadly, "And today is Sunday again. O what Sundays. There is nothing that seems like the Sabbath."

As civilization receded, some of the ways in which women thought about themselves changed. Eastern values suggested that true women were feminine and attractive. However unlikely the attainment of this ideal on the journey west, it shaped women's views of themselves and served as a normative goal. But it was a losing battle to be concerned about appearances, and most women stopped thinking in these terms altogether. "As the days lengthened into weeks, our self-respect suffered somewhat in the matter of clothes," wrote one, who described her skirt as "a piece of wide fringe hanging from belt to hem." Another explained, "We were so worn out that we were not particular how we were dressed but presented a mixture of fashions." Only when the trip was almost over did Luzena Wilson suddenly realize how thoroughly she had forgotten the female norms she had observed in Missouri. As her party neared its destination, a man dressed in a clean white shirt came out to meet the travelers. The sight of someone in respectable clothes jolted Wilson and, as she recalled, "revived in me the languishing spark of womanly vanity." Realizing how she looked in her fraying sunbonnet and tattered skirts, "worn off in rags above my ankles," with her face sunburned, her hands "brown and hard," and, of course, gloveless, she shrank modestly away from the man's observation. By the end of the journey, Lavinia Porter agreed, "I doubt whether any of us could have been recognized."

"Getting tough, I can tell you," Mary Warner noted in her diary, after describing driving one of the wagons. If some familiar norms were forgotten, new ones were useful, for it was just as well if women got tough. As the trip progressed, women continued to be responsible for washing, cooking, and caring for children. But under the strain of travel, of parties splitting and hired hands quitting, women also took on jobs once reserved for men. They pitched tents, loaded, unloaded, and drove wagons, and yoked cattle. Some even drove stray cattle on horseback, and one surprised man noted "a couple of ladies" galloping full speed ahead after the beasts. Another disapprovingly noted that ladies rode astride, "the greatest curiosity I have seen yet." Women whose husbands became sick or died on the trail, of course, assumed all the responsibilities for the family's survival and welfare, unless they were lucky enough to fall under the protection of another man. For many travelers, the line dividing the activities of men and women became less distinct and, in some cases, disappeared.

As women did men's work, men did women's. Single men shifted for themselves, but even married men sometimes helped with the washing and, when their wives were sick or out of humor, did the cooking. Some women suggested that helpfulness was a regional characteristic. As one wrote in her journal, she was lucky to have a Yankee for a husband, "so am well waited on." But another wife, from the South, felt that male courtesy and sharing was rare. "Men on the plains . . . were not so accommodating nor so ready to serve or wait upon women as they were in more civilized communities." Although men helped with female work from time to time, they did not do so regularly. Most of the disintegration of traditional work roles affected women: a man assuming female responsibilities was doing a favor; a woman performing a male job was doing what was necessary.

Because of the many difficulties of the journey and the exhausting grind of steady work, most women cooperated with shifting requirements. There seemed to be no alternative. But some women welcomed the widening of the female sphere. Rebecca Ketcham, a single woman from New York traveling west with friends, reported her riding adventures with glee. Others wrote that they enjoyed driving wagons and were proud of their ability to handle animals. They noted incidents that they felt revealed courage and skill. In one party, women "actually joined in the chase" for buffalo. Some went so far as to adopt the symbol of masculinity, the gun. "I keep close to my gun and dog," commented one woman from Illinois.

But even when women seemed to enjoy their new responsibilities, few speculated on the significance of their actions or capitalized on their increased importance within the family, for most women found the trip neither exhilarating nor liberating. Far from welcoming the expansion of the female sphere, a few found fault with it. "There were occasional angry debates while various burdens were being adjusted," noted one diarist. "Warner says I am cross for the first time," wrote a young wife. "Well none of the women think it their duty to help the cook, and he

is cross if he doesn't get help, and of course he gets tired also."
Women complained to their journals and to one another more
about their fatigue, the monotony of the daily routine, the dirt
and dust than they did about their unaccustomed duties, but
the point was the same. "This gy[p]sy life is anything but agreeable." "It is impossible to keep anything clean, and it is with
difficulty that you do what . . . you have to do." The meaning
of this catalogue of grievances is captured in a typical passage
from the journal of a woman who had already moved once, from
Ohio to Iowa. "Oh dear," she confessed, "I do so want to get
there it is now almost four months since we have slept in a
house. If I could only be set down at home with all the folks I
think there would be some talking as well as resting." Most
women hoped not to expand their sphere once they were settled
in the west but to recapture it.

As the trip progressed, it became clearer and clearer that the
wilderness was an alien environment. It was also "the domain
of the dreaded Indian." Conditioned to believe the Indians dangerous and savage, women viewed them warily and fearfully at
first. Although some thought the Indians noble in appearance,
most agreed with Margaret Hecox that, underneath it all, Indians were "just Indians." "I doubt if the savage instinct can
ever be eradicated from the wild man's breast."

The Pawnee, whom women encountered not long after leaving
"civilization," usually posed few threats to the emigrants and
"proved better than represented." But if they were better than
expected in one sense, they were worse in another. Women
noted disapprovingly that the Pawnee and members of other
tribes "were insistent beggars, often following us for miles and
at mealtimes, disgustingly stood around and solicited us."

Many women became adept traders, even as they condemned
the behavior that facilitated the exchange of food and clothing
for whatever Indians could provide. Very few connected begging, or for that matter the stealing they blamed on Indians,
with legitimate hunger, a shortage of clothing, an environment

under attack. Yet their diaries describe some of the forces that
were gradually reducing the Indians to penury: the teams of
oxen and the herds of cattle and sheep that devoured the
grasses so essential for the buffalo and the way of life based on
the huge beasts; the demand for wood that denuded what timber
existed on the plains and prairies; the wasteful hunting. Virginia Reed described only her father's forays, but they were
destructive enough: "Paw goes a bufalo hunting most every day
and kils 2 or 3 buffalo every day."

Rachel Fisher, who noted how the Sioux she encountered
were "thakefull of the smalest gift," gave some sense of the
Native American perspective. The Sioux, she said, "complain
that the Buffaloes has all left from near the road they have to
go 30 mils for their subsistence there fore they expect a smal
contribution from each company of emegrants." This knowledge
did not prevent her from labeling them "beggarly and thieve-
ish." One wonders how the Sioux woman who exchanged moc-
casins and beads for bread with Amelia Knight a few years later
might have explained her situation. Was she "pinched with
want" with her "children constantly crying out with hunger," as
were the Indian women Thomas Fitzpatrick saw in 1853? Did
she see not only her family without the necessities of life but
also her economic role as the producer of bison robes disappearing along with the herds? Surely she looked at the wagon
trains "with an unquiet eye . . . the harbingers of the approach
of a dismal future" even as she tried to save her family from
starvation.

Although the Indians responded to the threat of emigration
by burning grazing lands (in the 1850s) and attacking wagon
trains (in the 1860s), few women encountered the violence they
expected. Nonetheless, it was often difficult to overcome anxiety. "Secret dread and alert watchfulness seemed always necessary," remarked one woman; another wished "all of the
Indians in Christendom were exerminated."

The fear that women often expressed had a sexual component. Women constantly commented on the nakedness of Indian men, who were "guiltless of clothing, . . . very many . . . in the state of our first parents before they committed their first sin." Popular captivity accounts hinted at Indian sexuality when female victims described savages whipping their "almost naked" bodies. Readers could easily imagine what other foul acts Indians perpetrated on the "almost naked" female form. Events on the journey seemed to reinforce the idea that Indian men lusted after white women's bodies. A number of journalists recounted episodes in which Indian men tried to trade ponies for white women. The women's response was one of stark fear. Some described hiding in wagons to avoid the savages' flattery. Others became the butt of their husbands' senses of humor. One revealed that her husband pretended to strike a bargain with an Indian, his wife for two ponies. The Indian, little realizing the joke, generously offered three, "then he took hold of my shawl to make me understand to get out. About this time I got frightened and really was so hysterical, began to cry."

The journey offered other distasteful sights that challenged the values white women held dear. Particularly disturbing were the "renegade" white men, former fur traders and trappers, who had taken Indian wives, produced families of mixed-blood children, and even forgotten English. These men symbolized the possibility of racial intermingling and cultural compromises on the frontier. Their choices suggested the allure of another way of life. When Catherine Haun met up with one such person at Fort Bridger, she was shaken by his rejection of civilization. His "appearance was loathesome in the extreme," she wrote, "it being hard to distinguish him from his brother Indians." Indeed, that he had known and willingly abandoned a superior way of life was so shocking and threatening to all her beliefs that Haun "regarded him with more fear and abhorance than . . . a manly buck." Instead of sharing his culture and uplifting "his squaw and family of half-breeds," he had sunk to their level. His wife and children were "unfortunates."

Women had somewhat more ambivalent reactions to the Mormons, who, on the one hand, were white and civilized but, on the other, had rejected central tenets of middle-class culture. Emigrants admired Salt Lake City, a stopping-off point for California emigrants, for its beautiful plan, its cozy, snug homes, its prosperous and bustling air. But more often than not, women saw the similarities between their own culture and that of the Mormons as superficial. In the eyes of the overland emigrant woman, Mormon men were "very hard looking" and the women ugly.

Female writers assumed polygamy exploited women sexually without giving them anything in return. "These demons marry some girls at ten years of age," wrote one horrified observer, who emphasized that the demons often took on "a mother and her daughters and marr[ied] them all." To get "only one third or perhaps one twentieth share of a man" was hardly worth the hard work Mormon men expected of their wives. Indeed, Mormon wives were "all . . . a poor heart broken and deluded lot and are made slaves to the will of these hellish beings who call themselves men . . . They have not so much liberty as common slaves in the south." The fear of sexual license and the conviction that Mormon women, like Indian wives, were men's slaves suggest the confidence emigrant women had in their own values and social place, as well as their fear of change.

These confrontations with an alien world and the hardships of travel, which increased so dramatically during the second part of the trip, caused women, at times, to feel fearful and bitter. Under stress, some women turned against their husbands and blamed them for the whole unhappy undertaking. "I felt as though myself and little ones were at the mercy of a madman," Mary Powers reflected, while Margaret Hecox, who had retreated into the family's wagon with her children as the rest of the party watched an Indian war dance, agreed: "I wondered what had possessed my husband, anyway, that he should have thought of bringing us away out through this God-forsaken

country. I feared that we all were to be scalped or taken pris-
oners before morning." After a moving description of her
younger brother's sickness and death, Ada Millington tersely
observed, "Ma thinks if we had been 'at home he needn't have
died.' "

Despite her bitter thoughts, it apparently did not occur to
Margaret Hecox to confront her husband. Nor did it to Mary
Powers, who noted in her reminiscences, "I said nothing." The
ways women handled their frustrations most often testifies to
their attempts to live up to norms of female behavior, at least
in front of their men. Lavinia Porter confessed she often cried,
wished herself at home, and then returned to chores with an air
of assumed cheerfulness. For others, keeping journals must
have served as a legitimate release of tension and as a place
for cataloguing grievances. "This journey is tiresome . . . it is
perilous, the deaths of many testify, and the heart has a thousand misgivings, and the mind is tortured with anxiety," explained one weary woman in her journal. Women also expressed
their grievances to one another. "Husband is scolding and
hurrying all hands (and the cook), and Almira says she wished
she was at home, and I say ditto." And occasionally all the
women gathered together to share their feelings. "The female
portion of our little train are almost discouraged," observed one
writer. "We sat by moonlight and discussed matters till near
11 o'clock."

On August 3, 1854, Mary Burrell wrote, "Worse than all,
stuck my nose in where I had no business." Though she did
not reveal what she had done, the entry suggests that, though
women most often tried to act as women should, they did not
always succeed. Nor did men always live up to standards of
manly behavior. Both sexes indulged in disagreeable and petty
conduct. "All out of humor," noted one woman, while another
revealed she had hardly expected "to see so much selfishness
and bad temper." "Being jolly when you are so tired yourself
is no picknick," observed one woman still well enough social-

ized to feel it was her duty to cheer the "tired and cross" men. Men admitted in their journals to "heavy hearts," quarrels, and complaints and described shockingly inappropriate masculine behavior. John Minto told of coming across a father of four, "lying on his back upon a rock, taking the rain in his face, seemingly given up all thought of manly struggle." The cry of Indians sent some of the men of another train scurrying to hide in the wagons, courage fast forgotten. Vignettes of inept husbands unable to control their wives suggest how hollow were the claims of some to male authority.

Given the difficulties of the journey, it is not surprising that social restraints occasionally broke down. As tension built up in one party, the observant Rebecca Ketcham noted how the behavior of all her fellow travelers changed: "It does seem as though we might have everything pleasant, but is all the other way. Mr. Gray [the captain] scolds when he is around, and when he is away the rest scold and find fault with him." As time passed, Rebecca detailed how the women finally stopped complaining to one another, abandoned all sense of woman's place, and "talked pretty plain [to Mr. Gray,] me more so than ever. I don't know how he liked it, but I cannot help it." Other examples of what could be called female insubordination crop up in the diaries: women refusing to cook, women refusing to camp at an assigned spot, a few trying to bring the trip to an end altogether. One set flame to the family wagon; another beat her husband with a horsewhip. These were the extreme, but subtle resistance was, no doubt, more common and also less likely to be recorded. Lavinia Porter, who disapproved of her husband's barrel of whiskey, described what she did. Sure that complaints or reasoning would fall on deaf ears, she resorted to indirection, certainly a tactic that women found useful. "I patiently bided my time, and one day when no one was around," she proudly recounted later, "I quietly loosened . . . the barrel . . . and by nightfall there was nothing left."

A 250-pound woman berated and abused her husband,

"charging him with bringing his wife and children out into the God-forsaken country to starve and die"; she was, however, the exception, and Lavinia Porter probably more typical. But apparently, neither open insubordination nor indirect resistance resulted in clear rethinking of the female role or of gender relations. Rather, women struck out blindly, angry at the tedium of the trip and the prolonged disruption of their female world. They were, perhaps, too tired to do otherwise. And as the journey neared its end, there seemed less and less need to rethink, as women's thoughts turned more and more to the future and the reestablishment of their world, now so sharply contrasted with life on the trail. What had initially been vague now loomed close. "I am very weary of this journey, weary of myself and all around me," wrote one woman in late August. "I long for the quiet of home where I can be at peace once more."

The journals and reminiscences show the rich variety of responses women emigrants had to the overland experience. They noted cheerful and lively moments, as well as those of suffering and death. Many testified to the new and strong ties they had formed with one another, a good beginning for a new life. "I feel that the good friends we have made on the journey more than make up for the hardship," noted one woman. The trip had been a mixed experience for white women, and, as their journals hinted, a far darker chapter for the Native American women who appeared so fleetingly as emigrant women made their way west. But for the white women it was a passage to a hopeful time, a time to start anew. At the end of her journey, one woman wrote this artless poem, which captures so much of the response of women to emigration.

> *Day after day*
> *We wend our way; Through sage and sand,*
> *In hope to find,*
> *To please our mind,*
> *A home in a happy land.*

3

"A Maid of All Traids"

In the early years of migration to the Pacific Northwest, some
weary travelers caught their first glimpse of a western home at
the Protestant mission station at Waiilatpu in eastern Oregon
Territory. Motivated by stories of the western Indians' interest
in Christianity and by a zeal to save heathen souls, Narcissa
and Marcus Whitman had left New York State in the 1830s to
labor as missionaries among the Cayuse Indians. Traveling
westward with a company of fur traders, the Whitmans and their
colleagues were some of the first Americans to settle in Oregon
Territory. During their early years in the West, they erected
mission buildings, began agricultural operations, and tried to
teach the Indians the rudiments of Christianity and the American way of life. Their initial attempt to build a family ended
in tragedy when their only child, Alice, born shortly after their
arrival, drowned at the age of two. It was years before Narcissa
recovered her equilibrium and rebuilt family life around her
adopted children—first, two of mixed racial background, and

then, in 1844, a large family whose parents had died on the Overland Trail.

When most emigrants approached Waiilatpu, they judged the couple's mission a success. The missionaries had a comfortable house, all the trappings of middle-class life, and neatly dressed, well-mannered children; the numerous buildings, fields, and gardens gave the site the appearance of a bustling village. Although the Cayuse had not abandoned their seminomadic way of life and only a few were cultivating crops for themselves, they appeared at Sabbath services when they were camped near the mission and sang hymns enthusiastically in their own language.

This vision of a West where whites and Indians coexisted harmoniously was a fleeting one. By the time more and more emigrants had arrived in Oregon Territory, the Whitmans' enthusiasm was waning. The Indians were reluctant to abandon their traditional ways, and none had converted to Christianity. Many of the Indian men considered farming women's work, similar to gathering roots and other edibles. Cayuse women were unwilling to replace the labors that brought them respect and power within the tribe with some version of white female domesticity. Indian resistance to their teachings frustrated the missionaries. As the mission buildings themselves made clear, the Whitmans looked forward to a West civilized along familiar lines—not a West where "barbarism" flourished.

Narcissa's own child, born shortly after she and her husband arrived at the mission, had interacted comfortably with the Indians who lived nearby. By the 1840s, Narcissa was trying to keep her adopted children separate from what she considered the contaminating influence of tribal culture. She avoided working with the "poor Indians" and focused instead on the children's welfare and on the physical and spiritual needs of the emigrants who passed through Waiilatpu.

Although Narcissa reported that the Cayuse did not know "what to make" of the throngs of emigrants "coming into the country," the Indians made it clear to the Whitmans that they were alarmed by white emigration, which threatened their control of tribal lands, and tired of the missionary presence. When their attempts in the 1840s to convince the couple to leave the mission failed, they resorted to violence, killing the Whitmans and several emigrants who were living at the station.

Few settlers would face such a fate, for the large numbers of emigrants in the late 1840s were tipping the balance in favor of the newcomers. Indeed, most white emigrants gave little more than a passing thought to the peoples they were displacing. When they did, they saw themselves on the side of justice and progress—they never doubted that the West would belong to the white race and its civilization.

Certainly, toward the end of the trip, women had little interest in contemplating the fate of the Indians. Their thoughts turned to their own futures. "I can scarcely realize that we are so near our contemplated home," Esther Hanna wrote in her journal a few days before ending it in September 1852. "My heart arose in gratitude to God that we were spared to reach this land." For women like Esther Hanna, the journey's conclusion was a joyous event. Misgivings about the frontier evaporated as families began their new lives. As Anna Maria King remarked, "I was much apposed to coming . . . [but] if I were back there and know what I know now, I should be perfectly willing to come."

Others found the period of adjustment to new surroundings trying. Physical exhaustion from the trip's rigors, a reduced emotional resilience, and meager family resources contributed to a sense of desolation in the days after arrival. Clothes were tattered, and many treasured possessions lay discarded back along the trails. No matter how carefully emigrants had planned the trip, few arrived with much cash, and even the lucky ones found their reserves could not replace what they had thrown away in desperation. "There were no luxuries to be had even if we had ever so much money," one early pioneer recalled. But just as important as emigrants' physical and financial condition was the shock of confronting reality. Many women had survived the trip by fantasizing about their future "happy home in a happy land." If they had passed by the Whitman mission station, they had seen one version of that fantasy fully realized. When they reached their own destinations, however, there were no homes waiting. "After the way we had suffered and struggled to get here," a Missouri woman wrote to her mother, "I had all I could do to keep from asking George to turn around and bring me back home." As dreams collapsed, some gave in to feelings. One band of women arriving in Puget Sound by boat in November 1851 spent a long, dreary afternoon helping their husbands carry possessions up the beach beyond the reach of the tide. Then, overwhelmed by their situation, one of the husbands later recalled, "the women sat down and cried." It was not long, of course, before some sort of shelter, however rudimentary, was constructed. But a permanent home often proved elusive. Journals, letters, and census data suggest several moves during the early years of settlement, as families sought the right claim or the right job.

Women settling farming frontiers, far from the Pacific coast, also found adjustment difficult in the months and early years after their trip. Although they were not so fatigued after a journey ending in Nebraska or western Iowa, their initial situation could seem bleak. The flat landscape struck many women as depressing. "As long as I live I'll never see such a lonely country" was how one woman described her reaction to the Texas plains, while a Nebraska pioneer reflected, "These unbounded prairies have such an air of desolation—and the stillness is very oppressive." Like settlers of Oregon and Washington, emigrants pushing onto the plains frontier arrived at their destination with little capital to soften the burdens of homesteading. Like their counterparts in the Far West, these emigrants often found their dreams of a permanent home illusory.

The early years of settlement on farming frontiers differed according to time, location, and settlers' backgrounds. The mid-century plains and prairie frontier offered emigrants coming from Europe and the Mississippi Valley not only fertile soil and sufficient rainfall, for example (unlike the arid plains, sweeping from the Dakotas south to Texas, settled later in the century), but also special problems stemming from the region's geography and climate. Although emigrants could use familiar agricultural methods, the weather, with its extremes of temperature and high winds, could mean low yields, crop failure, and the destruction of valuable livestock. Timber for building and fuel, so abundant in the Far West, was rare on the prairies and plains, and its scarcity compounded problems of settlement. Hunger, poverty, and ruin hovered closer to the pioneers of this frontier than to those of the Far West. There, however, though subsistence was assured, poor transportation and inadequate markets meant a continuing shortage of capital, which affected the quality of life.

Although each new farming region offered settlers unique challenges, white women shared certain experiences. During the initial period of settlement, they began housekeeping in primitive circumstances. Because of the shortage of capital and labor, early farming efforts were on a small, diversified scale and demanded the participation of the entire family, especially adult women. The first years of settlement, therefore, continued the trail experience by demanding that women overstep cultural and social norms for the sake of family survival. The sense of dislocation some felt initially stemmed from this enforced departure from familiar behavior. The early years of settlement, in fact, would test many facets of the cultural framework that women had brought west with them. The test suggested that women found value in that framework despite its seeming lack of suitability for frontier conditions. Both the framework and the women proved flexible and resilient in the face of adverse circumstances.

As one Oregon woman noted, the frontier was "a hard country for woman" because "things . . . [were] rather in a primitive state." Certainly, whether a dugout or sod house on the plains, a small shack, cabin, or hole in the Far West, early housing was crude and crowded, offering neither comfort nor privacy. Families lived for months in these dwellings, sometimes for years, as money and time went into other improvements. These homes challenged domestic ideals and the concept of gentility, and women sometimes became discouraged. "What a contrast . . . with our home in Ill. one year since," sighed one.

The preparation of food, an important female responsibility, was difficult without familiar ingredients and utensils. An Oregon pioneer of the 1840s described setting up housekeeping with her new husband with only one stew kettle (for making coffee, baking bread, and cooking meat) and three knives. Since the stoves with which many pioneer families had started over the Oregon Trail had been abandoned to lighten the load, this woman, like so many others, did all her cooking over an open fire. No wonder some pioneers looked back on this period with distaste. "I assure you," Maria Cutting wrote, "we had many privations and Hardships to endure and O such makeouts sometimes having to use shorts instead of flour, sometimes sugar sometimes none."

Yet others took great pride in preparing tasty food despite the obstacles; women's response to difficult living conditions often seemed related to their early attitude toward emigration. As one Iowa pioneer explained, "I came here willingly believing it to be for the best and am determined to try with the assistance of Providence to make the best out of it." In any case, they knew they had no options beyond making "the best out of it." There was no returning home. As Margaret Wilson told her mother in an 1850 letter, "You will wonder how I can bear it, but it is unavoidable, and I have to submit without complaining."

No matter how women reacted to primitive living conditions, few were delighted if they had "primitive" neighbors. "I suppose Mother had more trouble there [in Oregon], really, than she had on the road; because we were surrounded by Indians,"

one daughter explained. On the trail, the wagon train had offered fainthearted women the protection of numbers, and offensive natives were always left behind as the company moved on.
Now settled, however temporarily, those who found Indians living nearby had to adjust to their presence.

Abigail Malik was remarkably open-minded about her Indian
neighbors. She had one to help with the housework and proclaimed her "a very good girl." When Indians turned up "a
beging for work," she and her husband set them digging for
potatoes. In her opinion, "The Indians are very good and kind
here. And they Would Not do enneything to the Americans
here."

Despite her positive responses, Abigail did not link Indians'
behavior to their overall situation. She never connected their
desperation for work with the changes caused by white settlement. When white farmers took up claims on Indian lands, they
disrupted the Indians' food gathering and hunting. The shortage
of food led native men and women to beg and scavenge. Nor
did Abigail think about the ramifications of the smallpox that
infected her servant's sister except in terms of her own family's
health. "I told her [not] to dare to Come here untill her sister
would get perfectly Well or die." Smallpox, which had been
introduced to America by Europeans, certainly killed its fair
share of white children throughout the early years of our
country—but it eradicated whole tribes of Indians, who lacked
any immunity to it and other European diseases.

When some Indians declared in 1855 that "no More people
[shall] cross their Country enney More" and threatened to kill
those who tried, Abigail drew a careful distinction between local
friendly tribes and those who were "Awful Saviges." For the
latter she had no sympathy, for she did not, in her heart, believe
the land belonged to the Native Americans, nor did she think
they had any right to use violence to protect tribal territories.

Even when white women hired Indians or bartered with them,
few felt entirely comfortable. Friendly Indians had the unnerv-

ing habit of appearing silently, wanting food or just a look at a white woman and her children. Many white women believed that native men were particularly aggressive when white husbands were away from the homestead. They found scavenging for food frightening, especially when the men carried weapons, which white women assumed, usually wrongly, were meant to be used against them. Not surprisingly, women often reacted aggressively. Sarah Sutton was typical. If Indians came for food when her men were absent, she jerked "a tent pole and laying it about her with such good effect that she had her squat of Indians going on a double quick in a very short time." At other times, she wielded a pistol. Although the women might gain the upper hand in such encounters, they found these incidents unpleasant and unnerving. Susannah Willeford, an Iowa pioneer, spoke for many other women when she stated that the "native Indians" were "seldom if ever welcome visitors as far as I was concerned."

White women living on farming frontiers saw little value in native culture. As Mrs. Miller explained in 1852, the Indians who lived near her in Oregon were "dying here as elsewhere, where they are in contact with civilization . . . I used to be sorry that there was so much prospect of their annihilation . . . Now I do not think it is to be much regretted. If they all die, their place will be occupied by a superior race."

Lack of sympathy for and negative evaluations of native people doubtless contributed to women's sense of isolation. When Susannah Willeford recalled that "we had no neighbors nor company save a straggling land hunter, or the native Indians," clearly the native Indians did not count as company.

How Indian women responded emotionally to white settlers can only be imagined: the desperation that led to begging for food; the determination to survive that lay behind barter. Martha Gay provided some hints about the perspective of Indian women from an encounter with an Oregon "squaw" who spent a night in her barn. A few months later, the woman reappeared, selling berries she had gathered. "She looked at me and began to laugh. She said, 'You don't know me?' I said, 'No, I never saw you before did I?' Then she laughed more heartily and said, 'Ah, paleface soon forget. Indian never forget.'" For this woman, studying and remembering white faces was a necessary strategy for survival. For Martha Gay, there was absolutely no reason to remember an Indian face.

During the earliest period of settlement, the faces women remembered were those of their beloved female friends and relatives. Husbands and children were no substitutes for those left behind, as Nellie Wetherbee discovered. "I have been very blue," she wrote in her journal, "for I cannot make a friend like mother out of Henry . . . It's a bore—and Mother is so different and home is so different . . . Oh dear dear." The difficulty of finding female friends stemmed, of course, from the scattered pattern of settlement (the Oregon Donation Law, for example, provided each family with 640 acres, thus ensuring isolation) and from the fact that there were fewer women than men on the frontier in the first years. As Mollie Sanford noted in her diary, "I do try to feel that it is all for the best to be away off here [in Nebraska]—I can see and feel that it chafes mother's spirit . . . If the country would only fill up . . . We do not see a woman at all. All men, single or bachelors, and one gets tired of them."

But the gender imbalance was not so great as many popular accounts have suggested. The 1850 male-female ratio for the country as a whole was 106 men to every 100 women, while in rural Oregon that same year, there were approximately 137 men to every 100 women. By 1860, however, the sex ratio in frontier counties approximated that in the East. The frontier, then, was not overwhelmingly male. But given the role female friendship played in women's lives and the obstacles to their meeting, the loneliness they felt was understandable.

Real isolation was, however, a short-lived phenomenon, usually lasting only two or three years on most parts of the frontier. Some of the men turning up in the census or in Mollie Sanford's diary were preparing homesteads for their families. The immigration pattern of Whidbey Island, near the coast of Washington, suggests the rapidity of the settlement process. Attracted by its fertile prairie land and pleasant climate, Isaac Ebey, an 1848 pioneer from Missouri, selected the island for his future home. By the time his wife, Rebecca, and their two sons joined him three years later, there were several other families on Whidbey and more coming. In June 1852, Rebecca was writing, "We have plenty of company four families of us here 12 children." Although her guests eventually moved to their own claims on the island, Rebecca's diary catalogues numerous visitors, both new emigrants and old. After Rebecca died in 1853, newcomers to Whidbey included the Ebey cousins, her husband's father, mother, brother, two sisters, some children, and a single man who married her daughter the next year. Nor was the Ebey clan the only one on the island, for other families as well as some unmarried settlers migrated to Whidbey during these few years.

While women shared certain physical and social conditions on the farming frontiers, their family environments differed somewhat both from national norms and from one another. Census data show that throughout the nineteenth century the size of American families was shrinking, not because of reduced mortality rates but because women bore fewer and fewer children. In 1800, white women who reached menopause bore on the average 7.04 children. Forty years later, the figure had fallen to 6.14, reaching 4.24 in 1880.

Scattered studies of family size on the farming frontiers show patterns that reflect different family strategies and values. Pioneer families in early Oregon, facing the need to clear land and start farming operations, had large families, perhaps averaging as many as six children or more. The desire was to have enough children to help out on the family farm but not so many as to harm the farming operation itself or the children's inheritance. Married couples living on a later farming frontier, in

Middleton, Idaho, in the 1870s, were engaged in entrepreneurial farming that had little need for child labor. They did not
see themselves as establishing a landed patrimony for their
children, as had the early farmers on the Oregon frontier. As a
result, they had smaller families.

"Will I be a happy beloved wife, with a good husband, happy
home, and small family," Mollie Sanford had mused, "or an
abused, deserted one, with eight or nine small children crying
for their daily bread?" Scattered studies of parts of the trans-
Mississippi frontier suggest that Sanford's chances for marital
satisfaction in the terms in which she posed them were good.
Despite differences in family size, the popular view of frontier
families with ten or twelve children is clearly exaggerated. The
typical frontier household, while larger than those in the East,
was composed of parents and several children living together.
An analysis of the Iowa frontier showed families with one to
four children living at home, while a detailed study of a Texas
pioneer area with 896 families turned up only twelve families
with ten or more children. The average household in this part
of Texas contained four children, but fully *half* of the families
had three children or fewer living at home. While none of these
figures reveal actual family size because they do not take into
account children who were grown and on their own or those
who had died, they do suggest that western households were
not dramatically out of line with American households elsewhere.

Women on farming frontiers were, then, most often wives and
mothers. While on some farming frontiers women had more children than on others, they limited family size. Even the fecund
women settling Sublimity, Oregon, controlled fertility. Temperance Downing (the mother of seven) and Elizabeth Hunt (the
mother of six) bore no children after their mid-thirties even
though they had several years of possible childbearing ahead
of them. While it is impossible to know the methods they used
to limit family size, information on contraceptives was available.

Newspapers between 1820 and 1873 advertised both contraceptives and abortifacients, while pamphlets, birth-control cir-
culars, popular health books, and other books told women how
to control conception. Contraceptive practices were long described in folklore. Although personal testimony concerning the
use of birth control on the frontier is rare, a few references
show that frontier women knew of and practiced birth control.
An Oregon midwife, for example, described an abortion, a
method of family limitation that increased during the nineteenth
century. "I went to the woman's place several times," she rec-
ollected. "She had staged several sham battles. You see, they
didn't do what was right, and had tried, too soon, to have the
baby and get rid of it. When it was far along, it was a killing
job. Hot salt water was what they used, and it sometimes
passed. After the woman herself would be about to die as well
as the baby, they'd call for help."

If pioneer women were not the fecund breeders of popular
history, nor were they or their husbands the excessively youthful
group so often described. Most studies of pioneer families show
husbands typically in their thirties or forties, with wives several
years younger. Nor did girls in their early teens usually marry,
despite the shortage of women on some frontiers and the appeal,
in Oregon, of the 1850 Donation Act, which offered more land
to married couples than to bachelors. One pioneer woman recalled a proposal when she was thirteen. Perhaps it was from
a suitor with an eye toward the land she might represent. "I
said, *no*! Why I'm only a *child*. I have never given marriage a
thought yet." She, like other women on the farming frontiers,
would not face the challenge of creating a new life in a new
place burdened by youthful inexperience of swarms of young
children.

The family provided the context for women's emotional and
work lives during the initial years of settlement, when interaction with outsiders was limited. Many pioneer women resolved
consciously, as did Susannah Willeford, "to devote my time,

life and energies to the welfare and interest of my family." This was no small resolve; women's work for and with their families was extraordinary. Since few pioneers arrived with substantial financial or material resources, and since hired help was rare, every family was thrown back on itself in the struggle to get started. All cooperated in the work of establishing the farm, but because women often were the only adults besides their husbands, they had to contribute more than a woman's share.

"I am maid of all traids," one woman remarked in her diary in 1853. As had proved true on the trail, necessity changed the relationship between men's and women's work. The tasks seemed endless. Women did heavy outside "male" chores, helping to dig cellars, build cabins ("as there was no other man . . . [Father] could get to help him"), plow, and plant ("there were neither man nor boy that we could hire in the county"). Then there were the conventional female jobs—sewing, "sweeping dusting churning ironing baking bread and pies dishwashing &c." And always there was laundry, an arduous undertaking that many women seem to have particularly disliked. "Dreaded washing day," wrote one, who added, "And as Mr. Taylor is not well he brings me water I finish by noon then scrub in the after noon feeling quite tired." Women cared for vegetable gardens, cows, chickens. As farmers, cooks, seamstresses, and laundresses, their labor contributed to the family's well-being and survival in almost every way.

But women did more than these tasks, since they shared "a strong desire to provide the necessary comforts for our family." In many cases, they became small-scale economic entrepreneurs. One resourceful but not unusual woman, for example, started out by cutting up wagon covers to make shirts to sell to the Indians. Then she moved on to making gloves for soldiers stationed nearby, a task with which her husband helped. "So, before spring, they were turning out very handsome gloves, also buckskin money belts." Later, as emigrants began to come into Oregon, she baked bread, pies, and cookies to sell. Female enterprises changed as opportunities changed, though the sale of butter and eggs seems to have provided a fairly steady source of income for women. These funds were especially important because of the chronic shortage of capital on the frontier. And as one observer pointed out, women often supported their families while their husbands learned how to farm. Occasionally women viewed their earnings as their own, but most often they were not a source of economic independence but rather a means of supplementing the family's income.

"Female hired help was not to be obtained," one man pointed out when reflecting on his pioneer years. "I assisted my wife all I could—probably did as much housework as she did." Continuing the pattern emerging on the journey west, men performed some female chores. Letters and journals show them helping with the washing, the cooking, and caring for children. But as on the trip west, men usually assumed these responsibilities only occasionally, when their wives were tired, ill, or in childbirth.

Much of the heavy labor women did initially could also be categorized as helping husbands out in the absence of male assistance. But wives more routinely assumed male responsibilities than their husbands took on female responsibilities. When men left their homesteads, as they did when gold was discovered, or when they went off to fight Indians, conduct politics, or herd cattle, they were often gone for months at a time. The women were left in charge. "As we live on a farm," wrote one, "whatever is done I have got to attend to and so I have a great deal of out doors work." As she listed her chores, they included caring for hogs and hens, milking cows, and running the dairy. A hired man worked on the grain. On the plains, men often hired themselves out for cash, leaving their wives to oversee the crops and animals for weeks.

As their enterprises and their letters and journals indicate, women were both practically and emotionally involved in economic matters when they sought to improve the family financial status. Even Kate Blaine, a Methodist minister's wife from the Northeast, wished she could be making some money. "If I were not the preacher's wife I should take in [washing] . . . It is very profitable," she confessed. Despite the conventional depiction of woman's world, the home, as separate from man's world, the workplace, the two overlapped on the frontier. Nor were women "disinterested" in economic matters. As women shared men's work, they began to express male perspectives.

Home was not the quiet and cozy retreat that nineteenth-century culture envisioned, but a busy center of endless chores and economic ventures, as it is for those with home-based businesses or telecommuting jobs today. Moreover, women were determined to defend it. One who recounted how a flood destroyed her family's investment explained, "It did seem almost hopeless to start practically from the beginning again, but I was willing to do it." Destitution on the plains in the 1870s produced the same kind of resolution when women refused to admit economic defeat. A spectacular case of courage and devotion to property was provided by the illiterate widow of a California squatter. When the rightful claimant to the land (who had killed her squatter husband) tried to drive her off the property, gun in hand, the widow seized her own pistols, approached her opponent, and dared him to shoot her dead. Her defiance proved too much for him, and the woman retained the land to which she was so devoted.

If the frontier blurred gender distinctions in the world of work, it also tolerated other departures from female norms. Women were occasionally involved in politics. Widow Mary Ann Sims of Arkansas noted, "The papers are full of Politics as this is the year for the Presidential election . . . Of course I take sides as every one does so I espouse the cause of Filmore." At least one woman did more than talk. "During these years," David Staples, an early West Coast settler recalled, "Mrs. Staples cast as many votes as any man. Voters from Arkansas and Missouri, who could not read would walk around . . . and ask her for whom they should vote. She would take the ballot, and running her pencil across certain names, would say I would not vote for that man. By this means, she very materially altered the complexion of results." Women occasionally conducted religious services in the absence of preachers. They filed claims, took care of business, and, as one wrote, "I had a gun and could shoot with any of them."

The activities of these self-reliant pioneer women defied a number of nineteenth-century stereotypes. But this did not necessarily mean that they abandoned the larger conception of women's nature or that they ceased to value female culture. Nor did it mean that they attempted to work out a new definition of woman's sphere. Their behavior and their attitude toward their family, their attempts to replicate eastern female culture, suggest that their new environment, although it changed what they did, had only a limited impact on their views.

One might expect, for example, that women's economic importance to the family enterprise would result in a reordering of family relations and a reallocation of power within the family. Ideology, of course, characterized the nineteenth-century male as the decision maker. Actually, many American women participated in decision making and exerted power in subtle and not so subtle ways. As foreign visitors to the United States noted, "Woman is the centre and lawgiver in the home of the New World." Ideology never tells all.

Because ideology does not describe reality, the true nature of power relations in families of the past is elusive. Power is difficult to measure at any time. Who wins or loses family confrontations reveals something about the allocation of power and can more easily be observed than the ways in which family members influence or modify decisions. Yet any judgment about who wields power and how much depends on influence as well as power. In studying the nineteenth-century frontier family, the normal problems of analysis are compounded by the lack of direct information about the day-to-day decision process. The privacy of family life, symbolized by the notion of home as retreat, worked against recording situations that might reveal power dynamics. As Elizabeth Lord, reminiscing about her pioneer life in Oregon, pointed out, "Of many things connected with our family I do not care to speak in these pages, such as my marriage, the loss of my first child and the birth of my second, which meant much to all of us and was a great event in our lives, and is something that especially belongs to ourselves."

Conclusions about the power structure of frontier families are thus drawn from hints rather than from direct evidence. Census data provide a few uncertain clues. They show, for example, that there was no great disparity of age between frontier husbands and wives, which may suggest some limitations of male authority. The small surplus of males on the frontier gave single women some freedom to pick and choose before marriage, which could have affected the nature of the marriage relation. And control of fertility may signify female power or a process of mutual decision making. Divorce records reveal the belief that marriage should be a loving partnership, not a lopsided patriarchal arrangement. Certainly, when husbands were away in the mines, at the legislature, or on the range, women had real authority in their families.

Evidence suggests, however, that though women were co-partners in the frontier adventure husbands still made the major decisions. Men seem to have determined whether the family would move on to a better piece of land or pursue a business opportunity, just as they had decided to bring their families west. Yet, in both cases, men initiated discussions but did not dictate. They consulted their wives, and it may be that female power was really the right of consultation. Both men and women testify to the interaction. Milo Smith, a Colorado pioneer, pointed out, "There is not an enterprise that I have ever gone into that I have not talked the details over with my wife before hand," while another pioneer described a lengthy period of negotiation between herself and her husband, who wanted to take up a new claim. "Finally, after much deliberation on my part, and persuasion on the part of my husband, I consented to taking up a . . . claim," she reported, but only after learning that there would be a colony of thirty settlers from Baltimore nearby.

Women on the frontier did make many minor decisions, although they still deferred to men, negotiated with them, and often worked for their goals indirectly. An account of an Iowa pioneer family reveals how many women must have operated. Although the husband planned to support the family by doing carpentry, "Mother had different ideas. During his absence she had accumulated nine cows . . . She was able to support the family nicely . . . But milking cows did not appeal to father; one week from the time he returned there was only one left." Yet this was not the end of dairying after all, even though a male decision appeared to have been made. The woman did not confront her husband, but with an inheritance she again invested in cows. With the proceeds from dairying, she bought winter clothing and supplies and made her point. Eventually the family acquired hogs to help consume the milk; stock raising ended up being the family's main economic activity. Female deference and patience succeeded.

Throughout, women were careful to maintain the idea of male superiority. As Kate Robins explained to her mother in New England, "Abner would not like it if he knew I sent for you to send me things." The implication was that women would work behind men's backs and avoid direct confrontations with male authority. Frontier women were not attempting to upset the traditional male-female relationship; they did not consciously covet male power. Women's letters and journals describing the ways in which they managed when their husbands were away make this point explicitly. "My husband was absent so much of the time," wrote one woman, "engrossed in mining or in politics, that the care of the family and the farm was left entirely to me, and I was physically unequal to this double burden."

Since her reminiscences show her to be a woman with great physical energy, one suspects that it was the constant responsibility that she disliked. Women were reluctant to take on the burden of decision making alone, and when they did, it was with the expectation that they would do so only temporarily.

Mary Ann Sims, a widow at twenty-five, expressed her anguish at having to play a man's role on a more permanent basis. "I have been busy all day casting up accounts and attending to business," she wrote in January 1856. "I had no idie that it was as much trouble to superentend and take care of a family as it is I feel tired sometimes." A few weeks later she added, "Allway beeing accostum to have someone to depende on it is quite new to attend to business transactions and it pesters me no little." Two years later she observed, "I see a woman cannot fill the sphere of a woman and man too." By 1859 her thinking had crystallized: "It has often been a source of regret to me that my daughters were not sons a man can change his station in life but a woman scarsely ever arrives at more exalted station than the one which she is born in if we ecept those whose minds are mascaline enough to cope with men. a woman whose mind is supirior and whose feelings has been cast in a more exquisit mould to be compell to associate with *courser* minds who cannot understand is compill to feel loanly." Cultural prescriptions were so strong that the widow found herself physically and emotionally exhausted by male responsibilities. On the other hand, despite many offers of marriage, she remained single for several years. A study of frontier Texas illustrates a similar reluctance on the part of propertied widows to remarry. Perhaps the burden of decision making lessened as women learned "to live alone and act for [themselves]."

Possibly women's fundamental importance in the early years of settlement set limits to female deference. "The women were not unaware" of their role in helping to support the family, one reminiscence noted, "and were quite capable of scoring a point on occasion when masculine attitudes became too bumptious."

Though there may have been limits to deference, and though women may have felt an underlying tension because of the contrast between female norms and their own lives, most tried to observe cultural prescriptions concerning familial behavior. Direct confrontations occurred but appear to have been unusual. The evidence is, of course, weighted toward literate women, the very ones exposed to cultural role definitions. But studies of peasant women, who prove less independent than educated women, suggest that a dramatic reallocation of power within humble pioneer families was unlikely.

An examination of letters, journals, and memoirs that touch on marriage and courtship also indicates how many women carried conventional ideals west with them. Although it has been suggested that frontier women were drab work partners with few sentimental illusions, many of them nourished romantic views. Nineteenth-century society had glorified romantic love as a necessary precondition for marriage. Advice books, novels, and schooling described the rapture that a potential husband could be expected to inspire. The rigors of frontier life modified but did not undercut the value of romance.

In fact, the situation of single women on the frontier encouraged romantic fancy. Scattered studies of pioneer families indicate that single women married not in their early teens but in their late teens and early twenties. Frontier demography made romantic ideas and love and courtship meaningful, for a woman could wait for a "purely spiritual and intelectual" suitor to appear rather than accepting a humdrum and unworthy admirer.

Sixteen-year-old Rachel Malik found herself besieged by suitors after the passage of the 1850 Donation Act. "There is a great many young men loves me about Hear," she noted in March 1852. Speaking of two of her admirers, she announced she was interested in neither: "They dont suit my taste." Despite gifts that included gold rings, a watch, and a silk dress, she chose to marry John Biles, who courted her with romantic letters.

The selection of a mate was not without a functional aspect, however, which it may have lacked in urban areas (but probably not in farm communities). "Young women were really sincere when they sought to excel in the preparation of household articles," one pioneer woman commented. "Their teaching was such that such excellence brought its reward in desirable matrimonial favor and the final fulfillment of woman's mission in life." Both sexes agreed that industriousness and competence were desirable for a marriage. A series of letters from a young Nebraska pioneer to his mother reveals this perspective. "You wanted to know," he wrote, "when I was going to get married. Just as quick as I can get money ahead to get a cow and to get married. I want to before I commence shucking corn if I can to Aunt Jennie's oldest girl. She is a good girl and knows how to work . . . A fellow cant do much good on a place when he has everything to do both indoors and out both. She says if we marry right away, she is going to do the work in the house and shuck down the row when I am gathering corn, but I will be glad enough to get rid of the housework." After his marriage, he reported with satisfaction, "She makes everything look neat and tidy and is willing to help me all she can."

The realization that marriage represented a working partnership hardly precluded romantic ecstasy, at least on the part of women. Capable as she was of seeing through some romantic ideology ("How pleasant it would be to have a comfortable little home with one I *love*. I am afraid the anticipation is more pleasant than the participation would be"), Elizabeth Wardall faithfully recorded her raptures in a courtship lasting several years. "O: what a blessed thing is *love*," she wrote, while Harriet Strong told her future husband, "How glad I am *love* is indiscribable. I would dislike to think anything that *could be fathomed* could effect you and me as it does."

Nor did marriage necessarily dull tender feelings. Women did not see their husbands merely as work partners, although this aspect of the relationship may well have provided a solid basis for their affection. Susannah Willeford described her husband as her beloved companion, "my first and only choice. The man to whom I had first given my heart and confidence. The man with whom I had sacrificed my home and friends, the man with whom I had shed tears and shared his gladness and with whom I had shared many difficulties and by whom I had borne eight children." Her words convey their warm relationship, as do the testimonials of many other women about their marriages. Pioneer wives both expected and experienced the feelings that nineteenth-century literature suggested were part of married life. Separation often led women to express these emotions in romantic terms. Roselle Putnam called her husband "the idol of my heart" and remarked, "Never did I know what it was to sufer anciety untill I knew what it was to be seperated from [him]," while the long-married Mrs. Stearns spoke of her husband's "dear face." When husbands finally returned, women like Rebecca Ebey captured the emotional tone of their marriages: "And one thing which made [the day] . . . seem more exceedingly delightful, My dear husband arrived safe at home."

Nor was love without a sexual component. Although some historians have argued that nineteenth-century women neither wanted nor enjoyed physical affection, scattered evidence from married and single women on the frontier shows that passion had its place. Since nineteenth-century women were reticent about sex, these references are all the more remarkable. Wrote one woman to her husband in 1867, "Dear Husband you say you think that I could get plenty to hug me well I don't know whether I could or not I don't think I look very hugable now at least to any but your self as there is no-one knows how well I can hug but you." That a chaste hug was perhaps not what she meant is suggested by a letter written a few weeks later when she revealed, "I dreamed of seeing you last night and I thought I had a pair of twins." In a similarly suggestive manner, Kate Blaine told her mother she missed her absent husband as a bedfellow: "Now when I sleep alone the bed is so cold and my feet will not keep warm." A few women were less ambiguous than Kate. The widow Mary Ann Sims lamented she had not met a suitable marriage partner and acknowledged the sexual satisfactions she missed. "I know that there is not a woman . . . that is capable of feeling a more devoted affection than [I] I am naturely impolsive and affectionate and I loved my husban[d] with all the intencity that my nature was capable of feeling but I must confess it was more the passionate ideial love of youth," she wrote. Though she implied that passion should disappear with maturity, it was not so for her. Her final diary entries show her struggling to overcome her feelings for a man she described as wild and dissipated.

It is certainly true, as Phoebe Judson observed, that "the inconveniences of our environment and the constant drudgery eventually took all the romance and poetry out of our farm life." Though Phoebe was talking not of marriage but of her idealized vision of farming life, her comment raises a valid point. Pioneer women worked hard most of the time, and their difficult life put limits on flights of romantic fancy. But they were more than work drudges, and their occasional references to love suggest that the belief that romantic love was the basis for marriage had affected their attitudes and expectations.

The majority of frontier women were wives and mothers during the early years of settlement; primitive conditions and women's workloads complicated motherhood. But women still were able to form the intense emotional connections with their children that nineteenth-century culture proclaimed were so central to motherhood. Furthermore, they took their role of mother seriously and attempted to live up to its demands. "How forsably I feel the responsability of a Mother," sighed one.

Only rarely did frontier women reveal how they felt about pregnancy and birth (which they called a time of sickness). Giving birth was, however, part of a "female ritual" that called for the involvement and support of other women on the frontier as it did in the East. To be alone at such a moment was a dreadful fate. "I do not know what they will do when she is *confined* not having any Neighbours," wrote one woman, expressing the common fear of being without female support at such a moment. When it was at all possible, frontier women gathered round during childbirth, with little thought of monetary reward. The ritual had rules. "A woman that was expecting had to take good care that she had plenty fixed for her neighbors when they got there," explained one woman. "There was no telling how long they was in for. There wasn't no paying these friends so you had to treat them good."

If women were reticent before birth and gave few indications of what their views of motherhood were, this was not so afterward: "Well, old journal," Almira Beam exclaimed in 1861, "you have been rather silent these few months past: but it could not be helped. You have great cause to be thankful that we ever met. Arthur is asleep in his cradle below, and mother is getting dinner." In their letters east, women indicated their deep emotional concern for their children, recording the smallest details about their babies—their clothes, habits, small achievements. "I would tell you that he is the prettiest baby in the world," wrote Sarah Everett from Kansas, "if I was not intending to send his likeness." Occasionally mothers expressed ambivalent feelings about their female children. Two years earlier, Sarah had described another baby as "the newcomer who seems to cause more rejoicing among her distant relatives than those at home —we think of calling her Clara Elizabeth . . . It isn't of much consequence however seeing it's nothing but a girl anyway."

Yet four months later, Sarah reported the death of *"sweet little* Clara—She brought a great deal of sunshine into our homely cabin this summer, and when she was carried out of it, it certainly seemed very dark to me." Whatever Sarah's earlier comment meant, Clara's death revealed that her mother saw the maternal relationship as central and emotionally absorbing. A child's death robbed the mother of one "more dear to me than any thing ever had been." Such testimonials strike the twentieth-century reader as overly sentimental, but they were typical in the nineteenth century. The commonness of children's death on the frontier (twenty of the thirty-five reported deaths in Cass County on the Nebraska frontier in 1860 were children six or younger) did not lessen the impact of such losses.

The nineteenth century defined the regulation of children and the formation of their characters as a mother's central tasks. Life on the frontier complicated them, as Mollie Sanford suggested: "Mother . . . fears I am losing all the dignity I ever possessed." "I know I am getting demoralized, but I should be more so, to mope around and have no fun." The pressure of other duties and the lure of the outdoors made regulating children difficult. Abigail Malik worried that her daughters "will Not Mind me eny." Children remembered running "wild in the woods without any restraints," "carefree all through the woods and . . . hills." Chores also took children away from the watchful eyes of their mothers.

While life on farming frontiers made a mother's duty toward her children more worrisome, few mothers rejected their responsibility. Children also remembered punishments and disciplinary measures. One daughter recalled criticism of her language and other maternal strategies designed to encourage ladylike behavior: "If I carelessly put my sunbonnet strings into my mouth, I got my tongue burned from the vinegar and cayenne pepper into which they had been dipped for the express purpose of making the process disagreeable." In later years, pioneer women often pointed to their children as symbols of their lifework, testifying to the importance they attributed to their labors as mothers.

When they could, then, pioneer mothers molded and educated their children. Rebecca Ebey, a pioneer from Virginia, taught her children lessons, but not just in reading and writing. "We . . . spend our time in training the young minds of our children in the principles of Christ and creating within them a thirst for moral knowledge," she explained. While knowledge of Christian principles was one goal, inculcating the habits of steady industry was another. Women expressed disapproval of idleness and indolence in children and sought to encourage them to be useful. On the frontier, mothers expected their children to work, as recollections of pioneer childhoods make clear: "You will gather from what I have related that work and plenty of it was the lot of pioneer children," said one pioneer, remembering his early life.

Tasks were not assigned solely on the basis of sex. Girls recalled plowing, herding cows, carrying wood and water, while boys helped mothers wash clothes and dishes. "I think the boys ought to do something," explained one mother. Just as responsibilities of the sexes overlapped in the adult world, so, too, did they in the children's world. But as time passed and children grew, gender distinctions were stressed. Daughters recalled mothers clarifying appropriate female behavior. Both sexes acquired knowledge of boundaries, as records show. One reminiscence tells of "Margaret Isabell's sons, . . . teenagers . . . [who] had held their mother up so she could milk the cow. She was still weak from the birth of the baby, but milking a cow was 'woman's work' so they would not do it." Girls recalled their introduction to domesticity as they acted as a "mother's right hand." This was an apprenticeship for marriage, as Amanda Gaines explained: "I assist Mother in household duties which are various. She is preparing me for a Farmer's wife." Another daughter wondered whether she had any existence aside from the domestic routine, for her life was "so prescribed for me by my family environment that I do not know who I am." She did know what she did, however: washing, cooking, and assisting "dear old mother." Even recreation could be gender specific, with girls riding, visiting, and picking wildflowers, while "boys swam with Father . . . and trapped animals."

Since the frontier family worked together, it was natural that women shared child care with their husbands, a departure from nineteenth-century norms. Women expected and wanted assistance, not only because of the work involved, but because of the need to clarify standards. Women assumed that their husbands would introduce sons to the male world and take responsibility for their development at the appropriate time. This might occur relatively early. As one woman explained, one of her boys was a problem: "His pa is gone so much that he is becoming a great deal of trouble to me I have often heard it said that little boys would not be industrious about everything under their mother's controll . . . I find it so, They become so accustomed to their mother's commands . . . that they get so they do not mind it." She concluded, "When little boys become old enough to do some work they need a father to show them and to push them forward to make them industrious."

In the first few years following emigration to the West, frontier women helped create a new life for their families. The ways in which they approached their duties and related to family members revealed both the new environment and the influence of culture. Tired and overworked as they were, many of them still had the energy to worry about standards and norms. Of course, they made the necessary accommodations. The realities of bringing up children to survive and flourish in their new homes encouraged women to foster behavior not so important in safer environments. "Children here have to learn self reliance and independence," explained one parent.

But the truth was that female culture shaped the ways women perceived the frontier experience and provided a means of orientation to it. Even though frontier conditions forced them into manly pursuits and led them to modify some of their standards, they hardly pressed for liberation from female norms and culture. Much of the "freedom" that women experienced was the freedom to work even harder than they had before, with dramatic results. "I am a very old woman," wrote twenty-nine-year-old Sarah Everett. "My face is thin sunken and wrinkled, my hands bony withered and hard." Why should women lay claim to male tasks in addition to their own? The domestic ideal was a goal toward which women could direct their efforts, the promise of a day when their lives would not be so hard, their tasks so numerous. Domesticity, with its comfortable definition of woman's place, helped women bear what they hoped were temporary burdens and reestablished their sense of identity and self-respect. It served as a link with the past.

Frontier women often indicated their desire to hold on to the conventions of female culture no matter how unfavorable the circumstances seemed. "Home," crude and impermanent though it might be, received the kind of attention that would have pleased the proponents of domesticity. Though the cabin or sod house might not be the cozy nook pictured in stories of western life, women hoped to make it one as they papered walls with old newspapers or tacked up cloth to make the house snug and cheery. Old rags became rugs, old dresses curtains. A keg might become a footstool, upholstered with an old pair of pants. Thread turned into lace doilies. Outside, women planted flowers and trees from seeds they had brought with them and generally tried to maintain the standards of domesticity and hospitality with which they had been familiar before emigration. Although they often wore rough and rugged clothing, even buckskin trousers, pioneer women found "all these things . . . dreadfully annoying." As one pointed out, "We were always wishing for enough money to buy better clothes." The interest in fashion and the attempts to dress in style symbolized the intention to remain feminine. The "career" of a mid-century Oregon pioneer is revealing. "Although I had now been absent from civilization—otherwise Ohio—for more than a year," she wrote, "I was still considered an authority on the matter of dress and fashion. I was consulted and acted as adviser whenever a new cloak or gown was made . . . I trimmed hats, literally, for the entire neighborhood, and I knew less than nothing about millinery."

The determination to maintain ties to the traditional female world and to create a female community where, in fact, there was none was apparent in the energy with which frontier women sustained old friendships and associations. Mrs. Coe remarked in a letter to a friend in 1863 that she had written hundreds of letters, so many "that my Diary has dwindled away to almost nothing—All my romance has become reality—and as for poetry—it has vanish'd, resolved itself into and, mingled with the landscape around me." Pioneer women wrote letters to eastern female relatives and friends, detailing their lives, providing all the vital information that formed the basis of an intimate female dialogue. They enclosed material of their dresses, described dress patterns, sent pictures of their children; they asked scores of minute questions about the health of family and friends, marriages and deaths, fashion, religion. "The most trivial things that you can mention about each other have a great interest to us way out here," Mary Ann Adair explained to her mother and sister.

Bonds of affection sustained the dialogue between settlers and their eastern friends and relatives, but that dialogue had emotional costs. Slow and irregular mails, which could take up to a year, contributed to the natural anxiety women felt for the health and well-being of those far away. "My dear mother," wrote one woman, "you do not know how miserable I feel about you, for I have not received a line from any of my family." And as years passed, a new fear appeared. "Everything has changed so much at home since I left, that I expect I should feel like a stranger now." And with time, it was also possible that those at home would cease to care. "I have waited almost a year and a half hoping to receive a letter from you," Elisabeth Adams wrote from Iowa to her sister. "Why do you do so? Do you not wish to have intercourse with me? Do you not *love me*? I am sure I love you, and the longer I live the more I feel the want of affection from others, the more my heart yearns for kindness and love from my own family, I mean my *father's family.*"

A common theme runs through the correspondence. "I want you to come if you can and as soon as you can for no doubt I shal feel my self very lonesome." Women's letters are filled with urgent invitations to friends and relatives to emigrate. Often over a period of years, encouragement and advice about the trip poured out of the West in hopes that friends from the old life could become part of the new. "I want you all here, then I would be perfectly contented," explained Louise Swift, while another woman told her sister, "When we get together again we will not be parted so easy."

If relatives and friends did not come west, women sustained ties with them by nourishing hopes of an eastern visit. Eventually this hope was realized for a lucky few; other women remembered that, in the end, all would meet in heaven. Although some of their discussions about a heavenly meeting sound strange to modern ears, the emotional well-being of many pioneer women was sustained by their faith that the network of friends and relatives could be eternal. There is, perhaps, no greater testimony to the importance frontier women placed on female culture than the conviction that parts of it would be replicated in heaven.

While many women on the frontier devoted considerable energy to keeping alive the home network, feeling, as one young woman put it, "Tis true we may have friends among strangers; but, ah, they are not parents, brothers nor sisters," most emigrants attempted to establish new ties with other women as soon as possible. The trip overland had provided one opportunity for a new beginning. "Ever since I saw you in camp at Iowa (in '54)," Anna Goodell told Mary Bozarth, "you have looked and acted like my good Aunt Sarah." Proximity (which was a relative term) also determined friendships. Although the nearest neighbor might be miles away, women made a special point of visiting one another. Reciprocity was understood. "Mrs. Terry came this morning," wrote Almira Beam in her diary. "She says she will not come again until I come to see her." Soon Mrs. Terry had become "the best neighbor I ever saw, or heard of." Although women might go for days or even weeks without visitors, when they came, they stayed. The visits provided a relief from work and the opportunity for mutual support and sharing experiences. Rebecca Ebey's diary revealed the many rewards of female friendship: "I have been busy all day ironing cleaning up and mend the children's clothes Mrs. Alexander came over this evening to spend the night I was very much pleased to see her and had been look[ing] for her for a long time . . . Mrs. Alexander is very cheerful and makes me feel much better than I have done to be awhile in her company."

Yet creating a web of new friendships on the frontier was difficult. Distance was an obstacle, at least at first. And cultural or social differences, usually overlooked, could stand in the way of intimacy. "Oh how I pine for association [of] some kindred mind," a young widow in Arkansas reflected. "All of my neighbours are good honest kind people but they seem to have no idie beyond their little sphere of action they do not appear to have a feeling nor aspiration higher than the things of life satisfying their physical wants." Aware of such distinctions on the frontier, she decided, "I had rather be aloan for I feel aloan." Loneliness for another woman made her "meditate upon former scenes in my life when I had doting loving relatives all around me."

With time, however, the new network took shape. Ties became warm as marriage bound families together and family, relatives, and old friends emigrated to swell the circle of love. A study of kinship in Oregon suggests that this process could be relatively rapid. At least 40 percent of the households listed in the 1850 census had kinship ties with one other household and perhaps more. Census figures can only hint at the emotional significance of these relationships.

Despite the trials the frontier posed for them, many frontier women continued to see themselves within the mainstream of nineteenth-century culture. Although their courage, persistence, and physical endurance seem extraordinary to a later time, none of these women viewed themselves as extraordinary. Their diaries and letters show they expected to labor hard and long to

achieve their goals. Though notes of weariness often creep into
their accounts, they appear to have grumbled very little, at least
on paper. Some complained of the monotony of farming life,
though others seemed to enjoy the fact that there was "no bus-
tleling crowd as in City or town to marr our peaceful happiness." They expressed discontent if family fortunes wavered,
but they did not see themselves as drudges. Comments about
their Native American neighbors invariably contrasted their own
lot with that of the long-suffering Indian woman, who toiled like
a slave for her husband.

The attitude of women during the early period of settlement
was conditioned not only by their belief in hard work but also
by limited expectations for personal happiness. Writing to her
mother about a young niece's birthday, one woman advised telling the girl to remain a child "as long as she can, for the
troubles of a woman, will come upon her soon enough!" The
phrase "troubles of a woman" suggests something of the female
frame of reference. Nineteenth-century ideology promised
women fulfillment through marriage and motherhood, yet most
knew the physical pains and dangers associated with bearing
children and the disruption of female culture that marriage so
often brought about. In a highly mobile society, they witnessed
the anguished separations that frequently parted family and
friends for life. The disparity between ideology and reality made
it risky to assume happiness in any setting. The religious knew,
of course, that God assigned both blessings and trials in life;
Christians had to expect both. With such life experiences and
Christian beliefs, nineteenth-century women were equipped to
deal with the realities of their lives on the frontier.

Their letters to friends and families in the East are good
evidence of their plucky attitude toward pioneer life. "Tell father I am not discourage and am not sorry I came," wrote Kate
Robins to her brother, while Kate Blaine told her mother, "I
could not have believed that I should have been as well contented as I am situated and must needs be here. We are de-

prived of all the conveniences I had considered indispensable before we came." Although most women were candid about the work required (Kate Blaine said, "A woman that can not endure almost as much as a horse has no business here, as there is no such thing as getting help") and acknowledged their homesickness, they often were satisfied with their situation. "If our friends were here, we should be very contented, notwithstanding as we are deprived of many conveniences and comforts we might have enjoyed at home." Domestic triumphs, home improvements, new clothes, and preaching in the vicinity were duly described and appreciated in the context of creating culture in a new place. The ultimate objective of many of the letter writers was, of course, persuasion. Still, the satisfactions cannot be discounted nor can the women's underlying assumption of steady progress on the frontier. For white women, the future looked promising. So Phoebe Judson recalled, "The letters written back to our eastern friends gave such glowing descriptions of our fair dwelling place that some of them were encouraged to make arrangements to cross the plains the following year."

Women also told friends of the beauty of the West, of its good climate and healthy way of life. They noted the disappearance of old ailments and the feeling of bodily well-being they derived from the activities of outdoor life. To their single relatives, they described the "western gallant"—perhaps not "dressed up gentlemen" but perhaps "better than anything you ever saw or heard of before."

Of course, it was in the interest of these women to attract friends and family to the West to aid in the task of building society anew. "I promise you a hearty welcome to my house" was a refrain of female letter writers. Yet the lures were real. As Pop from Arkansas pointed out, "If she was back and new as much as she dos she would endure as much more as she has to get back to Oregon."

4

"Am Beginning to Feel
Quite Civilized"

In their early years on western frontiers, women made their major contributions to and through their families. As the period of isolation ended, women's social contacts multiplied. The organization of churches, schools, and voluntary associations, the development of rural towns and cities, gave many white women a new and more public forum for their activities and opened another phase of female experience in the West. With growth came the opportunity to carry out the civilizing mission implicit in the concept of domesticity. The ambitious task proved both satisfying and frustrating. In their role as mothers of civilization, frontier women most clearly faced the tensions between culture and environment and confronted the complexities inherent to establishing society in a new setting. In some places and at some times, they also came up against the power of other cultures that did not conform to their vision of the future.

The growth of rural communities, which provided one basis for women's activities, proceeded in stages that might pass rap-

idly or stretch out over five or ten years. At first settlers lived
far from one another, sometimes only with Native Americans as
unwelcome neighbors. Any other white household, even one at
some distance, became part of the social circle. "We were . . .
'all told,' " Phoebe Judson remembered, "eleven families within
a radius of six or eight miles, widely separated by our holdings
of 300 and 20 acres to each family. In those days anyone residing within 20 miles was considered a neighbor." Because
there was no central meeting place, group activities like preaching took place at various locations.

With the arrival of more emigrants, white families were soon
living closer together and building stronger communities. The
troublesome Indian presence usually disappeared as Native
Americans succumbed to disease and starvation or were forced
onto reservations. The initial spatial fluidity of the community
gave way to established centers of activity. The local store, the
schoolhouse, the post office became foci of social, commercial,
and religious activities. With time, differentiation increased.
Congregations built their own houses of worship, and eventually
school districts with their schoolhouses were established. Small
villages and towns developed. As the process of growth continued, the spatial and social simplicity of an earlier time disappeared. Families naturally created ties with the people they
found most compatible and supported activities that corresponded to their vision of community life. Class and social distinctions, which most settlers thought were absent in the early
years, emerged. The very act of selecting churches and school
sites created divisions and alliances. "Each is afraid that the
other will have some preference shown him or will derive more
than his share of the benefit from the locality of the church,"
one woman explained.

Western cities provided another basis for women's civilizing
mission. While popular views of the westward movement highlight rural people as typical emigrants, the percentage of the
western population living in cities nearly matched that of the

nation as a whole. Many who went west moved directly to the urban frontier.

Some western cities emerged to service the needs of agricultural areas, but others, like San Francisco and Denver, sprang up in advance of rural settlement and grew at a pace that surpassed their speculators' wildest dreams. Other sites became cities because they supplied the emigrant trade. St. Joseph and Kansas City fitted emigrants for the trek across the plains, Salt Lake City functioned as a rest stop for travelers, Portland as a destination. Writing from Portland in 1865, Harriet Williams vividly characterized the speed of urban growth when she reported that one thousand people had arrived one Saturday with not a house to be had for rent. Santa Fe, San Antonio, and Tucson represented yet another type of city, first Spanish and then Mexican centers, that became a part of the United States through conquest. With their Spanish-speaking populations, they represented environments very different from the cities founded by Anglo settlers.

Whatever the forces behind the development of a particular city, commentators provided the general explanation. American frontiersmen were not only farmers but also enthusiastic town builders, planners, and speculators. Foreigners marveled at the swiftness of western urban development. "Nothing earns our admiration as much as the rapid rise of towns in those parts of the American Union . . . twenty-five years ago . . . still inhabited by Indians," wrote one in an 1854 Missouri immigrant guide. Urban growth was like "a stroke of magic." Phoebe Judson conveyed the drama of the urban frontier, starting with the "nightly spectacle" of "glowing fires" that cleared the land. "New buildings," she wrote, "spring up in all directions, and everything wore that indescribable air of excitement and thrill that accompanies the carving out of a town in the wilderness."

As the first stages of frontier development passed, women participated in shaping their communities' identity and character. While each settlement had its own opportunities and challenges, certain trends facilitated or hindered the process of community building.

One of the most striking features of developing agricultural frontiers that affected both individual women's lives and their attempts to create culture was the transiency of the population. Wapello County, Iowa, offers a typical picture. Less than one-third of the settlers listed on the 1850 census were there ten years later. Single men appear to have been more transient than married men, as an investigation of another Iowa county during the same ten-year period suggests. There, 91 percent of the single men but only 73 percent of those with families picked up stakes. Only 27 percent of the pioneer families there stayed put over the ten-year period.

Census data give no information about why settlers on the rural frontier moved so quickly. The Wapello County data show that those who stayed until 1860 had been more successful than those who left. (Moving in itself, however, was not necessarily a mark of failure. Of emigrants to the county in 1850, for example, those who had moved several times owned more valuable property than first-time emigrants.) This picture of a geographically mobile lower class on the frontier resembles, but is more extreme than, the pattern of urban lower-class transiency that historians have described for eastern cities in the nineteenth century. Other studies of frontier farm laborers, tenants, and land consolidation support the picture of frontier communities rapidly departing from the egalitarian, homogeneous model so often described.

Transiency, social and economic inequality, and community conflict shaped rural development. On the one hand, they suggest the ways in which experience differed according to class (although the written records that reflect the experience of the more successful and prosperous settlers yield little evidence about life at the bottom). On the other hand, they also point to the barriers those who wished to establish stable institutions and moral habits on the frontier faced.

The urban frontier differed from rural areas in a number of ways. Demographically, western cities had more youthful populations, fewer and smaller families, and sometimes small concentrations of blacks. During Portland's twenty-year pioneer period, for example, 41 to 50 percent of the women were childless, and 20 to 30 percent had only one or two children. At least half the women were under thirty, most were married, and probably most were white (Oregon forbade settlement by enslaved or free blacks). And they were surrounded by young men. The actual sex ratio depended on the nature of the town or city. In 1850, Portland, a commercial center, had more than three men for every woman; mining and cattle communities had proportionately more men than Portland, rural villages fewer. Although the ratio evened out with time, the implications for urban female life and activities were manifold. One woman commented, "There is plenty of men here. They cast sheeps eyes at Lib and Lucy's girl but they have not popt the question yet." Courting was only one leisure activity for a predominantly male society that also drank, gambled, and supported prostitution. Middle-class female concerns might not fare so well, as the editor of the Houston *Morning Sun* pointed out: "It is a source of much astonishment, and of considerable severe comment . . . that while we have a theatre, a court house, and a jail, and even a capitol in Houston, we have not a single church."

With few families and numerous single young men, the urban frontier departed radically from the middle-class ideal of a family community. Many of the men lived in boardinghouses or hotels that were, in essence, male dormitories. Though most married women did not work, they sometimes chose to live in hotels and boardinghouses rather than set up their own households. Hired help was in short supply, while "city" dwellings could be just as rough, crowded, and hard to maintain as a rural cabin. Housekeeping all too often signified drudgery, and many young women wanted none of it in the early days of urban living.

Like rural communities, towns and cities also had unstable populations. Roseburg, Oregon, a county seat and center of trade in the Umpqua Valley, was described by an 1862 visitor as "a gem of a village." He remarked on its well laid out streets, its "neat, white, frame cottages." On the surface, Roseburg was a stable frontier town of some charm. Yet census data suggest that beneath the surface, the picture was one of instability. The 1860 census revealed that over half the youthful adult work-force was composed of restless single men. Few of them stayed long in the charming town. Eighty-five percent of those appearing in the 1860 census were gone within five years. Some wives shared male mobility, but marriage was a factor that seemed to diminish men's urge to move on. While only a third of the single men stayed for more than five years, approximately two-thirds of the married men did. Still, the majority of the town's men settled in Roseburg only temporarily, and economic information suggests their stay was not a very successful one. Those with little or no personal property were the least stable.

Economic data point to social and class distinctions on the urban frontier. Although the early days of Roseburg's growth saw little in the way of economic specialization, a sense of social differentiation soon emerged. The newspaper's identification of "respectable" or "leading" local figures was echoed in private correspondence. By 1876 the *Plaindealer* was referring to an *"elite,"* mainly composed of merchants and professional men. These successful residents were politically and culturally active in town affairs; they were men of prestige. Their wives shared in their social position. Longtime residents like artisans and laborers were also considered respectable, solid members of the community. Paupers and minorities were at the bottom of the social scale.

On the urban frontier, which Roseburg exemplified, marriage seemed to retard transiency, while length of residence was associated with wealth. These correlations suggest that some married women were in a favorable position to participate in community growth, for as wives of respected men they had power and prestige. They also stayed long enough in the community to contribute to its culture. And these women were most likely to be familiar with cultural imperatives because of their social status and, in Roseburg's case, because of settlers' New England ties. But a New England background was hardly necessary. The rapid appearance of eastern papers, magazines, and novels on the frontier ensured that literate middle-class women would be reminded of their mission as mothers of civilization.

The civilizing task was far from easy. Women residing for a lengthy period on the urban frontier, like their counterparts on agricultural frontiers, constituted only a minority of the population as a whole and also a minority of their own sex. Community differences divided urban and rural areas. The large floating population of young men in a western city or town had little stake in that place's future, while families on agricultural frontiers also were often only temporary residents. Attempts to establish standards of behavior and to shape culture confronted these conditions time and time again. Mrs. Stearns, a prominent Roseburg resident, gave a graphic picture of the atmosphere that made her task difficult in a series of letters to her husband. Their sons were "running in the streets," and she trembled for their safety because of "this drink and gambaling . . . the chief Amusements night and day." The teacher played billiards, the town was agog at the latest scandal. Mrs. Kearney's baby was born and announced full term by the doctor, early by the mother, and illegitimate by the husband, who talked of divorce.

Anglos settling in former Mexican towns and cities faced somewhat different problems as they tried to impose their own standards on society. In San Antonio, the influx of Anglos overwhelmed Hispanic residents and their way of life. Until the arrival of the railroad in 1879, however, relatively few Anglos (most of them male) resided in Santa Fe. In 1880, the population of Santa Fe stood at 6,635; of these, only 797 were non-Hispanic.

The predominantly male character of the Anglo population

encouraged intermarriage between Anglo men and Hispanic women. Indeed, a majority of Santa Fe's Anglo married men in 1870 had Hispanic wives, many light-skinned and from the city's elite families. Intermarriage fostered social and cultural change, but often that change was gradual and affected both marriage partners.

Anglo women were few and, as a minority, found it difficult to transform the character of a place in a way that they believed was necessary. Even the landscape was distasteful. As one woman pointed out, "There is nothing pleasant to cast the eye on for a moment not a tree or shrub or flower." Santa Fe itself was "the most miserable squalid looking place." The preeminence of the Roman Catholic Church rendered the place disagreeable to Protestant women. Even the appearance of the city's Hispanic women was offensive, for they wore clothes that seemed too much like undergarments to be decent. Their habit of raising their skirts when crossing creeks struck one Anglo woman as "truly shocking." Rather than being industrious and moral mothers, they were "indolent" and morally lax. They smoked cigarettes and gambled.

Middle-class standards gave Anglo women an easy way to evaluate Hispanic culture and prevented them from seeing the realities. In fact, middle- and upper-class Hispanic families strictly regulated their women, although common-law marriages among the lower classes and illegitimacy were not unusual and were, in fact, increasing.

Hispanic women would find the arrival of Anglos and incorporation into the American polity a mixed blessing at best. On the one hand, the new culture that Anglo women were so intent on fostering had little tolerance for Hispanic traditions. With the incorporation of the Southwest into the United States, Hispanic women lost legal and property rights they had enjoyed under Mexico. As Anglo settlement grew, Hispanic women had fewer and fewer economic and social opportunities, perhaps one reason why illegitimacy and female-headed households were on the rise. On the other hand, Hispanic women who entered formal or informal unions with Anglo men found some advantages. Anglo men tended to be literate and more prosperous than Hispanic men. Felipa Montoya, a domestic, married a Civil War veteran who was employed as a stagecoach driver. Another woman obtained a job as an army laundress when the soldier with whom she lived attested that they were married. When the laundress's "husband" left the army, he left her as well. His indifference to his "wife's" fate suggests the long-term negative consequences for Hispanics of the Anglo presence.

Some Anglos, too, struggled in the mixed society, frustrated when their efforts to establish cultural hegemony fell short. Missionary wives, some of the earliest married Anglo women to tackle the civilizing task in the Southwest, encountered deep resistance. Alzina Read and her husband came to Santa Fe in 1849, sure that the city was their "portion of . . . [the Lord's] vineyard." The Roman Catholics to whom Alzina handed out tracts were certainly as "heathen as earth contains," although she acknowledged they had "immortal souls." But it was uphill work to be a minority in such a setting. When the Reverend Lewis Smith and his wife began their school in 1852, Hispanic Roman Catholic parents kept their children away from the Protestant missionaries. Harriet Shaw, who also tried teaching, eventually decided making and selling butter and cheese and rearing her children were more rewarding than a frustrating attempt to keep school.

In Roseburg, Oregon, Mrs. Stearns was more hopeful about the future, despite the gambling, drinking, and illicit sex in which the city's white residents indulged. Most settlers did not abandon the vision of a good society just because conditions seemed unpromising. Mrs. Stearns reported that the town had taken the first steps toward establishing a free school, but she was not directly involved in formal efforts to organize it. In Roseburg, as elsewhere, it was the men who usually established political, social, and economic institutions and founded official cultural groups like lyceums and debating societies—or at least it was the men who took credit for these activities. Newspaper accounts, recording the process of community growth, focus on male achievements but provide little information on women. Occasionally, however, there is a glimpse of married women who helped to organize and staff formal social institutions. Mary Staples, for example, recalled, "Through the efforts of the ladies in 1860, a purchase of 150 volumes was made as the beginning of a Free Library," while Esther Pillsbury recorded her participation in the Okoboji Literary Society and her election as its vice president. But women more often lent support to formal institutions rather than founding them.

The social ties that women made with one another, though not formalized, were nevertheless instrumental in establishing culture on the frontier. Though few newspapers commented on such activities, letters and reminiscences attest to the early and spirited efforts of pioneer women to create their social world and its standards. Lois Holman told her mother that no sooner had she arrived in Sergeant Bluff, Iowa, than "the lades have all called on me that live here in the City whitch concists the whole of six." She went on, "I have not retirned them yet but I must begin soon or I shant get round this summer." Although the male world might regard visiting as frivolous, it created a female support system and assisted women in their attempts to regulate society. As suggested in the previous chapter, early female networks probably included women from different backgrounds, but with time, women became more selective in their choice of companions.

One function of the informal network was to share information about fashion and styles. Although it might seem puzzling as well as superficial for women in frontier communities to talk of fashion, these discussions bolstered their sense of identity and increased their feelings of control over their environment. Appropriate clothes helped to encourage and reinforce correct behavior and establish a proper society.

Informal social exchange also consoled women and clarified

group norms. Louisiana Strentzel reported spending part of a
day with Mrs. Chase, who was "in great trouble" because of her
husband's drinking. Kate Blaine listened to a homesick woman
pour out her unhappiness. The "little frail creature" loved her
husband, Kate explained, and "will smother her homesickness
and other trials, rather than permit him to know she is not
happy. It really seemed a relief to her to be able to tell me how
she felt." Female confidences helped women who were discouraged and frustrated in their roles as wives by allowing them
to express their feelings to a sympathetic listener. As they did
so, they could reaffirm the correctness of their worldview,
whether it involved the necessity of female submission or the
importance of temperance.

Female companionship also helped relieve the tedium and
burden of female work. Women helped one another cook festive
meals in preparation for community social occasions. Sewing
and quilting were often done among a circle of friends. "I went
to Mrs. Low's quilting There was 15 to quilt had 2 quilts and
there was indeed meery faces about them," reported one young
Iowa pioneer. While they worked together, women also "gos-
siped." "This afternoon," wrote Elisabeth Adams, "I go to Sewing Society at Mr. Pierces. I suppose the affairs of the town will
be discussed over the quilt." Gossip made work go fast but, like
individual exchanges, probably also served as a means of expressing anxieties, reasserting standards, exchanging important
information, and even covertly or overtly attacking male society.
Unfortunately, gossip rarely gets recorded, but the few references to it suggest these were its functions.

The group setting made necessary work more enjoyable and
also provided an occasion for sharing the creative skills fostered
by female culture. There was "commendable reciprocity in the
exhibition and distribution of new patchwork quilt designs. The
display was made with quite as much pride as is the showing
of artistic fancy-work today," one woman reported. "All plans,
patterns, ideas or innovations were pleasantly passed along . . .

This was true, likewise, of clothing cutting. Exclusiveness in the cut or trim of apparel was unthought of."

As a community developed, the informal pattern of female interaction might take on a wider social purpose. Voluntary female associations, staffed by women who had decided along with Mary Jane Hayden that "the time had come when I must do my part socially," provided a variety of services for the community at large. Even quilting became a means of social assistance, as Ellen Strang noted when she described a surprise quilting at the Lewises': "They being in great want of a [quilt]," with the guests providing the materials.

Women's cultural contributions were not limited to these informal group settings with other women. Although women were not listed on school boards in the West, or on the boards of trustees that founded early schools, they played a significant part both in establishing and servicing educational institutions. Private educational efforts were important on western frontiers, since many communities lagged in establishing common schools. Even bustling Kansas City, for example, had only one public school in the late 1850s, which could not accommodate all city children. A school census indicated that 90 percent of school-age children were not in school, though other estimates offered less gloomy figures. Although a writer for the *Journal* pointed to what seemed an obvious truth, "If our city would employ the most effectual means for a steady growth . . . let her do for education what other cities have done," not until 1867 did the city's children have classes, and then in rented quarters.

The failure of western communities to provide early public education for children reveals much about the state of western society and the process of community building. A majority of men and women failed to see free public education as an important enough social goal to press for or to pay for in the early years of a community's development. Only a minority of the pioneers (often of New England backgrounds) worked to set up public, quasi-public, or private schools, thus ensuring that some children at least would be exposed to the moral, religious, and educational values central to the nineteenth-century curriculum. Their efforts, while important, were often hindered by financial crises and temporary failures. Their influence was limited, all too often, to those children whose parents would pay. (Even as late as the 1870s and 1880s, only about 40 percent of those eligible to attend school in Jackson County, Oregon, did so. The five-dollar charge helped to deter the others.) In the long run, of course, their efforts succeeded, and free public schooling became the norm in the West as in the East.

Although men served on the boards of early community educational institutions and played a crucial part in raising money, women helped to staff them. If the frontier was anything like the East, as many as one-fifth to one-quarter of the women taught at some time in their lives. In many cases, women started the educational process. Reminiscences and letters almost always point to a mother or female neighbor as the first teacher. Early on, married women often set up simple schools in their own homes, realizing, as did Mollie Sanford's mother, "that the children ought to be in school." These impromptu schools had little permanence, serving neighbors and family for a few months a year when nothing else was available. Later, as communities built schoolhouses, women were drafted to teach. "Next arose the question of teacher," one woman wrote, describing the informal process of selection in her frontier community. "Somebody suggested that Mrs. Lewis, the wife of our community doctor, would be a good teacher. I do not know how it was determined that she was qualified, but she was chosen by a show of hands, and accepted the post." As the process of selection became more sophisticated and as public education finally became a reality on the frontier, women continued to staff city and country schools; most often they were confined to the primary department as either teachers or directors.

Although women's ability financially to support education

was limited, they did provide some monetary assistance for hard-pressed schools. Tabitha Brown, who was instrumental in establishing an early private school in Oregon, showed generosity that was exceptional, not only for the size of her gifts but also because her benevolence was recorded. The widowed grandmother donated land, a house, $550 of her earnings, and a bell before her death in 1857. Perhaps just as important as these contributions were women's attempts to support boards and trustees in their difficult educational ventures. Brown's contributions are again instructive. One account of her life reveals that male trustees decided to discontinue the school, "but the resolution had been heard through the cracks in the ceiling of the cabin by Mrs. Clark, Mrs. Smith, and Mrs. Brown, and they plead with the men to reverse it, with the result that the school continued."

For married women, teaching could be viewed as a natural extension of motherhood and, thus, an eminently respectable occupation. Some also saw teaching as a means of capitalizing on women's moral and religious influence, as Catharine Beecher had suggested, while others stressed the importance of maintaining social and cultural standards in the West. In advertising for the second term of her early log-cabin school in Oregon City, Mrs. Thornton assured prospective students and their families that "strict attention will be given not only to the intellectual improvement of the pupils, but also to their morals and manners." Even on the frontier, female teachers offered instruction in "all the branches usually comprised in a thorough English education, together with plain and fancy needle-work, drawing, and painting in mezzotints and water-colors." The early appearance of female academies run by women and teaching the "female arts" in rough towns like Houston suggests their determination to pass on female culture.

Of course, moral and cultural goals did not preclude pragmatic concerns. Agnes Sengstacken found "my school teaching quite a relaxation" from "my family and my housework," while

Sarah Everett hoped to make money for her dairying by teaching. Sarah even considered leaving her baby with a neighbor and taking her five-year-old "boarding around" with her so that she could take a teaching job. Whatever the motives that led them to teach, married women helped both to establish and to support educational institutions in their communities in the years when support was most needed.

Single women, though always a minority of adult women on the frontier, made up the majority of female teachers, and it was as teachers that they helped shape their society most directly. Teaching represented, as Catharine Beecher had pointed out, a woman's "road to honourable independence and extensive usefulness where she need not outstep the prescribed boundaries of feminine modesty." Women gradually came to dominate the teaching field in the West, as in the East. In the early days, even though women set up schools at home and taught spring schools, men usually taught winter schools, which teenage boys, busy with farmwork in the spring, attended. In Iowa Territory, for example, only 23 of the 124 teachers were women in 1848; in less than two decades, however, women had taken over the profession. An 1854 report suggested the reason for the change: women would work for half what men demanded. Teaching, then, became women's work as the community matured and men found better-paying opportunities.

At least two sorts of single women decided to teach in the West. Women like Mollie Sanford wanted jobs to earn money and pass a few years until they married. Teaching was their most attractive alternative, but it was viewed as temporary. As Fannie Case confided to a friend, "I cannot say that teaching is perfectly congeniel to my taste—but—well, I might as well say it, but it is very confidential, you know, I think there is nothing so nice as housekeeping, in a little home of one's own, and I have no hopes that there is such bliss in store for me, think teaching second best." Others, however, came from the East as part of the crusade to civilize the West. Teaching was their vocation. The Board of National Popular Education sent over a quarter of its teachers to the trans-Mississippi West. Most of them stayed in the West; some married, an event "incidental to the main purpose of sending teachers . . . West" but one allowing them to "form connexions which will increase their power of doing good."

No matter why women chose to teach, the job itself had little security. When schools failed to materialize or collapsed through lack of support, would-be teachers found themselves unemployed. When they worked, many discovered, often to their dismay, that they were the focus of community interest. Some of this was to be expected. Settlers had raised the schoolhouse and saw it as both an educational and a community center. Their proprietary sense was evident in the process of teacher selection, in their attendance at periodic school exhibitions, and in the practice of having teachers board with members of the community. But the constant surveillance in and out of school, the need to prove competence and character, the bad food, poor quarters, and even household chores sometimes involved in boarding around led some to bemoan their situation. "I find among strangers we are judged by outward appearances," one Iowa teacher sadly observed, "and that we cannot be to careful in giving the world's people occasion for slander."

Classroom conditions hindered teaching. Short terms of three months were educationally limiting. The wide range of students' ages forced a teacher to do a little of everything. One Ashland, Oregon, schoolhouse, for example, had twenty-eight pupils, all in one room, during the 1859–1860 term. Seven were between five and nine, thirteen between ten and fourteen, four between fifteen and twenty, and another four between twenty and twenty-nine. Not only were students of different ages, they were differently equipped. Each student brought books from home, thus complicating instruction even more. Finally, a casual attitude toward school made attendance irregular and unpredictable.

Teachers' letters and journals stress the effort and unpleasantness of teaching in the authoritarian manner that conditions and pedagogical theory suggested. "I have only 11 scholars," wrote one woman to her aunt, "but I am glad I have no more for it is all I can do to manage them. I have to use my ruler pretty often." Mollie Sanford's response to the requirements of the classroom was similar, and she appeared torn between an image of woman as nurturer and the reality of teacher as disciplinarian. "I was thinking the other day how nicely and smoothly I was getting along," she wrote in her journal. "Not an unpleasant event had occurred at school . . . But a day or two ago I had to inflict my first corporal punishment. After exhausting my powers of moral suasion with little Johnnie Morton, to establish my authority and make an example, I chastised him very mildly."

When Johnnie didn't come to school for a few days, Mollie, conscious of possible criticism, visited the troublesome boy at home. Discipline, necessary as it was, might provoke community disapproval. An irate father suggested limits to the teacher's authority. "I am very sorry to informe that in my opinion you have Shoed to me that you are unfit to keep a School," he wrote, "if you hit my boy in the face accidently that will be different but if on purpos . . . you are unfit . . . I shall in forme the Superintendant in which this Scool has been commeced and how it Seames to go on." An Iowa schoolteacher fared even worse and was brought to court, charged with "assault and battery by punishing in an immoderate and cruel manner one Peter John Matthew," and found guilty. No wonder one of the teachers confessed, "I wish this term was through. I am becoming tired of teaching." Few probably stuck with teaching for more than two years.

Teachers whose goals included attention to their pupils' "precious undying souls," and the advancement "of culture and refinement among the female of the regions," faced similar problems. Moreover, their high sense of purpose and their unmarried status often made them feel lonely in their new communities. Perry, Arkansas, was a "benighted portion of the west," Maria Atwater commented to the Board of National Popular Education.

The perceived "stupor" of pupils and parents undermined attempts to provide an education that would "soften the asperities of tempers, check the waywardness of . . . appetite and train . . . [the] habits of industry." Ambitious goals may well have made students appear even more backward than they were and progress slower. Parental indifference sometimes hampered efforts to establish Sunday schools, too. As one Missouri teacher reported, "They have plenty of time to buy and sell, and many of them desecrate the Sabbath by drinking, horse racing and gambling." Another described her successful Sunday school, which attracted mothers and children. Even so, she found herself not altogether pleased. It was hard, she admitted, to adjust to mothers' nursing their babies during her instruction.

Sensitive to their Christian responsibilities, these teachers confronted their own inadequacies. "I do feel very incapable" of doing good, wrote one teacher from Missouri in 1853. "I have had so little religious experience myself. Pray for me that I may be taught of God how to teach and that my feeble efforts to serve Christ, may be blessed." For all the difficulties they encountered, however, most of them were aware of a great opportunity to extend culture. And their communities responded with occasional raises and even appreciation for their good "influence in the community."

Somewhat unexpectedly, these missionary teachers found themselves departing from the very norms they expected to maintain. In the absence of permanent churches, they took on religious responsibilities themselves. "It seems rather hard that neither of these men are willing to open the [Sabbath] School by prayers," one teacher reported, "but since they are not, I feel it my duty to do so." Another teacher, similarly situated, indicated how fast she forgot proprieties when duty called. "The question whether a woman should pray in such a public place was . . . easily answered in my mind," she wrote.

Their comments highlight the paradoxical side to women's

civilizing activities. Devotion to "duty" and efforts to build community could result in unconventional behavior in the same way that early burdens of pioneer farming had done. Yet few of the women went beyond the rationalization of duty to claim that their new activities were appropriate for all women. As a group, they were conscious of conventional female norms, eager to observe and spread them.

Although the highest hopes of these teachers may have been dashed as they embarked on their ambitious program of molding minds and souls and of spreading civilized values, although they were often depressed, many eventually saw signs of progress on the frontier. Perhaps the culture they were able to communicate was diluted, but as the prejudice of the communities disappeared, as teachers succeeded in imparting even simple standards to children, they felt they had achieved something worthwhile. The proof was that so many sent out by the Board of National Popular Education stayed. "I like the West so much, and see so much need of teaching here, that I have no intention of ever going home to stay," wrote one, while another confessed, "I do *not* feel like a stranger in a strange land." For all its frustrations, teaching seemed to offer firm evidence to some women that their civilizing mission was succeeding.

Certainly teaching offered the most satisfying career for single women. Although most adult women on the frontier were married or would marry, there were increasing numbers of single women who needed or wanted to work. In Portland, for example, single women constituted 22 percent of the adult female population in 1860. By 1880, the percentage had risen to over 29 percent. Working women often expressed the desire to be useful and to avoid being an economic drain on their families. "Next winter *I must* be where I can make some money for myself," Irene Calbraith wrote to her father, "instead of being a dead expense on you. I *must* and I *will*."

Rural communities offered few opportunities for paid employment aside from teaching, and so needy or enterprising young women, like Mollie Sanford, went to urban areas to "look about for something to do to help myself . . . duty and necessity call me." They found respectable jobs as domestics, nurses, teachers, seamstresses, clerks, or decided to leave the respectable world behind and take up prostitution. None of these occupations paid much, nor were they particularly rewarding in other respects. Mollie, working as a dressmaker and seamstress, reflected, "I do often wish that I might be something more than a mere machine. There is something dull in sitting here day by day, planning this garment and making that." Despite her pluck and initiative, she considered the unappealing job "my destiny just now. There does not seem to be much that a girl *can* do here." Census data support her complaint. The 1870 census showed 45 percent of the single women in Portland, for example, working, mostly as domestics. For white women, these jobs were temporary, their monotony to be ended by marriage. For the few black women in the West (never more than 1 percent of the population of the Rocky Mountain and Pacific states), domestic service was a lifelong occupation because their husbands did not earn enough to support their families. With the coming of industrialization to the West within a generation, the number of job opportunities multiplied, but women's position did not improve much. Working women in Kansas in the late 1880s hardly made enough to break even. Working women in the West were undervalued and underpaid.

It was as wives, then, that most women contributed to their communities. Reestablishing Protestant institutions on the frontier represented one of their greatest challenges. From the beginning of the vast migration west, many had feared that the frontier would become a center of religious indifference. By 1850, eastern missionary societies were spending $500,000 a year on western missionary work and had sent out and helped support over twenty-six hundred ministers for "destitute" frontier communities. By aiding missionaries and by preparing the way for them, women helped to establish religious institutions on a firm basis. As they did so, they, too, discovered unexpected opportunities for autonomy, although, like the teachers, these women rarely capitalized on these opportunities.

Westward migration posed many problems for Protestant denominations. Creating and sustaining new congregations when members of the community were scattered, held different denominational loyalties, and were out of the habit of regular churchgoing and giving were difficult. Buildings had to be constructed, maintained, and then used. As the Reverend Milton Starr lamented, "Even the New England element among us seem in some measure to have forgotten their early training," while the Reverend Oswold in Kansas agreed, saying, "It has become entirely easy and natural, to remain at home all day Sunday."

Apparently, however, women in the West, like their eastern counterparts, remembered their religious duty better than men, so much so that the frontier "congregation is mostly *(femenine).*" These steadfast women were particularly important at the beginning of missionary work, when ministers were trying to establish the habit of regular worship. Perhaps just as crucial as their attendance was the encouragement women gave to missionaries, who were often deeply depressed by their apparent failure. So Mrs. Thornton lifted the spirits of the Reverend Gray, who recounted how she "assured that the *result* was greater than I was able to perceive. She said she had observed a marked increase in the piety of some of our church members since I came here; that the young people were more interested—that I was well fitted for this place &c." It was this kind of support that comforted missionaries as they sought to Christianize the West.

By mid-century, ministers judged success by conversions and membership figures. Women not only swelled membership rolls but were quickly recognized as recruiters and forcibly reminded of their responsibilities. The Reverend Reuben Gaylord, an Iowa missionary of the 1840s, "took occasion before the meeting closed to make some remarks upon the duty of mothers and the power which God had given them over their children. Several wept freely." Circuit rider John Dyer pointed out that maternal recruiting must even be done at life's last moments, for a mother's parting religious advice "often brings the children to Christ." Women were also encouraged to exercise their influence on their husbands and gain them and incidentally their assets for Christ. "Some of the female members have husbands," wrote one candid Oregon missionary, "who are not professors —who might give much more than they do—that is allow their wives to, which they would willingly do—but they feel a restraint in that particular—of course the wife must always exercise prudence in such a case."

Many women found that church membership and activities satisfied deep spiritual needs. But their support for religion also related to their role as community builders. During the long trip over the Oregon Trail, numerous women had noted how they missed observing the Sabbath. The reestablishment of services linked them to the world they had left and symbolized their determination to make the West like the East. Christian fellowship reinforced and publicized social and moral standards and clarified values. Skimpy church records show how congregations tried to uphold norms by disciplining errant members and rejecting them if they refused to mend their ways. Such incidents must have provided the substance for many lively community discussions. The Pleasant Grove Presbyterian Church, for example, recorded the case of Mrs. Pira Rudolph, who "having absented herself from the stated ministration of the word for the past year or more and various reports derogatory to her character as a christian coming to the ears of the Session she was visited by them, and she expressed a desire to have her name striken from the roll." The West Union Baptist Church records described an unseemly altercation between Sister Zachary and Sister Constable. Sister Zachary, the minutes noted, "having circulated Slanderous reports against the character of Sister C and having failed to prove them and having refused the call of the church when cited to attend and wilfully so, is considered disorderly, and unworthy [of] the fellowship of the church." Mrs. Constable was later in trouble for a party given at her house. While these policing activities perhaps strike the modern observer as excessive, they defined the highest standards of conduct for the community. They gave believers the courage to struggle on. Jane Walrud's diary shows the impact religious fellowship could have as she reported how she had been able to resist "the tempter [who] came and gave a hard try."

Religion also offered some women the opportunity for leadership. In the days before formal churches were organized, women, like those in Sublimity, Oregon, who offered their parlors for services became key figures in providing religious exercises for their communities. In Kansas, Lois Murray played a much more important part than hosting preachers in her home. She became church school superintendent and began to read sermons in the community Sabbath school. Although she was careful to seek her husband's approval, the "mission" God had given her led her to speak at numerous meetings and even to officiate at funerals. It was "from a sense of duty I complied; and felt I had merely filled a servant's place," she explained. Though few women probably interpreted their religious duty so expansively, others did work in Sunday schools, often the only continuing religious activity in a community served by itinerant preachers. Women instituted these schools, recruited students, taught them, and even attended regional conferences to report on their progress.

Camp meetings, revivals, and prayer meetings also provided leadership possibilities. Whether open to both men and women or to women only, the fluid format of the prayer meeting encouraged participation, and women took advantage of the opportunity to act freely. "Everybody who wished to do so could take part by offering a prayer, making a talk, or singing a song as the spirit moved." The Reverend Atkinson gave a good picture of female activism in his description of an 1848 prayer meeting: "I preached, after which a prayer meeting was held. The impenitent were invited to the anxious seat. Some women spoke. Two screamed very loud and grasped hands, uttering many things incoherently." Although Atkinson's Congregational background made him uncomfortable with the women's behavior, they provided a dramatic focus for the meeting. And though he might disapprove of emotional women, Atkinson was shrewd enough to realize how instrumental they were in bringing about conversions and membership. They could hardly be discouraged.

Female church groups also provided women with some power. The Reverend Knight attested, "As is always the case in the infancy of Christian efforts, we have been greatly indebted to the ladies of our congregation for material aid. By their sewing society &c. they have furnished fuel and lights and kept up repairs." The sums women raised to support religious causes were often substantial; the money was desperately needed on the frontier, where eastern support for missionary work was inadequate and where expenses were so high. Women's fund-raising abilities thus gave them a real, if limited, power. Although the minister might point out specific needs, the women made the money and the decisions. Records of the Ladies Guild of St. Paul's Episcopal Church in Oregon City, for example, reported that the rector requested help in building a rectory porch. "After some talk on the subject," the minutes revealed, "it was concluded to lay it on the table until the next regular meeting." Not until the following year did the rector get his porch. And that same year, the vestry begged the women for $150 to meet year-end expenses.

As Ephraim Adams evaluated the contributions of women to frontier religion, he commented, "What wonder if there were some praying and talking then, and voting too, other than that done by the brethren?" His comments suggested the freedoms and implied the boundaries of the church world for women.

Although religion in the West offered women scope and influence, in the end it also confined them to their socially established role. Instrumental as Lois Murray had been in supporting the religious life of her early community in Kansas, she wrote the letter "requesting that ministers might visit us, when God might direct." Formal church organizations excluded women. Despite her position as assistant superintendent of the Sabbath school, and her appearance at the quarterly conference to report on it, Ketturah Belknap found herself not on the church board but driving "home with perhaps two or thre Lady visitors for we al ways expected friends from distant parts of the circuit to be entertained." And when in Keokuk, Iowa, a few Episcopalian women gathered into a society in 1850 and determined to form a church, the vestry was composed entirely of men who were not even Episcopalians.

On western frontiers, churchwomen as well as churchmen continued to operate according to prevailing gender expectations. Most women viewed the minister as "sent of God" and expected men to regulate the larger affairs of the church. Ministers, for all their dependence on women, shared the prevailing ideas of society. And, financially pressed, they still anticipated that men would provide the bulk of the monetary support. The Reverend Chamberlain was only expressing a typical attitude when he wrote, "We greatly need a few *faithful laboring* male members. I sometimes feel I stand almost alone in the great work."

It may be that the religious activities of women in their frontier communities eventually contributed to a broadening understanding of female religious roles. But women's records show little evidence that they overtly resented their displacement or their secondary position. Subconsciously, some of them may have harbored rebellious feelings. Certainly, that Lois Murray continued some of her informal services even after the circuit rider served her Kansas community is suggestive. Her justification indicated she was unwilling to accept the common definition of woman's place. "From a sense of duty, I complyed [and attended to religious services] and felt I had merely filled a servant's place," she explained. And the decision of St. Paul's Ladies Guild to keep the rector dangling on the matter of his rectory porch may imply a similar resentment of limited female power within the church. But the signs of discontent are few.

Of all the women involved in establishing Christ's kingdom in the West, missionary wives were doubtless the ones with the highest religious and cultural purposes and the highest standards. Their efforts suggest both the problems and successes involved in building frontier communities. The women constituted a small but influential group. Most of the 2,679 missionaries sent from the East to spread the gospel to white settlers on the frontier probably were married, for they were counseled and counseled others to bring wives with them. An Iowa band received typical advice when it brought up the marriage question: "Wives are the cheapest things in all Iowa. Bring wives! Bring Yankee wives, that are not afraid of a checked apron, and who can pail the cow, and churn the butter."

Women who went west as missionary wives initially viewed themselves as missionaries first and wives second. If young Cushing Eells's marriage proposal lacked some of the standard romantic trappings, it was certainly appropriate for a woman who had written in her school copybook, "I go, my friend, where heathen dwell; / Then if on earth we meet no more, / Accept this cordial, short farewell, / Till we meet on Canaan's shore." Asked if she were willing to be a *missionary* (rather than a wife), Myra replied, "I doubt whether you could have asked any one who would have been more willing."

Few anticipated the potential conflict between the two roles. Nor did their religious enthusiasm and lofty idealism prepare them for the reality of missionary work.

Although often initially impressed by the frontier's potential for fruitful church work, couples soon discovered how hard it was to attract steadfast supporters. The realization of the importance of female support led wives to take on heavy recruiting and social responsibilities, which had both emotional and physical costs.

Ministers' wives played an important role in attracting other women to church activities. As the Reverend Tenney testified, "The only reputable social circle rallied about the church as a center, though the town ladies did not enter the church organization. The pastor's wife became the center of female influence." As a woman of influence, the minister's wife assumed the duty of visiting, taking "every opportunity to invite sinners to come to the Saviour." In her own home and in the community, she served as a model of Christian womanhood. She also was an informal recruiting agent for her husband. The Reverend Atkinson realized that recruiting demanded entertaining. "It is very important for me to have visitors," he remarked.

As teachers in Sunday schools and regular schools, as organizers of prayer meetings and other church groups, the women also labored to create Christian society in the West. Saving souls turned out to be no easy matter, but at least the task was central to the religious mission. Few wives, however, had realized that religious duties might take second place to their efforts as fund-raisers. They were pulled into fund-raising for the church, organizing and canvassing for operating funds. One Methodist minister's wife collected the money needed to pay off the church mortgage. But the women soon discovered they must also help support their own families. Missionary subsidies were woefully meager, no matter what the denomination. Men had the responsibilities of preaching, visiting, and traveling; women were left to earn money. So women taught not only because teaching might serve a religious purpose but because it paid. The Reverend Milton Starr, reporting from Tacoma, wrote, "Our first effort here was to instruct a few of our neighbors children in our own house. My wife is now teaching . . . about 12 schollars on an average . . . This helps a little by way of support." Missionary wives also took in boarders for cash, even sold butter, and almost always did their housework without hired help, all the while practicing rigid economy. Their husbands' letters are full of descriptions of the workloads of their wives and breakdowns caused by fatigue.

The trials of missionary life increased as women discovered the necessity of playing several roles simultaneously. At the beginning of missionary work, most of the women were young and childless. But with the coming of children, domestic demands clashed with religious vocation and with a wife's duties as helpmate. The life of Elkannah and Mary Walker in the 1850s was punctuated with strife as he sought to persuade her that her first obligation was to him. As an itinerant minister, he wrote, living "without you is the greatest earthly sacrifice I have to make and if I could have you with me, I should regard it as the greatest earthly comfort. You have no idea how strong is my feeling on this point. You gave yourself to be a minister's wife before you became a wife & mother." Mary Walker was not to be persuaded; other women sadly set aside their original hopes. "How forcibly do I realize that my husband has got to be the laborer for the church . . . for the Lord," wrote one wife in the early 1850s, "whilst my duty is to take care of him and make *home* my paramount field of action. I fear I am not reconciled to this my views being so different from the duties of a minister's wife especially a missionary's wife I have literally as much as I can do to take care of myself, my husband, my dear babes, whereas I thought my duties would be almost wholly spiritual I have felt unhappy because I have not been able to teach. I came here for that purpose. I love to teach but if domestic toiles are to be my care I will yield obediently." Though the appeal to duty may have helped, submission was difficult and at times tinged with resentment. Mrs. Eells, who "yielded with regret" to her husband's dutiful decision to move to the rough frontier of Walla Walla, announced flatly when their house burned after ten years, "We can leave now; we have nothing to leave." Her son's comment that those years "were ever uncongenial to her" suggests her embittered feelings.

Mrs. Eells disliked Walla Walla because of "the life, the

lonely farm work, and the want of society." Perhaps she disliked it, too, because, in that remote place, it was difficult to realize the many goals of missionary life, which sought to create a West populated by industrious, faithful people living moral, pious, and temperate lives. Such a social vision was noble and corresponded to the nineteenth century's understanding of woman's civilizing mission. But this was not the West that emerged. Although western society did not lapse into barbarism, drinking and other social vices flourished. Many people stubbornly refused to attend church. Secular amusements continued to attract a spirited following despite denunciation by the godly. One young woman captured the flavor of the confrontation between the secular and the religious. "The Church members did not like [dancing]," she wrote, "and some of them got a little 'huffy' about it, but we did not care a fig for them. One of the young ladies told the minister that if he would preach a sermon, we would not dance, but we must either have a sermon or dance. The minister took his hat in hand."

By so narrowly defining the nature of a good society, missionary women felt defeated at times, even though they played a significant part in the development of the West. As ministers' wives and as teachers, they occupied positions of visibility and respect in their communities. They used their status to make others aware of the highest standards of nineteenth-century culture and provided a clear frame of reference for evaluating frontier life. Their work made it impossible for new communities to forget their links with American society as a whole.

Yet, for years, the women could see only failure. Religious commitment appeared to be weak in the West, and missionaries and their wives seemed unable to do much about it. Denominational rivalry tempted the "faithful" to transfer allegiances, but no denomination had impressive growth statistics. One study of church membership suggests that only one out of every three or four persons was a formal member of any church in the West.

No wonder missionaries and their wives were often deeply discouraged. Yet the frontier was not as irreligious as they thought. Formal church membership nationwide included no more than 23 percent of the population in 1866. But missionaries judged their achievements by their ambitious hopes and contrasted their gains with an idealized picture of religion in the East. And they correctly noted the different atmosphere of western society. Many of the props that maintained the semblance of religion in the East—churches, bells, the quiet Sabbath—were absent in the West, while the competition from visiting, horse racing, and relaxing was all too strong. The West was a godless place for the godly.

Consolation from the home missionary board sometimes lifted the depression that missionary couples seemed routinely to experience. But low spirits soon returned. Because they were certain their objectives were righteous, they came to question the vitality of their faith. Finally, some shifted to more promising fields of endeavor. "The question I asked my self," the Reverend Kellogg wrote, "was this: in which sphere can I do the most good?" For Kellogg it was college teaching, for Atkinson a major church in Portland, where he gained affluence and a Chinese houseboy by 1870. For others, the answer was to return to the East. Although men ostensibly made these decisions, evidence suggests that exhausted and frustrated wives played a part in motivating career changes.

"It is not wise to overdo and thus sacrifice the future to the present," Atkinson noted. "Many do this and die before their time." Eventually, many who, like Atkinson, stayed with their religious vocation reinterpreted their mission. Rather than turning to conversion and membership figures to assess their effectiveness, they counted the number of church buildings, clergy, and financial assets. Institutional growth assuaged consciences. What part women played in redefining the religious mission is not clear. Yet as early fund-raisers and church builders, women may well have been involved in the increasing emphasis on institutional expansion. Certainly, their recollections of their husbands' careers tell a story not of defeat but of gradual success.

Of course, most women did not define success as narrowly as missionary wives once did. Those who flocked to church and joined sewing circles but never became church members sympathized with some but not all the goals missionary women espoused. Yet even less ambitious attempts to establish social institutions on the frontier ran into obstacles. Activities that women supported were only partially successful at first. Most institutions had a fragile existence as a shifting population undercut attempts to create stability: schools were not maintained every year; literary societies and sometimes newspapers disappeared within months; even churches disappeared. Habits like drinking and gambling persisted.

Yet, by and large, there is an accumulation of evidence that women fulfilled important aspects of their western mission. First of all, family life survived. Reminiscences of pioneer women were often cast in dramatic terms, picturing their families triumphing over the wilderness. Domestic ideology and the hard work of women deserve much of the credit. Communities were established and grew, with goodly if not godly institutions offering opportunities for social interaction.

The mere existence of Sabbath services, whether they produced conversions or not, symbolized community progress and provided the congregation with an opportunity for friendly intercourse. Rachel Applegate's enjoyment of the Sabbath was social not spiritual. "To day is sunday," she wrote, "and I have just got back from Church—seen every body." Likewise, dances, frowned on by the clergy, and parties indicated a goodly society that was "very enjoyable compared to our earlier pioneer life," as one woman pointed out.

As such comments suggest, women, in time, used a new frame of reference to judge the progress of their pioneer communities. Instead of comparing the new life to the old in the

East, settlers compared the present to the past on the frontier. From this perspective, the advance of society was clear. Isolation had disappeared, and institutions had emerged. Women could see the part they had played in initiating, supporting, and maintaining community growth and found a sense of satisfaction in their contributions. As material conveniences became more readily available and better communications with the East were established, women began to "feel quite civilized" and even told themselves that their pioneer experiences and the pioneer stage of society had ended.

Census data suggest that only a minority of women lived in one community over an extended period. At first, their efforts to establish and sustain social institutions and civilized habits may have seemed inadequate and unsuccessful. They may well not have imposed their views on temporary residents, although the institutions they supported must have influenced them. But they, too, could see progress when they contrasted their present situation to their earliest days on the frontier. Moreover, the few who remained within one community eventually had the satisfaction of seeing their standards established as the community's, just because they stayed and because they belonged to the most prominent and prestigious social groups, with visibility and the means of expressing their point of view. And, as one study of frontier culture indicates, later emigrants, attracted by a community's character, tended to reinforce early cultural patterns and strengthen dominant values. The transients became less important as the number of like-minded settlers grew. Community histories that describe growth from the perspective of the stable minority tell a story of success.

That the frontier experience reinforced many conventional familial and cultural ideals is apparent in an examination of domestic ideology in the West. Frontier images of women were closely tied to images of middle-class women current in the East. The concept of woman as lady, the heart of domestic ideology, survived; it was vivid in songs and poems. However hard it was to live the genteel life, the image's persistence indicates the continuing desirability of the ideal and the efforts made to attain it. More common was the characterization of woman as wife and helpmate. This view deemphasized gentility and stressed the desirability of initiative, resourcefulness, and energy. The image reflected the qualities needed on the frontier, but essentially the image was still a domestic one, and, in keeping with conventional nineteenth-century ideas, women were perceived as selfless creatures living to serve others rather than themselves.

Although the frontier experience resulted in an emphasis on certain "masculine" qualities as desirable for western women, the necessary domestic framework remained intact and was, in fact, strengthened by frontier life. Women were extolled as mothers, wives, and civilizers. Their confrontation with the wilderness reaffirmed their image as molders of civilization, through church, school, and social activities. The reality of the frontier, far from rejecting the civilizing mission, reaffirmed it.

5

"The Rarest Commodity . . .
Are Women"

In 1849, a disease that had swiftly assumed the proportions of a national epidemic struck the pioneer inhabitants of a simple log cabin on the Missouri plains. Mr. Wilson, a farmer in his early forties, exhibited all the telltale symptoms of a sickness affecting males most virulently: an unquenchable thirst for fortune, a firm conviction that he had nothing to lose by abandoning his home, and a compelling desire to be off to California at once. What was unusual about the course of gold fever in the Wilson household, however, was that his young wife was equally infected and was determined to accompany her husband west. "I would not be left behind," she recalled more than thirty years later. "I thought where he could go I could, and where I went I could take my two little toddling babies." Undaunted by their relative ignorance of California and gold mining, the Wilsons set off across the plains to make their fortune. Thousands of Americans and Europeans flocked to California by land and sea. For, as Luzena Wilson explained, "the gold excitement spread like wildfire," not only sweeping through Missouri, but through all the other states and Europe as well.

California, with its promise of instant riches, rapidly attracted a motley crowd of newcomers from diverse cultural backgrounds. On the eve of the gold rush, the territory was a quiet backwater with a population of 150,000 Native Americans and about 14,000 white and Hispanic inhabitants. Many of the Anglos were married to Hispanic women from elite families and had adapted to the Californio way of life. A year later, the amazing transformation was well under way. California's non-Indian population approached 100,000; of these, 80,000 came from the states, 3,000 from Europe, 13,000 from Latin and South America, and 4,000 from China. By the end of 1852, the number of newcomers had more than doubled, while the Native Americans had begun a dangerous spiral of decline, their numbers dropping by 80 percent during the 1850s. The Wilsons were thus part of a vast migration of fortune seekers, but they were unusual because they came as a family. Only about 5 percent of early California gold rushers were women and children.

California was the first and most spectacular of several mining frontiers in the trans-Mississippi West. Although flush times rapidly petered out and gold production declined, continuing dreams of striking it rich provided emigrants for subsequent rushes to other areas. In 1858, rumors of gold in British Columbia sent twenty-five thousand to thirty thousand to Canada, many of them from California. In 1859, reports of gold in Colorado triggered what was to become the second largest mining rush in the West, attracting experienced forty-niners as well as tenderfeet from the Midwest and South. Within three or four seasons, fortune seekers had depleted the easily mined deposits, and the central Rockies mining frontier collapsed. But discoveries in the Pacific Northwest during the early 1860s and in Montana and Idaho toward the end of the decade kept the fantasy of riches alive and miners on the move. In the mid-1870s, prospectors thronged to the Black Hills of South Dakota, lured by gold once more.

Over several decades, then, the mining frontier shifted its location as metal deposits were discovered, exploited, and exhausted. In the earliest stages of a mining rush, fortune seekers worked alone or in small groups, hunting for "placer" gold (miner slang for loose ore that had eroded away from its original rock formation). As these deposits ran out, it became apparent that retrieving gold or silver embedded in solid rock or in deep gravel demanded a sophisticated technological approach and capital. In time, the necessary expertise developed. Later mining frontiers were exploited less by individuals operating independently or in small groups than by corporate and industrial concerns with miners working as wage earners. Even as early as 1852 in California, the financial demands of mining had transformed most of the miners into wage earners.

Dramatic stories of the gold rushes, the dazzling riches, the life in the mining camps caught the imagination of contemporaries, and the lore of the gold rush became a part of American popular culture. With the exception of the mining-frontier prostitute, pictured either as a woman with a heart of gold or as a predatory female ("Hangtown Gals are plump and rosy, / Hair in ringlets mighty cozy, / Painted cheeks and gassy bonnets; / Touch them and they'll sting like hornets"), women, especially nonwhite women, were not remembered. In some ways, this was hardly surprising. In 1850, California's white population was over 90 percent male; in the mining camps, the figure was probably higher. Yet while women's participation in the mining rushes did not catch the popular imagination, women like Luzena Wilson were there. Although Eliza Farnham advised her readers in her 1856 book, *California, In-Doors and Out*, that "none but the pure and stronghearted of my sex should come alone to this land," both strong and weakhearted, single and married women came to California first and to other mining frontiers later.

Because there were so few white women on the mining frontier, they were highly visible. In 1853, the appearance of four women in Nevada City "caused a great sensation . . . [for] there has never arrived more than one lady at a time before." As one of the women reported, "the men stand and gaze at us with mouth and eyes wide open, every time we go out." While the arrival of women gave men the opportunity to feast their eyes on the female form, women's presence had a symbolic significance for the new and rough society. Despite the skewed sex ratio and the volatile mix of ethnic groups vying for riches, and despite the belief that gold fever reduced rootless men to a condition far more debased than that of ordinary men, nineteenth-century society still expected middle-class women to tame and refine the mining frontier. As Farnham pointed out in her influential publication, "There is no inviolate fireside in California that is not an altar; no honorable woman but is a missionary of virtue, morality, happiness, and peace, to a circle of careworn, troubled, and often, alas, demoralized men." Farnham believed that only "the presence of women" would provide an "efficient remedy for these great evils" that California was experiencing. But she realized that the mining frontier tested female influence. "It is hard to natures, that have not more than common strength," she wrote, "to live uprightly and purely, when they feel that there is no sympathy with their life, in those who surround them—and, still worse, no faith." California and the later mining frontiers posed one of the nineteenth century's greatest challenges to the conventional wisdom that women were shapers and civilizers of society. Would white women mold the new society on the mining frontier, as Farnham hoped, or be molded by it, as she feared? This was just one of the questions California and the other mining frontiers raised for the women who came there and for the culture that accorded them such significant moral influence.

While Farnham hinted at the presence of disreputable women in California, notably absent from her book is any real consideration of women who did not belong to the white middle class. Indian women, Hispanic Californio residents, South American, Chinese, and European emigrants represented different and competing models of womanhood. In Farnham's eyes, such models were inadequate to the challenges of taming the California frontier and morally and socially deficient. Although, in the long run, none of these women were able to impose their version of womanhood on mining society, their presence made the task of creating a model middle-class society in California difficult.

How various women participated in the mining rushes and what the experiences meant to them and to American culture make a complex story. Its complexity is immediately apparent in white women's responses to the mining frontier. Luzena Wilson arrived in Sacramento to find that a miner was willing to pay her ten dollars for a biscuit made by a woman. The incident triggered fantasies. "In my dreams that night," she confessed, "I saw crowds of bearded miners striking gold from the earth with every blow of the pick, each one seeming to leave a share for me." Yet Martha Hitchcock wrote to her sister-in-law in 1851 that California disappointed her: "The more I see of men, the more I am disgusted with them—they are rather worse too, in California, than anywhere else—this is the Paradise of men—I wonder if a Paradise for poor *Women*, will ever be discovered—I wish they would get up an exploring expedition, to seek for one." Paradise or purgatory? What characteristics of mining communities help to explain such disparate reactions?

Perhaps the most striking feature of mining communities was the rapidity with which they developed. California's spectacular population increase demonstrated the pattern of instant growth that became typical of the mining frontier. While the agricultural and commercial promises of farming or urban frontiers might attract a thousand, the mining frontier would lure ten thousand. The White Pine silver-mining district, in Nevada, illustrates the pattern. News of discoveries in 1867 brought a handful of eager miners to the district by the summer of 1868. By midwinter, the population of the town of Hamilton had grown from thirty to six hundred, while the district as a whole had drawn about three thousand newcomers at the rate of about fifty a day. By the spring, seventy-five to one hundred were arriving daily; the total population of the White Pine district reached twelve thousand.

Another characteristic of the mining frontier was apparent in the White Pine area. Most "residents" were young men, for few women or family groups came during the early boom times. The demographic profile of Walla Walla, a typical mining camp in another area, shows an imbalance far more pronounced than on the urban frontier. In 1860, 59 percent of Portland's population was male, but 80 percent of Walla Walla's residents were men. The age distribution also differed. In Walla Walla, most of the men were between twenty and forty, while in Portland there were many men both younger and older. Many of the young men who thronged to mining centers lacked worldly experience. Gold seeking represented one of their first ventures out of the schoolroom and away from the confines of the female-regulated home.

Most mining districts were heterogeneous. Gold seekers came from every state and many foreign countries. About one-third of California's inhabitants in 1850 were foreign; ten years later the new boom area in Colorado's Comstock Lode region also had a high percentage of foreign miners. This heterogeneity set the mining frontier apart from agricultural frontiers, often settled by groups of Americans with similar regional backgrounds. Although mining society was, on the surface, cosmopolitan, it was not cohesive. Having varied backgrounds and few ties beyond the hope of striking it rich, miners were not members of a community but temporary residents, virtually transients.

The rapid influx of large numbers of fortune seekers resulted in ramshackle camps filled with fire and safety hazards. Little as these unsightly camps resembled eastern cities and much as they were temporary stops for a disparate group of transients, the camps had a definite urban character. Miners needed and demanded a variety of goods and services, and although few found the riches they envisioned, they earned enough to support numerous urban occupations and activities. Merchants, saloon keepers, cooks, druggists, gamblers, and prostitutes accompanied miners to provide for their needs and to share in their profits. Since farming usually followed discovery, freighters, bringing in both essential and luxury goods, joined this motley group. Even in the most feverish moments of the 1849 gold rush, only about half of California's residents were involved in mining. The rest serviced the miners. The pattern was typical.

Within a relatively short time after the discovery of gold or silver, mining camps and towns boasted a variety of urban amenities not found in same-sized communities in the East or on western agricultural frontiers. Newspapers, theaters, debates and lectures, sporting events, suppers of champagne and oysters broke the monotony of mining life and proved to the outside world that the strike had succeeded.

Because few communities established an adequate government, because drifters and ne'er-do-wells flocked to new centers, and because of the boom-and-bust cycle, most mining centers experienced disorder, too. "In the short space of twenty-four days," wrote Dame Shirley to her sister, "we have had murders, fearful accidents, bloody deaths, a mob, whippings, a hanging, an attempt at suicide, and a fatal duel." Although most camps were not as lawless as Dame Shirley's letter suggested and as stories later insisted, social standards and conventions broke down. Without a legal mechanism for settling conflicts in an environment full of young men, physical solutions to disagreements were common. Fistfights and murders occurred. Plentiful liquor spurred on the foolhardy and even the wise. Vigilante justice, glorified as a means of dealing with disorder, was itself often violent and brutal. In fact, it symbolized how much turbulence had become a part of mining life and how standards of justice and order had become perverted.

While white women might well be caught up in the violence,

it was Indian and Hispanic women who suffered most from the lack of order. In Downieville, California, a drunken miner broke down the door of the cabin where Josefa, a Mexican woman, lived with José in what was probably a common-law marriage. These unions were not unusual among working-class Mexicans, but few white miners saw them as legitimate. As was often the case with working-class Hispanic women, Josefa was considered fair game by white miners. She had heard rumors that "some of the boys wanted to get into my room and sleep with me." Although her intruder was too intoxicated to be a threat, when she and José tried to get him to pay for the door the next day, the miner called Josefa a whore. Infuriated, the woman stabbed and killed him. She was tried and hung within hours of the guilty verdict.

Josefa's fate, death by hanging, was extreme. Other women suffered less violent treatment or experienced only at second-hand the impact of white men's presence. Because most Hispanic women were illiterate, few left evidence of their personal responses to the changes triggered by the discovery of gold. But those rare sources that exist reveal fear, disapproval, and anguish. "It is necessary, for the truth of the account," one Hispanic woman recalled, "to mention the evil behavior of many Americans." Said another, "Our cattle were stolen by thousands," while a daughter remembered her mother's confusion with what Anglos called the rule of law. Her mother was "totally unprepared for the problems that came with American rule. Not only was the language foreign to her, but also the concept of property taxes, mortgages and land title regulations."

Whether directly or indirectly affected by the influx of fortune hunters, however, Mexican women received little sympathy from their white sisters. One rare comment from a newcomer to California acknowledged that "this *most unfortunate race*" was "ill-treated by our people. Possessing natural refinement of manners, their *diffidence* we entitle ignorance." White women, for the most part, however, shared the prejudices of miners

against women of color (often called "black Mexicans"). Said
one, "The lower orders of Mexicans are exceedingly illiterate
[and] in a religious sense elevated not far above . . . [their]
Indian ancestors." Such people needed to learn some hard lessons. As one woman living in a mining camp in the 1850s
commented, "It is true the miners had to put the fear of the
Lord, or His teachings, into the heart of the Mexicans and Indians . . . with a solid stick."

Since mining camps were often in areas with large Native
American populations, some of which had had little contact with
Spanish, Mexican, or Anglo settlers, Indian women were also
at risk. Although the situation of Indian women differed according to time and place, mining operations and the hordes of
prospecters tended to disrupt the economic basis of Indian life
and women's position as food gatherers. Inadequate food supplies drove some women to prostitute themselves. In a mining
camp in southern Oregon, one native woman exchanged her
body for bread and either sugar or a handkerchief. While prostitution offered some immediate relief from hunger, long-term
consequences included syphilis and sterility. A white man visiting an Indian settlement described women "so far advanced
with this disease that they were unable to walk." Other women
cohabited with white men, a strategy Indians had often used
to cement relations with outsiders. Few miners realized that
their Indian partners viewed the relationship in these terms.
White men considered these unions convenient and temporary.
Women who chose prostitution or cohabitation had some control
over their situation. Those who were raped had none. Indian
women were particularly vulnerable to unwanted advances
when their men were away from home working for whites. But
the rape of Indian women often provoked retaliation against
white miners, thus adding to the violent atmosphere in mining
areas.

Some gold seekers had set out for the West with every intention of maintaining standards, but their resolve often col-

lapsed under the realities of mining life. The story of one group from Boston epitomizes the breakdown. Bountifully supplied with Bibles and thoroughly instructed about the necessity of carrying New England culture west, the group's resolve evaporated almost immediately. After only two days in the placer mines, all the Bibles had disappeared, not given away in hopes of reclaiming sinners but exchanged in a Benicia, California, bar for whiskey.

Many miners felt that they were not accountable for their actions. They had no long-term stake in the camp and gave little thought to the consequences of their deeds. The *Denver Daily Tribune* printed a blistering article dealing with this irresponsible attitude and the behavior it encouraged. "Men of decent appearance seen elsewhere, as soon as they reached Leadville jibed, sang low songs, walked openly with the painted courtesans with whom the town teems, and generally gave themselves up to what they term 'a time' each one promising the other not to 'give him away,' " the article commented disgustedly. "Secure in the fact that their boon companions would not 'give them away,' that their women folks were safe and snug in their distant homes, that their children, prayers said, were tucked in their little beds, these whilom gentlemen announced that they were going 'the whole hog or none.' "

Joel Brown's letter to his wife, Ann, in 1852 puts the collapse of standards into perspective, however. "In fact when it is dig, dig, dig, work, work, work, there is not much time for immorality," he wrote. "Gambling and drinking is the worst crime I see here and this vice is carryed on nights and Sundays." Miners had neither the time nor the energy to carouse or brawl day and night. But there was usually nothing to stop them when they decided to have a spree, sought companionship in a saloon, or gambled away their gold dust.

Much of what the nineteenth century saw as vice came from the monotony and difficulty of mining life, the availability of cash, and the belief that morality was a woman's concern. Without good women, many men simply did not feel obliged to do a woman's job. "I attribute so much gambling and drinking to the fact there is no women in the country," wrote Brown. William Perkins agreed. "The want of respectable female society, rational amusements, and books, has added greatly to the demoralization of many whose natural character would have kept them aloof from temptation had there been other means but the gambling tables and drinking saloons, to have assisted them in whiling away the hours not devoted to labor," he wrote in his journal. "Notwithstanding the best efforts of a man," he continued, "it is impossible not to be more or less infected by breathing continually a tainted moral atmosphere." If proof were needed that the prevailing ideology had realistically assessed men's characters, the openly male temper of mining towns with the frank acceptance of vice provided it.

The appearance of the miners suggested the peculiarities of mining life. Shaggy hair, untrimmed beards, faces coarsened by exposure, old shapeless hats, baggy pants, flannel shirts, and high boots became the marks of the miner and fused into an image that entered popular culture. Just as women's interest in clothing and fashion on agricultural frontiers signified their determination to remain civilized, miners' sloppy clothing suggested they had in fact left civilization behind. The mining frontier was a world of its own, a world marked by singular uncertainties.

Unlike frontier cities and towns, which flourished either because of their strategic position or because of agricultural development nearby, mining camps, frequently in remote areas, mushroomed because of the promise of riches. Urban growth on the frontier usually suggested some stability and some future, but on the mining frontier it had no such meanings. Within three or four years, the cycle of boom and bust had occurred, the hordes of people had come and gone. A few districts avoided disaster by developing different kinds of mining operations or by finding alternative sources of prosperity to replace the precious metal. Their social and economic patterns came to resemble those of other urban areas. California, for a variety of reasons, never experienced the slump that most mining frontiers did. But the death rate of mining communities was significant.

The discovery of precious metals created two major cities, San Francisco and Denver, to supply the mining communities. Though they were instant cities (San Francisco had been a modest settlement in the 1840s, Denver a wilderness), they survived and grew. Still, like mining towns, their pattern of growth was erratic. Neither city, for example, had a stable population (even in nineteenth-century terms) but accommodated vast and fluctuating crowds of miners and suppliers. City residents themselves shared a mining-frontier mentality. They had little interest in building a city or creating a culture for its future but harbored dazzling visions of striking it rich by speculating in mining stocks or building sites, by providing supplies and services, or by doing anything else that might pay. They sought just enough order to protect their gains until they left.

In the early days, the two cities looked primitive and chaotic. In Denver in 1860, log cabins and shanties provided housing for "a sort of gypsy life." San Francisco in 1849 presented a picture of confusion and disorder, with most of the temporary inhabitants camping in tents. Its two-story buildings were either gambling halls or hotels. Within a few years, however, each city had elegant buildings, churches, libraries, schools, and shops offering a profusion of goods. As one resident of Denver explained, the city "socially . . . was a very gay place." A new arrival to San Francisco wrote home that it reminded her of Boston. But the transplanted New Englander was wrong. Buildings and urban amenities did not signify a civilized or stable community; in fact, many of San Francisco's improvements were made only after devastating fires, which so often swept through the carelessly built-up city. Little long-range planning occurred because few expected to remain. The profusion of buildings was no more a sign of stability than the size of the population.

Further indications of the impermanent character of San Francisco were revealed by the kinds of buildings that were constructed. While offices, hotels, theaters, restaurants, opera houses, and saloons were erected with alacrity, the construction of family housing lagged. The number of people running boardinghouses or hotels to house transients far exceeded the national figure. In 1850, for every thousand Californians gainfully employed, over nine were in the hotel or boardinghouse trade, more than double the figure for the country as a whole.

The population explosion that created the two cities also brought unavoidable urban confusion and stress. In 1848, a mere thousand inhabitants lived in the Bay Area. Within four years, thirty-six thousand more had flocked to San Francisco. By 1860, city dwellers topped the fifty-six thousand mark. Ten years later, one-third of the state's entire population lived in or within a few miles of the city. While it had taken Boston 250 years to attract one-third of a million people, it had taken San Francisco only twenty-five years.

The pace of urbanization magnified problems that had baffled city dwellers in more slowly growing areas, while the social composition of the cities contributed to a lack of interest in solving them. As one home missionary to Colorado explained, "Those who live in the quiet towns of New England, do not know what we have to contend with." The social hierarchy, initially based on the whimsy of fortune, was inherently fragile. Residents felt little responsibility to their communities. The heterogeneity of the population, as in the mining camps, probably contributed to social instability. Half of San Francisco's population in 1853 was foreign, many of the state's blacks clustered there, and the vast majority of all inhabitants were unattached men. Out of the total population of fifty thousand, there were only eight thousand women and three thousand children.

Yet city life in Denver and San Francisco was exciting, amusing, and novel. Early years were hard, but before long all the signs of culture appeared: theater, opera, restaurants, balls, churches for both black and white congregations. Visitors to the cities remarked on the numerous diversions and the relaxed way of life that had emerged. As John McCrackan explained to his sister in a letter of the early 1850s, San Francisco society was far less demanding than eastern society. "Here we are left to indulge our own peculiar views," he wrote, "dont attend church but half a day, believing that I can spend the ballance more profitably amid the beauties of nature." Drinking and gambling were two popular amusements that attracted more adherents, no doubt, than all the charms of nature or religion. The number of drinking establishments far outnumbered hotels and restaurants, and skimpy recorder's court statistics show twice as many arrests for drunken and disorderly conduct as for any other offense. Another diversion brought more to the hospital with venereal disease than with any other complaint in the early days of the gold rush.

A Denver woman recalled that her introduction to the city as a girl had been the witnessing of two murders: "These were terrible experiences to us, and we wondered what kind of a place we had come to." In fact, the nature of mining society raised the question whether women ought to participate in mining-frontier life at all. The leading San Francisco newspaper, the *Alta California*, thought the question not worth debating, since its policy was to attract women to California: "We are pleased to see that each succeeding steamer is bringing to California the wives and families of many of our merchants and mechanics who have preceded them and built for them a home among us . . . The happy influence of woman in a new country is a great one." In agreement that the presence of women was essential to the future of California, the 1849 political convention gave married women property rights, at a time when few other states had done so, hoping to lure them west. Yet even among boosters, there were mixed feelings about the presence of women. Nothing was done to establish a statewide system of public schools, and efforts to eliminate or license gambling failed.

Whether in Denver, San Francisco, or a remote mining center, men did not easily decide to bring their families west or to marry and settle down. They observed the characteristics of the mining frontier, which seemed to make it inappropriate for family life. As Robert Effinger explained, "I would much prefer that a wife of mine should board in a respectable bawd house in the city of New York than live anywhere in the city of San Francisco." Charles Tuttle highlighted "the privations and fatigues which females undergo" in a country with few women and told his wife she would be "deprived of the society of those of your sex and exposed to all the severities of the weather" if she joined him. Other men never considered bringing families west because they planned not to stay but to return east with a fortune. Most of them discovered that fortune was elusive. In the early 1850s, the average California miner was making only about three dollars a day—two dollars more than an eastern coal miner but hardly striking it rich. The pattern was similar elsewhere. The high cost of living ate up most of those modest earnings, but dreams die hard. Some gave up and returned to their families, but others stayed on, still alone, still determined to make the whole venture worthwhile. As one miner explained to his sister, "Everybody in the States who has friends here is always writing for them to come home. Now, they all long to go home . . . [But] it is hard for a man to leave here, when there is so much money to be made, with nothing . . . I have no pile yet, but you can bet your life I will never come home until I have something more than when I started." The longer they stayed, the harder it was to return or to settle down in California or anywhere else. They had become dreamers and footloose adventurers for life. Finally, the cycle of boom and bust discouraged men from bringing their families to the frontier. No one could know how long a strike would last or how profitable it would be. It often did not seem worthwhile to bring a family on a long, tedious, and costly journey when there was no certainty there would be anything but a ghost town when they arrived. Even miners living in those remarkable communities that survived the rush were reluctant to marry. Twenty years after the initial gold rush only 25 percent of the men in one California mining town and 33 percent in another were married and living with their families.

Yet the youthful miners were lonesome for mothers, wives, and lovers. "I expect that you will think . . . that I am crying to see my wife," Joel Brown wrote home. "Well suppose I am and what then? I am not the only one that is crying to see the wife and baby." The lines of anxious men waiting for hours for letters on Steamer Day in San Francisco mutely testified to homesickness and loneliness. Yet there were other reasons why men yearned for women. On their own, for perhaps the first time, miners had the unforgettable and unpleasant experience of doing women's work, and they found it monotonous and dreary. Then, too, some miners were quick to realize that if mining was an uncertain way to get rich, providing services was not. Some forty-niners returned home to get their families or brides and returned to begin a second and, they hoped, more lucrative career serving their brethren on the mining frontier.

Whatever the reason for bringing women west, most men believed that their arrival would signal the advent of respectable society. Yet their desire to have women on the mining frontier was ambivalent. As the legislators of California had given married women property rights but refused to curb gambling, so men on the mining frontier expected women to be agents of civilization but did not always want to give up the habits acquired in a time of relative freedom. Their ambivalence toward civilization was reflected in other aspects of mining life. As mining camps grew, for example, efforts were made to acquire symbols of eastern life: architecturally impressive buildings, stable social institutions, civil government. At the same time, however, there was often a profound unwillingness to pay for them.

If men had a variety of motives for sending for wives and families, women had many reasons for coming. Initially, many women had bade a reluctant farewell to their husbands for what they thought would be a relatively short separation. But as months passed, some realized that they had either to join their husbands or to give them up altogether. As Augusta Knapp told her husband, "Do not imagine that I want to come, for I do not, and think that you will be a real goose to stay, for all the gold in the mines; but if you do stay, I am coming, or else I will get a divorce . . . And whatever you do, Gid, do not *imagine* even that you can live without me, for you cannot and shall not." Gid eventually came home, but other men did not. And their wives went west to maintain their marriages. Many shared the expectation, however, that the sojourn in the West would be temporary and left their children behind.

Whether single or married, virtuous or fallen, most women also responded to the lure of riches. Maria Tuttle, one of the wives left behind, soon discovered she could not tolerate staying at home. Her anguished letter, written in early January 1851, conveyed her loneliness: "I have not heard from you since October and my mind is well nigh wrought up to a fit of desperation." Later in the month, she was carefully contemplating the financial advantages to be gained by going west. "I used to think to meet you at my father's door would be my choice," she wrote, "but now I have no desire that you should return if you can do well there, it would be better that I should go to you." Other women realized their own opportunities for making money by servicing miners. Margaret Frink, who was as fired up by visions of gold as her husband, described hearing tales of women's earning power. "I began at once to figure up in my mind how many men I could cook for, if there should be no better way of making money," she confessed. Once on the plains, the sight of the other emigrants filled her with dismay: "I was half frantic over the idea that every blade of grass for miles on each side of the road would be eaten . . . And, worse than all, there would only be a few barrels of gold left for us when we got to California." A few like Sophia Eastman responded to the sheer adventure of it all. As a schoolgirl in Lowell, Massachusetts, she realized, "I shall be obliged to go into the mill unless I get a passage before or by fall . . . I cannot submit to it, and I am willing to go with a small fitting out, or none at all, in the capacity of a servant, or any way, rather than be disappointed." As her brother-in-law noted, Sophia had "devoured all the reading about California," and finally, after borrowing money to pay for her trip, she set off for the West.

Some women, as one might expect, went to the mining frontier with the explicit intention of battling materialism and vice. Gold, wrote Sarah Gibbons, a missionary wife, was the god of adults in California, but she hoped to save the children. With similar idealism, Mrs. Harmon told a friend, "she thought it a pity for educated women to come to this country and spend their lives over a washtub and around a stove, and so she is going to teach." Even Mary Jane Megquier, a New Englander quite candid about her materialistic aspirations, still remembered a greater mission of being a "good influence upon society." Being a "good influence" in California was a heroic challenge.

Some of the first women to arrive on the mining frontier defied middle-class expectations. As prostitutes, they planned to better their economic situation by trading sexual favors for cash. Louisa Cook denounced those "who wear the form of woman, but o so fallen and vile, a living, burning shame to the sex they have disgraced." Shocking as Louisa found them, prostitutes lost little time once they heard the news of a strike. They came alone, in pairs, or, as Louisa observed, "sometimes a dozen in a drove." They may have constituted 20 percent of the female population in California in 1850 and outnumbered respectable women in early mining camps by twenty-five to one. Not all were American. Robert Effinger observed that "the cities of New York, Philadelphia, and New Orleans are pouring a portion of their prostituted population into our Market" but also noted "pretty French dancing girls" and Australian women who arrived to take advantage of the ready market of miners.

Some of the prostitutes were women of color who, because of racial prejudice, usually did not serve white miners but men of their own nationalities. Latin and South American women, procured by ship captains or agents, sailed to California to serve their period of indenture in cantinas. Young Chinese women came to California as virtual slaves. Some, like Ay Yee, were tricked into believing that they would be married or have a domestic position when they arrived. Ay Yee learned the truth in San Francisco when she discovered that she had been sold for $4,800. Most of the young women, however, must have had some glimmering of their fate, for they had been sold in China by their desperately poor families and transported by Chinese fraternal organizations to California, where they changed hands again. Lilac Chen was only six when her father disposed of her in 1893. "And that worthless father, my own father, imagine . . . sold me on the ferry boat. Locked me in the cabin while he was negotiating my sale," she recalled years later in anger. The initial shock or acceptance of a family decision was only the beginning of years of hardship. The *Alta California* in the 1870s described a scene reminiscent of southern slave auctions, with Chinese women "stripped and paraded onto a platform where prospective buyers could inspect and bid." Once acquired, these women served out their years in Chinatown as *boak haak chai*, a hundred men's wife. The predominantly male Chinese population, most either bachelors or with wives back in China, provided a steady stream of clients that brought profits to brothel owners but not to the women themselves.

William Perkins may never have ventured into Chinatown to see the situation of prostitutes there. Nonetheless, he noted an astonishing feature about white prostitutes in early mining society. A number of the "soiled doves" who paid "a nominal tribute to virtue," mainly by behaving decorously in public, were considered socially acceptable during early gold-rush years. At San Francisco's first piano concert, in 1849, the front seats were reserved for the "doves"; respectable men appeared openly in their company with little risk to their reputation, and

the women were "treated with the greatest respect and gallantry
the same as would be extended to the most respectable women
by men in general." The mining frontier's sexual demography
and the ability of some prostitutes to observe "all the exterior
rules of respectability" accounted for this social phenomenon
so upsetting to conventional moralists.

Some of the prostitutes did well on the mining frontier, especially during the boom days, when competition was limited
and prices were high. Edward Ely speculated that one madam,
"although she has not been in the place one year, . . . must be
worth a hundred thousand dollars. It could scarcely be otherwise considering the high price of everything . . . and more
especially where there is a monopoly. To speak plainly one
night's enjoyment of the society of the charming mistress of the
house, costs the man the moderate sum of one hundred dollars,
and the same indulgence with the girls, fifty dollars." These
women were high-class prostitutes working in good houses, and
early arrivals enjoyed many opportunities. Some acquired substantial possessions, as Ely suspected. Probate court records on
the estate of Mary Lee, who died in Sacramento in 1853, catalogued her white window curtains, two leather trunks, jewelry,
$1,520 in cash on deposit, and an opulent array of clothes,
including twenty-one skirts, eleven chemises, and thirty-one
dresses of linen, muslin, brocade, satin, silk, gingham, merino,
and wool, along with a white silk cape and a red jacket. Successful prostitutes considered their occupation a business, and
a prosperous one at that. A famous Denver madam, unusual
because her views were recorded, insisted that this was the
case: "She defended calmly but without emotion—the life she
had led. And she said at the first, 'I went into the sporting life
for business reasons and for no other. It was a way for a woman
in those days to make money and I made it.' "

The madam's response highlights the point that other occupations for women in the early days and even later were strenuous, unglamorous, and often paid poorly. Although prostitution
as a career represented female degradation in the eyes of the

moralists, for the prostitute the life represented economic opportunity. Although little is known of mining-frontier prostitutes as a group, the majority of them probably came from working-class families with few attractive economic alternatives. As the frontier symbolized a fortune to the miners, it no doubt suggested golden opportunities for women who may have already been in the business elsewhere. Certainly French and South American prostitutes were no novices. Neither was Mary Lee. Court records show that Mary, whose real name was Mary Butler and who was the daughter of Irish immigrants, had worked at Mistress Ann Wood's house in New Orleans. Some women may have drifted into prostitution after losing their virtue on the mining frontier. Moralists emphasized that adultery's inevitable conclusion was the brothel, and sometimes they were right. As one Denver madam explained, "I never took a girl into my house . . . who had had no previous experience of life and men. That was a rule of mine. Most of the girls had been married and had left their husbands or else they had become involved with a man. No innocent young girl was ever hired by me."

Yet prostitution was not always gilt-edged on the mining frontiers. Within the group as a whole, social and economic gradations quickly emerged. At the top were madams and women who lived in good houses with elaborate furnishings and a genteel atmosphere. The women who worked in dance halls and theaters, where the line between a courtesan and an actress was sometimes imperceptible, were of a different sort. Unlike high-class prostitutes, they could hardly afford to be choosy about their customers and counted on doing as many tricks a night as they could. On the bottom of the economic scale and far more marginal were women working out of their own cribs, small dwellings with a front bedroom, a window on the street, and a kitchen to the rear. These women's earnings were minimal, especially when youth and good looks faded. But even for the cream of the profession, downward mobility was a real threat as clients looked for fresh and younger faces and bodies.

No matter what the prostitute's class, age, or race, her profession was hazardous. As mining communities matured and respectable women came west, prostitutes were often harassed. The tempo of the campaign against prostitution picked up as a community developed and the number of its families increased. By 1860, in Nevada City, the respectable community's intention of cleaning up the town became evident when angry citizens raided the house of a prostitute. Not long after, other irate citizens were dragged into court, accused of wrecking the dwelling of a "notorious prostitute." In 1866, ninety people signed a petition requesting the government to ban all "bawdy houses." This hot issue landed in the city council, which passed it on to the police commissioner, who, typically enough, chose to do nothing beyond continuing an informal policy of occasional arrests. But as a result of this agitation, prostitution was confined to one area of town as if there had been some legislative action calling for it.

There were other hazards in addition to the consequences of outraged virtue. Syphilis or unsuccessful abortions ended the lives of many prostitutes. Mary Lee, despite her material success, died at the hands of another prostitute, who felled her with a bowie knife. Brawls between prostitutes and between their customers were part of the sporting life. In 1869, the Nevada *White Pine News* reported, "A man got on a spree Saturday night, went to a house of ill repute corner of Treasure and Dunn streets, and pitched into the nymphs after the most approved style of 'knock down and drag out.' He dragged two of the women into the street, knocked them down and trampled them in the mud. He was finally captured and locked up." Because the status of prostitutes under the law was so unclear, they were easy victims for crime. So Sarah Church, who worked at Mary Jane Carswell's house, made change for her client James Brown, explaining, "We had some business together that caused us to make use of some money." Then she claimed that he robbed her of over $5,000, "mostly in gold coin & some dust, also a lot of jewelry."

What happened to individual women over the course of years is unclear. Those who stayed with the trade followed the miners as they sought out new boom areas. Some of them, memoirs insist, escaped through marriage. "Sometimes a good citizen, wealthy and respectable," one woman maintained, "marries his wife from some one of these corrupt houses, and he seldom ever regrets his choice. He builds her up to be respected and respectable. I have heard of several cases." Unlike these women, who must have carefully concealed their past, Chinese prostitutes, many of whom found husbands in the 1870s, had nothing to hide. Often their families had sold them as young girls. Rather than being deviant, they were obedient daughters and hence desirable marriage partners. "Get out of this business while there's still time to reach paradise," one folk rhyme went. "The gaiety of pleasure houses in the past, where is it now? / You want respect don't you?" Other prostitutes were lucky and made enough, apparently, to retire. "Red Stockings," who appeared in Colorado in 1860, was supposedly one of the fortunate ones. Her background, whether real or fabricated, included a rich Boston family, seduction in Paris, and, of course, humiliation. A year after plying her trade in Colorado, however, she departed with thousands of dollars, supposedly reformed, and married respectably.

But the picture that court records and newspapers give of prostitutes suggests few happy endings. Violence, drink, drugs, and youth (some prostitutes apparently were in their early teens) were associated with prostitution along with growing social hostility. "Of all the human wrecks caused by the maelstroms of vice and dissipation," wrote the *White Pine News*, "there is none so sad to look upon as that of a young and beautiful woman. We saw such a one in Hamilton. She was young, perhaps not twenty, but intoxicated—beastly drunk. She had staggered in through the back door of a gambling den, and had been ejected from the room into the backyard . . . where she fell, amid the jeers and ribald jests of the rabble, the mass of whom were

doubtless less refined and no more virtuous than even the degraded target of their vulgar wit. In this helpless, maudlin mood,
she began singing, in sweet and plaintive tones, the very words
above all others most suited to her case: 'Once I was happy,
but now I'm forlorn.' "

Respectable single women or widows needing work, the
handful of married black women who needed to supplement
their husbands' income found less colorful and less dangerous
jobs, though their early opportunities for making money faded.
Like women on agricultural frontiers, mining-frontier women
performed "female" jobs. And despite the initial acceptance of
unorthodox females, a clear line divided reputable female work
from disreputable. In Sonora, California, William Perkins
pointed out, women could either become prostitutes or "osten-
tate a decent profession, such as sewing, washing, pastry
making and selling knick-knacks." At first, the respectable occupations paid well in a male society hungry for services. As
one young woman explained to an eastern friend, "A smart
woman can do very well in this country—true there are not
many comforts and one must work all the time and work hard
but is plenty to do and good pay. If I was in Boston now and
know what I now know of California I would come out here If
I had to hire the money to bring me out. It is the only country
I ever was in where a woman received anything like a just
compensation for work."

Married women, whose skills were far more in demand than
those of their counterparts on agricultural frontiers, found themselves in the early years doing the same jobs as single women.
They ran profitable boardinghouses, took in washing, hired out
as nurses, and sold pies and cakes, in addition to caring for
their own families. They shrewdly recognized their assets and
capitalized on them. For they tended not only to miners' physical well-being but also to their emotional well-being by creating the illusion of home. "A room in a private family was a
treasure," one woman pointed out, and men were willing to pay

for the comfort and the semblance of family life. By catering to men's needs and nostalgia, women often made more than their miner husbands and recouped family finances in times of misfortune.

In time, however, economic conditions changed for these women, as they did for their erring sisters. As the boom began to peter out, men abandoned the mines and flooded the job market. Competition brought lower wages, unemployment, and poverty to women who had serviced mining society. Some opportunities disappeared, others just paid less. As Sophia Eastman told relatives, by the summer of 1854 in California, "Wages are becoming low, and it is quite difficult to obtain a place. As soon as I can get my pay, I think I shall leave for Sacramento, or some other place." Yet a month later, she was still unemployed: "I find every day people are more and more unwilling to employ me." Although Sophia attributed her trouble finding a job to her refinement, which she thought made people reluctant to hire her, economic contraction and competition were the real problems. Cheap Chinese laundries, for example, threatened the livelihood of washerwomen. In Helena, Montana, Chinese laundries constituted such a serious threat that the town's laundresses warned the Chinese in a newspaper article to leave town or suffer the consequences. By the time the first phase passed in the mining West, few signs of women's early economic opportunities remained.

Even if the early years were financially rewarding, they were also hard on women and left them little time for relaxation or rest. Some claimed they hardly had time to leave their houses. It was not surprising that now and then they reflected that the monetary rewards were not worth the hard labor involved. After describing her primitive kitchen, the large meals she cooked three times a day, the washing, ironing, and odd jobs she performed, Mary Ballou concluded, "I would not advise any Lady to come out here and suffer the toil and fatigue that I have suffered for the sake of a little gold, neither do I advise any one to come. Clark Simmons wife says if she was safe in the States she would not come if she had not one cent."

The loneliness and fatigue that women experienced in the early years had compensations, however. The ability to earn money, far more than women could earn in the East, was satisfying, and working women enjoyed special status in early mining communities. They provided basic services that a predominantly male society desperately wanted. Their work as cooks, housekeepers, and seamstresses both enhanced their standing in the community and led to unexpected responsibilities and privileges. Some women reported that they became bankers for miners, while others noted that their word went unquestioned. And, of course, the attention that men paid to the women after they left their work could not help but feed their vanity. When Elizabeth Gunn went to church with her husband and children, all the men sitting on Sonora's main street rose to salute her as she passed by. Every available woman was avidly sought out for social occasions and became a belle. The middle-aged Mary Jane Megquier, who ran a boardinghouse in San Francisco, reported to her daughter that she was a social triumph at dances. Eliza Wilson, younger than Megquier but no beauty, remembered, "Even I had men come forty miles over the mountains, just to look at me, and I never was called a handsome woman, in my best days, even by my most ardent admirers."

Women who secluded themselves at home eventually found that domesticity was no protection from masculine attentions. Elizabeth Gunn in Sonora, Rachel Haskell in Aurora, and others initially tried to shut out the male world of the mining camp and devote themselves entirely to caring for their families. The free-and-easy atmosphere of mining camps made their task difficult. As one mother explained, "Virginia City [in Nevada] is a very hard city in which to bring up children, for all classes drink, high and low . . . Nearly all play and gamble. Two-thirds swear, and the other third uses bywords of every kind—some

very laughable ones—while others use coarse and rough ones."
Children not only had firsthand exposure to vice but also ran
the risk of physical harm in ramshackle, hastily constructed
mining camps and digs. In light of the threats to family life that
the mining frontier posed, Rachel Haskell's feeling of achieve-
ment in a simple evening at home is understandable. "How
comfortable and cozy the sitting room did look this evening by
twilight," she wrote in her diary. "The shelves laden with books,
specimens, minerals, shells. The Piano, the Sewing Machine,
comfortable sofa and easy chair, with healthy, happy, prattling,
chippy, little children."

But eventually, even these retiring women could not avoid
becoming centers of interest. On the streets, men stared.
Women who rarely ventured outside their houses were sought
out. Rachel Haskell's music attracted numerous evening visitors, while the Alverson girls' piano playing drew a crowd in
Stockton, California, in 1852—"scores of men in the street as
far as the eye could see, and some were sobbing." Women at
home had male visitors, some of whom spent the entire day.
Eventually the most domestic of women recognized that their
position in mining society carried social obligations. As Elizabeth Gunn remarked, "I have never attended concerts and lectures as I have done here! The folks are talking about a Lyceum
and I hope it will be formed; it will be something to draw the
young men from the gambling places and houses of ill fame
which abound here. The reason we go to everything good is to
set an example."

Since she was careful to fill her letters with " 'particulars' . . .
for I am 'a woman and a sister,' and am writing to women and
sisters," Elizabeth Gunn's correspondence vividly shows her
early experiences on the gold-rush frontier. The nature of her
life as a woman and her female perspective become particularly
clear when her letters are compared with William Perkins's
journal for the same years in the same town. Gunn described
family, religious, and cultural news, while Perkins spoke of the

teeming life of prostitutes, parties, and mining operations. Perkins, in fact, witnessed the Gunn family's arrival and captured Elizabeth and her perspective in a few vivid phrases. "What chance has virtue in the shape of tall, gawky, sallow, ill-dressed down-Easters," he wondered, "in rivalship with elegantly adorned, beautiful and graceful vice . . . It is too much to expect from weak male human nature in California, that a man ever so correctly inclined, should prefer the lean arm of a bonnetted, ugly, board-shaped specimen of a descendant of the puritans, to the rosy cheeked, full formed, sprightly and elegant spaniard or French-woman."

Perkins's comments were clearly more than unsympathetic remarks about Elizabeth Gunn's appearance and unfashionable clothes. Rather, Perkins was uneasy about the social role he rightly perceived that women like Elizabeth would eventually try to play on the frontier, especially when communities matured and respectable women found they were not alone. If, on the one hand, Perkins underestimated the power of these middle-class women to affect their communities, on the other hand, he accurately foresaw the limited nature of their victories. The character of the mining frontier, its population, lifestyle, illusions, and cycle of rapid growth and decay combined to prevent women from realizing their cultural mission in the way Eliza Farnham had envisioned in her book *California, In-Doors and Out.*

The editor of the *Montana Post* vividly sketched what respectable women, most probably the wives of the town's professional men, had confronted the year before on the mining frontier. "Public resorts there were none," he pointed out, "save for those where lawless men and shameless women made night hideous with their unlawful revels and midnight orgies." Unlike those settling agricultural frontiers, women in mining camps faced not an institutional vacuum but flourishing counterinstitutions and powerful and public models of unconventional female behavior. Gamblers, saloonkeepers, and prostitutes were always among the first in any new boomtown. By the time ministers, teachers, and wives arrived, they had to deal with these counterinstitutions, which were providing very real services for the mining community. The lure of another style of womanhood was strong. Although editors and merchants who realized the relationship between profit and permanence sympathized with efforts to establish a respectable society because it signified stability, this goal was clearly at odds with the values and tastes of much of the transient mining society.

How many women were involved in efforts to tame their mining communities is uncertain. Studies show links between marriage and class. The more affluent and successful tended to have wives with them. In one California mining town, for example, the families of professional men (6 percent of the total population) accounted for 24 percent of the families there. We probably can assume that the wives of these professional men were involved in building up respectable society, but we have no idea how much support other women lower down the social scale gave to their efforts. In any case, the uncertainty of mining life, the crowd of miners focused on getting rich and not on founding permanent institutions, hindered attempts to establish a firm social foundation. Campaigns to raise money for schools and churches faced general indifference, if not hostility. Church attendance was abysmal. The Reverend James Pierpoint reported a Sunday attendance of only forty out of a total mining population of three thousand to four thousand, and his report was not atypical.

Yet middle-class women enjoyed some advantages, the main one being their scarcity. Because there were so few women, there were always some men who would conform to female views in order to spend time with them. Whether they wished it or not, women's homes became the centers of a select social life as men lonely for female company dropped by to spend a few hours during the day or evening. Visiting was easy in a well-populated mining community, where much of the work was seasonal. Once visitors arrived, women could insist on proper behavior and maintain standards in the meals they served, the music they played, and the conversations they encouraged. "Had a spirited evening," Rachel Haskell remarked in her diary, as she recounted yet another night spent entertaining men at home. "It was exciting to meet two new gentlemen both good looking and interesting . . . Talked of books." Men, apparently, were careful not to lose visiting privileges by inappropriate behavior or language. As Dame Shirley explained to her sister, profanity was a way of life in California, but "the most vulgar blackguard will abstain from swearing in the *presence* of a lady."

If home constituted one small center of traditional social life, church was another. Missionaries to California bemoaned the materialism and godlessness of gold-rush society. What they, in fact, witnessed was the fragility of ties to organized religion when there were few social pressures to encourage conformity and many distractions. "Multitudes of young men who bore with them from their eastern homes the fairest reputation and the fondest hopes," wrote Baptist missionary Osgood Wheeler, "are here thrown into the whirlpool of confusion, this maelstrom of evil, to be heard from no more, unless by some fortuitous chance or Providential interference . . . they seem to wake up when I take them by the arm . . . But unaided by the restraints of an organized moral and religious community, they soon return to all their vice with renewed energy." The combination of breeding and religious indifference, even viciousness, shocked clergymen. The Reverend Tuttle, an Episcopal bishop, remarked how "men were kind personally, generous, . . . respectful and courteous; but I was appalled to discover day by day how almost universally given up they were to vicious practices."

Many apparently poised on the brink of perdition occasionally came to Sabbath services. Although the arrival of respectable women did not have a great impact on the size of church membership, it made attendance at church services and social functions more desirable. As one missionary candidly wrote to the American Home Missionary Society, "We must send no more unmarried men. California needs woman's influence . . . a devoted intelligent woman *can do more than two ministers*. A ship load of *female missionaries* would be the greatest blessing California ever had."

As women enlivened religion by their presence, they also took on their familiar but vital role of raising money to furnish and finish churches and to pay off debts on the buildings. Missionaries saw the building program as crucial because they believed that a steeple or the sound of a bell would revive the memories of religious obligations. James Waren, a Nevada City missionary, noted the importance of women's fund-raising. "We received very timely and efficient aid, by a *Fair* of the Ladies of this place," he wrote. Using $200 of borrowed money and putting in four or five weeks of work, the women netted $1,100 for the church. A miner, Charles Ferguson, also recalled some of these Nevada City church festivals. They offered few bargains. The men paid for the smiles.

Social occasions like fairs and balls became vehicles for fund-raising, entertainment, and the affirmation of proper behavior. Again the scarcity of women provided the opportunity to use social occasions for their own ends. As respectable women began to use these occasions to insist on polite behavior, they also began to demand proper clothing. William Perkins, along with many others, noted how, with time, "the epoch of flannel shirts . . . disappeared for townsfolk. We now dress like christians, and I smile to think of the change as I witness myself equipped in a silken lined cloth frock."

Because there were so few of them on the mining frontier, women moved beyond some of the social conventions of eastern life to adopt a more inclusive approach to female friendship. Elizabeth Gunn, who longed for more "good people" in Sonora and lamented because bad weather prevented her from visiting a New England woman who lived five miles from town, made friends with Mrs. Yancey from New Orleans, who "seems to have little education," although "she does not make mistakes in talking, and dresses and acts as though she had moved in good society," then with the minister's wife, and finally with Mrs. Lane, "a catholic. I like her as well as anyone I know here." Even more surprising, she had positive things to say about the neighboring French woman living with her mother, younger sister, and brother who made "her money by going to the gambling houses and dealing out the cards to the players." Yet, as women's insistence on decorum and dress at fairs and parties suggested, culture and class were hardly forgotten. Ellen Fletcher proudly reported that, despite the lack of formality, "it is said that there is the most respectable society of ladies in Summit City of any Settlement in the Territory." One of Elizabeth Gunn's friends had, she reported, counted "sixty virtuous females" in Sonora. The list was an ominous sign.

Since one of the objectives of respectable women on the mining frontier was to change its social atmosphere and particularly its open acceptance of sexual immorality, women used social occasions to make their disapproval clear to erring women and their gallants. Sarah Royce recounted with evident satisfaction a typical episode. The setting was an entertainment sponsored by women of four churches. In attendance was a wealthy man who had brought "a splendidly dressed woman, well known . . . as the disreputable companion of her wealthy escort." The couple made themselves comfortable and were probably more than willing to give generously to the churches. But the sponsoring ladies would have no tainted company or money and contacted a group of men to ask the sinners to leave. Sarah Royce concluded, "The events of the evening proved to him, as well as to others, that while Christian women would forego ease and endure much labor, in order to benefit any who suffered, they would not welcome into friendly association any who trampled upon the institutions which lie at the foundation of morality and civilization." Other women made the same point by refusing invitations ("I understand some are invited that are not fit for decent people to associate with," wrote Clementine Brainard) or by refusing to call. The identification of woman's sphere with morality and the seriousness with which many women took their cultural mission clarified the boundaries of the world of female middle-class culture and friendship and set the would-be civilizers apart from other women.

As these moral women counterattacked and sought to eliminate wicked institutions and the habits and attitudes that supported them, they soon discovered how few men shared their perspective. Prostitutes were social and sexual companions, and some men, at least, realized that it was impossible to lump them into the category "bad women." Some prostitutes were, indeed, disorderly and did little more than satisfy male sexual appetites. But, as many men noted, there were also "adventuresses of a better class, some of them educated; all of them accustomed to the forms of society; many with innate feelings of delicacy and womanly decorum, even after virtue has been discarded as an unnecessary appendage to California life." Conventional standards defining virtue and vice did not do justice to women who were, in fact, good companions and not vicious. Sexual transgressions did not result in an automatic collapse of character. Edward Ely's trip to the California mining frontier in 1851 led him to this conclusion. His initial view of prostitution was unfavorable, for it was, he wrote, "demoralizing to the community." But when Ely found himself on a coach with the madam responsible for the business he condemned, he found not only was "she . . . a really goodlooking girl . . . [but] had I not known her character would have thought her to be quite respectable. However we did not stand upon moralities in a California stagecoach and as she was witty and talkative the ride passed away very well."

Some men, of course, detested the prevailing acceptance of prostitution. The mere presence of prostitutes on the streets of a mining town "polluted" them, Charles Tuttle thought. Missionaries agreed and stood steadfast in their belief that prosti-

tutes were "shameless [and] . . . hopelessly irreclaimable." The
fall from virtue apparently cut prostitutes off, more or less permanently, from any hope of salvation. They were viewed as the
devil's agents, corrupters of innocent, if weak, men. As William
Taylor, a Methodist missionary in San Francisco, pointed out,
if the devil "can lead men into bad company, familiarize them
with debauchery, and fill them with rum, they fall an easy prey
to his diabolical designs." Where else could this scenario take
place as easily as in houses of ill fame, described by a missionary in Columbia, California, as "hatefully fixed up, with
gilded signs and wide open doors." Such men called respectable
women to the mining frontier and supported their efforts to safe-
guard values and institutions.

Clearly many, if not most, of the respectable women condemned prostitution, although its very openness suggested that
the men who agreed with them were very much in the minority.
The lure of another sort of woman with few pretenses to purity
or conventional morality was clear enough. Respectable wom-
en's attitude not only conveyed outraged virtue but also envy
and anger. High-class prostitutes in a city like San Francisco
and even in boomtowns enjoyed an opulent life and a freedom
of behavior probably attractive to hard-worked virtuous women.
In Sonora, Elizabeth Gunn wrote, "a judge . . . sold his house
to some women who came here from San Francisco." The
women had "a man servant to clean their house, and they eat
in a restaurant." In contrast, Elizabeth's life was epitomized by
her comment, "I am cleaning all the time." Generally, high-
class prostitutes were among the first to be able to buy expen-
sive goods like pianos or elegant clothes, while women like
Elizabeth Gunn and Luzena Wilson had "for several years [as]
my best dress . . . a clean calico."

Moreover, prostitutes were competitors. Instead of visiting
moral women in their homes, one outraged woman wrote, "young
men . . . nightly spend their evenings, like dogs, smelling out
all these vile excrescences, peeking through the cracks of doors,

windows, and blinds in our crowded thoroughfares, in the full
face of ladies and gentlemen going and returning from church!"
Even worse were young men who "pass the early part of the
evening in the society of virtuous females, discoursing upon the
charms of democratic life, and the solace of home, and virtuous
associations! and directly upon leaving, *cross the street and enter
a house of ill fame.*" The visibility of prostitution and the continuing support the male community gave it established the limits of not only women's moral authority but also their charms.
Women's pleased comments about the attention paid to them
on the mining frontier suggested the anger and jealousy they
felt when their charms were denied.

The saloon, often a gambling hall as well, was another target
for female anger. Once again male and female perspectives diverged. To lonely men, especially in the early days of mining,
the saloon was the place to find companionship and good cheer,
a place to forget failure and hard monotonous work. There might
be a good hot lunch there for free, and one might see "pretty,
saucy looking, active girls behind the bar." While saloons might
foster disorderly conduct and excessive drinking, these nega-
tives did not outweigh the real benefits to the men who fre-
quented them.

Women, however, knew that gambling destroyed habits of
industry and thrift, while drinking reduced men to the level of
"their own animalized selves" and bred irresponsibility and
violence. Furthermore, the saloon had a clear link with overt
sexuality. Not only did questionable women work there, but
abandoned women visited them. The decoration of saloons explicitly coupled drinking and sex. "In the gambling saloons,"
noted a horrified Elizabeth Gunn, "are pictures of naked
women, and women half dressed, dancing on the tables. I never
saw a place where there was so much need of teaching and
preaching and living as we ought to live." Finally, women saw
their husbands spending time and money in saloons rather than
at home. Rachel Haskell, a resident of Aurora, catalogued her

husband's visits to the saloon in her diary. "Felt very much
concerned . . . worried in mind a good deal . . . rather a forlorn,
angry feeling at heart" were phrases expressing her anxious
response to "those growing peccadillos," which included all-
night bouts. Saloons threatened the whole structure of domesticity that women like Rachel Haskell tried to create on the
mining frontier and, at times, even their physical well-being.

Women's strategies for modifying life on the mining frontier
included establishing desirable alternatives to vice and working
on an individual basis to reform sinners. Rachel Haskell's diary
shows how she dealt with the saloon problem at home. The
trouble was all too clear: "Papa came home very late with a
dreadful headache. He laid on the sofa saying 'He never was
so sick in his life.' Threw up. And I went to sleep with Ella."
Her tactic of making her errant husband sleep alone, "in his
cold bed for home penalty," seems to have been one of her
favorites, though she also reported "sharp" talks with him. Her
diary breaks off, so whether or not she reformed her husband
is unknown. She apparently did not, however, move beyond a
very individual response to the problem. Because "Mr. H. refused" to sign a temperance pledge, for example, she did too.
Other women, again most probably middle class, did organize
around the liquor issue. In 1855, for example, San Francisco
women lobbied for the prohibition of liquor. But women did
not easily move into the public world in their attempt to re-
shape it.

Because individual grumbling was ineffective, the issue of
Sunday closings of saloons and other businesses encouraged
well-organized collective efforts. Many middle-class women saw
the elimination of business activity on Sunday as a vital part of
the struggle to create order in mining communities. Few men
agreed with the militant women. For hardworking miners without families, Sunday was a day for mending clothes, washing,
and going to town for supplies and relaxation. It was the only
day of the week during the mining season when they did not

work. Merchants found Sunday one of their most profitable business days, as did saloonkeepers, restaurant owners, and prostitutes. Few of them could see much point in Sabbath closings.

So women in a few communities organized. The Reverend Hamilton, a missionary in Columbia, California, described one campaign for Sunday closings that women spearheaded. Complaints from what he admitted was a "minority" about business operations on the Sabbath were commonplace, but no one did anything specific to pressure businessmen until the women decided to mount a petition drive. Collecting more than 160 signatures on the petition requesting Sunday closings was but the first step; advertising a public meeting was the second. At the meeting, the women themselves read the petition "with a marked effect." Apparently the merchants were impressed by the "unanimity" on the issue and took "the matter into immediate consideration, and after strenuous efforts, on the part of those deeply interested in the object, secured concert of action and closed their stores." This victory was, Hamilton pointed out, entirely due to the women. Whether it would be temporary or not, he was not willing to say.

Women's growing eagerness to tackle vice openly was evident in San Francisco's famous "Cora affair." By 1855, the city had a nucleus of married women and families. Because these virtuous few had to walk through the parts of the city favored by prostitutes in order to reach the shopping area, they could hardly overlook the "offenders," who, they noted, had "splendid houses" and endeavored "to attract attention by sitting before their open windows and doors." The urban organization of San Francisco was typical in forcing this envious and outraged confrontation between virtue and vice, for lack of planning and rapid growth often brought the two together in mining communities.

Women met not only in the streets but in other public places as well. The Cora affair began at the theater. Charles Cora, a well-known gambler, accompanied his mistress, Arabella Ryan, or the Belle Cora, as she preferred, to the theater one evening. The Belle Cora's moral standing was clear in her status not only as Cora's acknowledged mistress but as a proprietress of a chain of bawdy houses. She was also notorious for the scornful glances she returned to virtuous women while walking the city streets. The same night, U.S. Marshal William H. Richardson and his wife were also in the audience directly in front of the infamous couple. Mrs. Richardson was horrified and urged her husband to have the gambler and his mistress thrown out of the theater. Though her husband tried to follow his wife's instructions, the pair would not leave. In the end, the Richardsons retreated.

The next evening, no doubt fortified by his wife's inflammatory rhetoric and more whiskey than usual, Richardson sought Cora out, provoked a quarrel, and was shot and killed. While Cora pleaded self-defense, the papers whipped up sentiment against him and the town's general immorality. "Let something be done," proclaimed the *Fireman's Journal*, "so that a man may be able to walk through the streets with a virtuous woman." Much of the journalistic campaign was directed at women, who responded enthusiastically by creating the heightened emotional atmosphere necessary for a moral campaign. As one angry woman wrote, "The ladies of San Francisco hold the power in their own hands . . . to purify this city, to drive hence the gambler and the harlot, and restore the tone of moral health and purity, and make it a suitable residence for the virtuous and the good."

Meanwhile, the Belle Cora hired the best lawyers she could find for her man. During the trial, one of them described the lovers' relationship as "a tie which angels might not blush to approve." San Francisco's respectable women responded indignantly. "Has the man who thus endorsed the sinful union between the gambler and prostitute, a mother living? Has he a wife or daughters, who can read his sentiments? Has he a son?" one woman wrote. Tempers continued high; the jury reached no agreement on Cora, hardly surprising since Richardson had clearly been the aggressor. Cora returned to jail. James King, leader of the editorial campaign, continued to bait "moral offenders," and in May 1856, one of his targets shot and killed him for his efforts.

In all the excitement, the women had aired their views in letters to the paper and enjoyed an influential forum in King's publication particularly, yet they did not organize. They left organizing to the men who formed a vigilante justice committee with strong female vocal support. "What is to be done with that villain, Casey [King's murderer]?" one wrote. "If the men don't hang him the ladies will!" The ladies did not need to worry that their bravado would be tested. The vigilante committee found King's murderer guilty along with Cora. The Belle Cora, who married her lover just before his execution, and others like her were warned that virtue would not tolerate vice. As the reform movement continued, different schemes were brought forward to eliminate gambling and prostitution or, at the very least, to decrease their visibility by confining them to certain districts.

The San Francisco *Chronicle* had declared it "the duty of the lawmakers to drive all such practices into the dark recesses of night, where the young and unsuspecting will not find them, unless they seek them out." By 1857, vice was less visible to the innocent young and their virtuous elders. Although neither gambling nor prostitution had disappeared or had even moved off the main streets, offenders were far more discreet than they had been in the past. On the surface, then, San Francisco seemed reformed, but underneath little had changed. The Belle Cora ran her house until she died in 1862.

The outcome of the Cora affair suggests that female efforts to change the mining frontier's atmosphere had, at best, mixed success. As flush times faded, some of the activities that depended on easy money departed. High-class prostitutes and gamblers left dying towns to search out vibrant ones, and many hardened miners followed. The moral improvement was the victory of decay. In those mining areas that found new sources of

prosperity and in cities like San Francisco and Denver, the
victories were more apparent than real. Sabbath closings worked
for a few weeks but often not permanently. Churches never
attracted the kind of support that committed believers thought
necessary. As late as 1890, 31 percent of San Francisco's residents were church communicants.

Women were capable of agitating and publicizing their position, though they were less successful in organizing to deal
with social problems. No matter what approach they took, they
were only superficially able to impose their views on a heterogeneous, transient male society. Their allies lacked the influence or the will to push through the reforms. Protestant
clergymen, of course, supported women's causes, but as Elizabeth Gunn pointed out, missionaries themselves enjoyed only
limited prestige on the mining frontier: "The minister is not
regarded with the reverence that was given him at home. They
respect his learning as they would that of any educated citizen
and think he is a good man, and that is all." Editors and merchants favored improving society, for they knew the illusion of
permanence worked to their financial advantage. But the illusion of order might well satisfy them; moreover, they differed
with women over issues like Sunday closings, which had financial repercussions and which the majority of the male population, many of whom were European and horrified by the practice
of the Protestant Sabbath, also opposed. City governments
proved more interested in making money out of vice than in
ending it.

Earnest women did succeed, however, in clarifying their standards. The lines between acceptable and unacceptable institutions and behavior became more distinct with time, and
certain conventions were observed in the presence of respectable women. Men left off their flannel shirts and wore topcoats;
their support of vice (if they wished to be received) was
carefully concealed. Social distinctions were sharpened. Then,
too, women established and supported institutions that com-

peted with vice as centers of attraction, and here increasing numbers worked in their favor. Ice-cream parlors, for example, favored by women, flourished. In San Francisco, ice-cream parlors served up to three thousand customers a day, "lovers with their sweethearts, and husbands with their better-halves." "No one visits here who is not willing to see and be seen," the newspaper pointed out. Balls and pleasure excursions, reputable theaters patronized by respectable women, were other lures. Churches served as both social and religious centers.

A woman emigrating to California, Eliza Farnham advised, ought to have "fortitude, indomitable resolution, dauntless courage, and a clear self-respect which will alike forbid her doing anything unworthy." Her list of virtues necessary for women on the mining frontier testified to her conviction that mining society had the capacity to shape women or to be shaped by them. How far her fears that women lost their female virtues on the mining frontier were justified is hard to say. Like the trans-Mississippi agricultural frontiers, the mining frontier did not encourage women to move very far beyond conventional social roles. Although men were not always willing to change mining society, they were as insistent about female nature as the most traditional woman. What California wants, one article in 1854 pointed out, is woman "in her highest and holiest nature . . . the companion, the friend, the co-worker with man in the great cause of humanity." Male conservatism in regard to woman's place was clear when men failed to give women the vote in early gold camps although miners in their mid-teens voted. Newspapers derided female radicalism and praised western women who "never talk of 'women's rights'—never parade the streets in bloomers and high heeled boots—never mount the stump . . . telling of the tyranny of men. In this respect [they] are angels in contrast with their strong-minded sisters in the East."

But if there were no radical innovations in female behavior or in nineteenth-century norms, there were changes. Women, just as men, felt the effect of loose or nonexistent community standards. The same voices that exhorted women to come to save the mining West often noted the numbers of women already there who had failed at that task. Certainly many women supported the familiar institutions like churches on the frontier, although the proportion of women who did so is unknown. But ministers pointed out that there were far fewer women in church than they had expected, and a variety of reasons lay behind this neglect. As Elizabeth Gunn explained, "We do not go to meeting now, as the preacher is a Southern man and favors slavery and there is no other meeting near." Certainly the presence of a cosmopolitan attitude toward Sunday as a day for relaxation and pleasure contributed to religious indifference. Another factor isolated by missionaries was secularism. There were fifty ladies in Crescent City, California, wrote one missionary in 1854, but only twelve church members. The influence of woman, he continued, "has not been *what is expected of her at home*; women of religious professions at home step into the deep stream of worldliness along with their husbands and instead of leading them out, *drag them down*." Worldliness there evidently was, but it was due as often to the weakness of organized religion as to the weakness of women. In the struggle to survive on the mining frontier, many churches also succumbed to worldliness. So Lura Smith explained that she had gone to the theater rather than church, for "it is cheaper to go there occasionally than to hire a seat in a *respectable* church." Whatever the reason, enough women forgot their duty to be noticeable. Wrote Mary Jane Megquier to her mother, "I suppose you will think it very strange when I tell you I have not attended church for one year nor even heard a prayer but I cannot see but every thing goes on as well as when I was at home."

Mary Jane had pointed out several years earlier, "You can do as you please about attending, it is all the same whether you go to church or play monte." Although distinctions between virtue and vice were clearly drawn, there was a certain tolerance for behavior as long as it was not socially dangerous and certain proprieties were observed. Prostitutes might not come to balls or church fairs, but as one Montana woman noted, "We never ask women where they come from or what they did before they came to live in our neck of the woods. If they wore a wedding band and were good wives, mothers, and neighbors that was enough for us to know. A marriage band with us had a way of stopping a lot of silly questions."

"It is so pleasant to have plenty of money, we cannot seem to get a thousand together but if I want ten or twenty it is always ready," Mary Jane commented. Women responded to the materialistic temper of mining society, as ministers had noted, and enjoyed spending easy (or not so easy) money. Their materialism manifested itself in a preoccupation with appearances. Visitors and residents both commented on the interest in female fashion that developed after the hardest days of the early mining frontier had passed. San Francisco papers criticized the luxurious clothing local women preferred, which drew its inspiration from France and the dress of the city's prostitutes. If the clothing was impractical and immodest, as papers suggested, women paid no attention. Nor were elaborate clothes confined only to a few women of means. "I have never lived in a place," one woman in Nevada announced, "where people dressed more richly or more extravagantly than in Virginia City. It is not only a few millionaires who indulge in it, but every woman on the Comstock who has a husband earning $4 or $6 a day." What some proponents of woman's place had feared came to pass on the mining frontier. Quiet domesticity was replaced by fashionable frivolity.

The variety and stimulation of life on the mining frontier also threatened the quiet domestic vision. Not all the excitement was welcome. The wife of a Grass Valley, California, minister who used her iron to fend off an amorous miner who drunkenly confused her with a prostitute named Fanny probably did not relish the incident. But women often enjoyed the drama. "I lead a life of great variety—full of agreeable, and stirring incidents," Martha Hitchcock declared. "I think that I should find any other country very dull after this." Mary Jane Megquier agreed and felt she would "never feel perfectly satisfied with . . . quiet ways again. Here you can step out of your house and see the whole world spread out before you in every shape and form. Your ears are filled with the most delightful music, your eyes are dazzled with every thing that is beautiful, the streets are crowded the whole city are in the street." Not every mining camp was a San Francisco, but every thriving mining town had money, numerous amenities and luxuries, and an atmosphere of excitement that rendered home back east and even the ideal home less attractive to many women.

Those welcoming women and families to the mining West had expected homes to become centers of good influence, and many of them were. But it was a sign of the impact of the frontier on women that homes there fostered customs that many moralists saw as scandalous and dangerous. Married women typically entertained married and single men at home. It was a short step for some women, sources show, from entertaining at home to going out with their men friends and even receiving presents from them. Innocent as such customs might have been initially, moralists believed they allowed young men to insinuate "themselves into the affections of married women." The devil surely lurked behind the custom. "He gives special attention to wives, more particularly the beautiful and young wives . . . He employs a great variety of means for their ruin; wine, flattery, and bribes, in the form of splendid presents," wrote the Reverend Taylor.

Although California and other parts of the mining frontier were not on the brink of a collapse of moral standards, as the jeremiads proclaimed, the criticism suggests that sexual mores were less rigid in the new environment. And it was not only the moralists who used the vocabulary of temptation and sin. Sophia

Eastman, a woman who had come to the frontier alone, was one
who agreed: "I would not let a friend come in the same manner
in which I came for unless they had a very strong mind and
well formed character they will even before they are aware be
led into temptation and at last be ruined."

Court records detailing causes for divorce reveal some aspects of women's sexual activities. A case involving a couple
in Union Town, California, in 1853 disclosed that the wife had
left her husband, not to live alone, but to share a house with
an unmarried male boarder. The community both questioned
the propriety of the arrangement and observed it closely. One
neighbor said that "it was improper that they should live in the
same house together," while another added that "they were
greater friends than they ought to be under the circumstances."
"Their conduct," he concluded, "would cause people to talk."
Yet a third witness revealed for the record how curiosity had
got the better of him as he passed the house one night: "I heard
some low talking . . . I stood there something like ten minutes
. . . I was standing as close to the house as one could get to
peep in through a crack by the door . . . I saw a light under
the door and stooped to look." An aggrieved husband described
his wife's adultery in some detail, testifying, "I see a man destitute of clothing save in his shirt come in & get into bed with
def[endant]. I shortly got up and went out to the well. I found
laying on the outside of the door a pair of pantaloons and
shoes." Women proved no more squeamish or less curious than
their male observers. Thus, one wife in an 1869 suit told her
husband she was off on a neighborly visit. "Instead of going, I
returned to the house, and saw this transaction with Mary W. I
stopped at the window several moments."

How many women strayed from nineteenth-century norms to
commit adultery, to pass as married when they were not, to
desert their husbands is, of course, impossible to discover. But
they did divorce their husbands. Unreliable as statistics are for
this period, they show that the divorce rates for states that were

part of the mining frontier were higher than for the United States as a whole (with the exception of certain areas of the South). Critics pointed out that divorce laws and residency requirements on the mining frontier were lax, and they were right. But the stringency or leniency of laws does not seem to be the main factor explaining these high rates; rather, transiency, prosperity, community tolerance, and plenty of opportunity for remarriage for those who felt their spouses had failed to fulfill their marital expectations do. Divorce was a viable option.

Mary Jane Megquier's letters written between 1849 and 1856 illustrate the gradual impact of the mining frontier on one woman by birth middle class, by training literate, and by nature free spirited. She liked the West because there was "not a word about such a thing is not respectable. As she told her daughter, "You know I always detested that." Yet at the same time, she was a New Englander, sensitive to her moral responsibilities. She, too, recounted an incident of ejecting a questionable woman from a social affair. Initially, Mary Jane had accompanied her husband to California, expecting, like so many other women, to earn a fortune and return to Winthrop, Massachusetts. And as her early letters show, she worked hard to make the fortune, talked of her old home, and missed her grown children. At the same time, she noted how much time she spent with men. Gradually her letters described parties and other recreations along with the work, visits to the ice-cream parlor with men friends, her failure to go to church. Her determination to return to the East began to weaken. "A few weeks ago," she wrote, "I could have left without a regret, but we are beginning to live like civilized beings." Finally, she and her husband made the trip to Winthrop; she went back to California without him. Her last surviving letters told her daughter of "Mr. Johnson of whom you often hear me speak . . . my gallant whenever I wish to go," and observed this "is the place to enjoy life."

Certainly not all women experienced the mining frontier as Mary Jane Megquier did, but many seemed to feel there was a freer and more enjoyable life there. As a woman in a silver-mining town characterized her neighbors, "The ladies of Virginia City are always ready for amusement, and I think enjoy it more than any class of people among whom I ever lived."

What, then, did the frontier mean for the women who went there? Women of "honest hearts, have fallen victim to the peculiar seductions [of] the place," one observer mused, but in spite of this, "paradoxical as the statement may sound, it is rigorously true that these women have improved the morals of the community." Such comments captured the complexities of female experiences on the mining frontier. Many tried to live up to the challenge described by Eliza Farnham in *California, In-doors and Out;* others, less worried by role prescriptions, found new enjoyments and freedoms. By their very presence, however, most contributed to the building of a family society and served to remind all of the cluster of ideas associated with nineteenth-century womanhood.

In the end, of course, those hard-core miners who so threatened order, morality, and stability were lured by a new strike and escaped these women altogether. The less adventurous, the towns in decline, the occasional communities that survived boom and bust to achieve some kind of permanence—all felt the impact of women. So, too, did the two great cities Denver and San Francisco. As the San Francisco *Bulletin* noted, the celebration of Christmas—"the time honored anniversary of family reunions, of feasting, fun and frolicking"—overshadowed drinking, gambling, and whoring. A victory indeed, but did a family-oriented holiday really symbolize real or apparent change?

This was the very question that white men and women asked themselves when they tried to understand what the mining frontier had meant to them. As early as the 1850s, William Perkins wondered what time would bring: "Ten years hence, perhaps, the standard of morality will have improved, and something more than a show of respectability will be required, but I ques-

tion if a jollier *Fandango* than ours, will then be produced."
And years later, Eliza Wilson also wondered, as she recalled
the old days. "Every lady was overwhelmed with attention," she
wrote, also thinking of a dance, "and there was probably more
enjoyment that night, on the rough pine floor and under the
flickering gleam of tallow candles, than one often finds in our
social drawing-rooms, where the rich silks trail over velvet car-
pets, where the air is heavy with the perfume of exotics, and
where the night is turned into a brighter day under the glare of
countless gas-jets."

❦ 6 ❧

"If Polygamy Is the Lord's Order,
We Must Carry It Out"

Emigrants passing Mormon wagon trains on the dusty trail west or resting in Salt Lake City midway through their journey observed, often with astonishment, the orderly, temperate, and industrious nature of Mormon society west of the Mississippi. Although the serious side of Mormonism was striking, there was also a certain gaiety. Dancing, acting, and making music played an important role in Mormon life, providing relief from the hardships accompanying settlement of the frontier. Here, emigrants realized, was a powerful alternative to the less structured pioneering experience encountered on the trail and expected at the trip's end.

Few felt comfortable with that alternative, and, if they listened closely to some of the music, they found plenty of reason to condemn the Mormon experiment. One song, a favorite at local festivals, started this way: "Now sisters, list to what I say / With trials this world is rife / You can't expect to miss them all, / Help husband get a Wife! / Now this advice I freely give, /

If exalted you would be, / Remember that your husband must / Be blessed with more than thee." The refrain provided further evidence of what was amiss in Utah, as it continued: "Then O, let us say / God bless the wife that strives / And aids her husband all she can / T'obtain a dozen wives."

The song's lyrics conveyed much about Mormon attitudes toward polygamy. On the one hand, the chorus gaily urged wives to encourage their husbands to marry for God's abundant blessings but, on the other hand, suggested the tensions of the marriage system with the reference to worldly "trials." To outsiders, the song's attitudes were puzzling, at best, and, for most, scandalous. Polygamy was nothing to sing about. It was a peculiar institution corrupting Mormon society, an institution easily compared to black slavery and open to the same solution: abolition. Harriet Beecher Stowe saw both the analogy and the solution when she insisted that the time was right "to loose the bonds of a cruel slavery whose chains have cut into the hearts of thousands of our sisters."

Clearly, the Mormon frontier with its distinctive marriage system and unusual social arrangements disturbed mid-nineteenth-century Americans profoundly. Like black slavery, Mormon "slavery" became the subject of a number of sensational tales purporting to reveal the nature of the Mormon system, especially its impact on women. Written not by emigrants or travelers who had viewed Mormon society firsthand but by daughters and wives of New England reformers and ministers, the popular books bore titles like Orvilla Belisle's *The Prophets: or, Mormonism Unveiled*, published in 1855.

Several themes appeared repeatedly. One centered on a pure and noble heroine who becomes entangled in Mormon life and subsequently reveals all its horrors and licentiousness. Closely related was the escape tale in which the main characters, in a series of thrilling chapters, elude the avenging and murderous Mormons. A third theme focused on polygamy. Novels revealed the husband in a plural household as lustful, materialistic, and coarse; for women, polygamy was nothing but a thinly disguised system of prostitution and economic exploitation. While writers did show a few plucky women who somehow had the intelligence and character to resist conversion and reject polygamy, they pictured most Mormon women as victims. Their stories assumed that only religious trickery, outright oppression, or female depravity could account for women's acceptance of a religion encouraging plural marriage.

These novels reveal more about the concerns of middle-class Americans than they do about life on the Mormon frontier. Harriet Beecher Stowe's description of polygamy as "a slavery which debases and degrades womanhood, motherhood, and family" was typical in emphasizing the threats Mormonism posed to women and the family. For a culture that defined the traditional nuclear family as the source of social stability and married woman as keeper of morals and culture, polygamy was anathema. Polygamy destroyed the family and woman's unique place in it and made women unfit for their moral and social responsibilities. With the family and female morality in ruins, social disorder and rampant immorality must inevitably result. Such a view fed the more general fears that the westward movement could bring about the collapse of social order and traditions.

It was no surprise that New England women produced much of the anti-Mormon literature. In the early nineteenth century, woman's sphere had been legitimized and imbued with significance through its identification with home. New England women had been active in propagating this new view of woman's role and subsequently in using it as the basis for a civilizing mission in both the East and the West. In less obvious ways, the novels may also have served to release tensions resulting from nineteenth-century marriage arrangements. The novels contain a surprising amount of eroticism and violence, suggesting that female writers were lashing out against male lust and the double standard and protesting norms that minimized sexuality in marriage and female sexuality in general.

Whatever subtexts were embedded in the tales of Mormon

life, the most explicit message was that all right-minded Americans should condemn the Mormon frontier experiment. Thus, Americans were puzzled and shocked at the rationale Mormon women, even those who appeared to be intelligent and virtuous, used to defend their way of life. Belinda Pratt's letter to her sister in 1854 presented typical arguments in support of polygamy. "Polygamy," she wrote, "tends directly to the chastity of women, and the sound health and morals in the constitutions of their offspring." Though the identification of polygamy with chastity was confusing to the outsider, it was a point Mormon women frequently made. Because all women might have husbands, children, and homes, none would be forced by loneliness or poverty to degrade herself by becoming a prostitute. As for men, Mrs. Pratt pointed out, those who were noble were worthy of a hundred wives. Presumably, if they had no legitimate outlets for their "nobility," they would find illegitimate ones. Polygamy, then, kept men virtuous as well as women.

Most nineteenth-century Americans, preferring the message the novels conveyed, rejected out of hand the claim that polygamy provided benefits for women. The truth about polygamy and the Mormon way of life, however, lay somewhere between the defense Mormon women mounted and the exposés irate female novelists presented. Polygamy was neither so degrading as the Gentiles claimed nor so liberating as the Mormon spokeswomen insisted. With its peculiar tensions and freedoms, Mormonism and the practices it sanctioned colored female realities on the frontier. Yet Mormon women also shared with other pioneer women experiences and even ideas about woman's place in the world. To be a Mormon woman on the Utah frontier was, therefore, to be both the same as, and different from, pioneer women elsewhere.

Without considering the Mormon settlement of Utah as a utopian experiment, it is difficult to understand the Mormon frontier and the experience of women there. The settlement of Utah was not merely another chapter in the westward movement but one of the numerous attempts in the mid-nineteenth century to build a new and more perfect society in the wilderness. Amana in Iowa, Bethel in Missouri, and Aurora in Oregon were other frontier settlements inspired by religious faith; members sought to build the City of God on earth. Communities like Communia in Iowa differed in having a secular ideological base but shared the goal of creating a more perfect society. Of all these frontier experiments, the Mormon undertaking was clearly the largest, the most important, and the most successful.

By withdrawing from what they saw as a corrupt eastern environment, groups like the Mormons intended to build a new society. Shared assumptions united these unconventional experiments. Basic was the conviction that human beings were perfectible. So, too, was the belief that social solidarity and cooperation stemming from a freely given commitment to the group as a whole could replace crass individualism and eliminate the need for social coercion. By its emphasis on the group rather than the individual, the utopian vision required planning and coordination to ensure material well-being for all and harmonious working arrangements.

Most of these mid-nineteenth-century experiments collapsed in less than sixteen years. As one study of ninety-one of these communities suggests, the mechanisms developed to reinforce commitment to the community differentiated the successes from the failures. Specific techniques, such as frequent small-group interactions and mutual criticism, modifications of social institutions like marriage, which divided people rather than united them, and the sharing of goods, increased the sense of community and often made it difficult for members to leave. Sacrifices like abstinence from liquor reinforced the sense of belonging, as did special rituals. Charismatic leaders who were able to justify group idiosyncrasies on exalted ideological grounds often guided these utopian experiments, but long-term survival depended on a strong organization to carry on after the leader's disappearance. Seen in this context, the success of the

Mormon experiment lay in its ability to create strong individual and group loyalty.

The denomination had its roots in the religious revivals sweeping across western New York State in the early nineteenth century and the genius of an inspired leader and self-styled prophet, Joseph Smith. At the age of fourteen, Smith claimed to have had a vision in which God the Father and Christ the Son appeared to him lamenting Christianity's decadence and stressing the need to recapture the spirit of the early church. Over the next ten years, his visions continued and resulted in an addition to the Bible, the *Book of Mormon*, and a growing conviction that his personal mission was to reestablish Christ's church on earth. In 1830, Smith organized the Church of Jesus Christ of Latter-day Saints, and the work of conversion began. Smith's prophetic claims were validated in the eyes of his followers by his apparently miraculous powers and his continuing dialogue with the divinity. Rejecting the Calvinist doctrine of original sin and predestination, he declared that all believers could be saved and called them to the task of creating God's kingdom on earth. Inspired by Smith's vision, the saints, as they referred to themselves, left their homes and headed for the frontier and the new Zion. Settling first in Ohio and Missouri, then in Illinois, where an angry mob of Illinois residents killed Smith in 1844, and finally escaping to Utah, the saints worked to build a physical kingdom under the close supervision of religious leaders. While the commitment to Zion involved sacrifices and suffering, the promised rewards more than compensated for the trials: "As man is, God once was; as God is, man may be."

Financial hardships, violence, and persecution dogged early attempts to build Zion within the boundaries of the United States. Most Americans justified hostility on the grounds that Mormons were theocratic empire builders and, thus, both a political and a religious threat. Mormon religious doctrines seemed both exclusive and excessive, while Smith's revelation that the day should come "when tribulation and desolation are sent forth upon the wicked" was unwelcome news to the wicked. The Mormons' ability to create self-sufficient political units was disturbing, and Smith's interest in running for the Presidency ominous. Rumors of polygamy, practiced secretly in the 1840s and early 1850s, led to charges of immorality. Despite the constitutional guarantee of freedom of worship, Americans had few qualms about driving Mormons out of one settlement after another and eventually a thousand miles away to the desert of Utah.

It was an indication of the cohesiveness of the new Israelites, as the Mormons liked to call themselves, that the group maintained itself in the face of such hostility. In fact, almost twenty years of persecution and suffering contributed to a strong group identity and encouraged Mormons to accept forceful church leadership and planning. United by memorable common experiences, organized by their leaders for common goals, and committed to the new order by peculiar social arrangements as well as by the promise of salvation, the Mormons in 1847 were at last free to claim "the land of promise held in reserve by the hand of God for a resting place for the Saints upon which a portion of the Zion of God will be built." Twenty years later, the dream of creating a utopian society was still strong, as Smith's successor, Brigham Young, made clear: "I have looked upon the community of Latter-day Saints in a vision and beheld them organized as the great family of heaven, each person performing his several duties in his line of industry, working for the good of the whole more than for individual aggrandizement; and in this I have beheld the most beautiful order that the mind of man can contemplate, and the grandest results for the upbuilding of the Kingdom of God and the spread of righteousness upon the earth."

In 1847, however, it took great faith to see Utah as the land of promise. The desert would not become fruitful without tremendous human labor. Church leaders, from the beginning, directed the effort, which was collective and cooperative. Settlers did not scatter to individual homesteads but lived in towns and villages. The church divided and distributed the land around the first settlement at Salt Lake, laid out the community, and directed irrigation programs to reclaim the land and provide water for all the farmers in the community on an equitable basis. In a similar manner, the church sent out groups to colonize other areas, where the same collective approach to settlement, farming, and irrigation followed. The bishop in a new settlement was a key figure, often supervising the digging of canals and ditches and even using the Sunday sermon to inform the congregation of the work schedules for the coming week. In a surprising contrast to other frontiers, Mormon settlers welcomed the assistance of Paiute Indians. Reflected one, "I cannot help but remark, that when I am very busy, Indians come and assist me in my work. I feel to thank my Father in Heaven for putting it into the hearts of those fallen people to come and help me Labor."

Such a favorable attitude toward Native Americans stemmed from the *Book of Mormon*'s identification of New World Indians with the lost tribes of Israel. Since the early days in New York State, Mormon missionaries had believed it their special duty to spread Joseph Smith's revelations to Native American tribes. In Utah, missionaries settled among the Bannock, the Shoshone, and others, taking to heart Brigham Young's instructions to spread their faith and way of life to the native groups inhabiting the Great Basin. "God would bless them and crown their labors with success," he promised them. Although conversion attempts were never as successful as Young had hoped, the Mormons' positive attitude toward Indians stood in sharp contrast to that of most other white settlers in the West and reflected the utopian goals for which they strove.

Although these early years were filled with hardships, Mormon settlers slowly but confidently conquered their environment. Their faith and the freedom from persecution made the difficulties of pioneering tolerable and reinforced group ties.

The church touched every aspect of life. The open support for polygamy after 1852 gave the church influence over the most intimate relationships in addition to general social and economic relations. The sense of identity grew stronger. The careful organization of concentrated settlements contributed to it and undercut the loneliness so common on other frontiers in the early years. Meanwhile, missionary labors, focused in Europe after 1852, mainly in England and Scandinavia, brought in scores of new converts with useful skills and talents and new enthusiasm for the social and religious experiment. Optimism and a strong group consciousness infused the task of turning the desert into a garden.

The sense of mission and collectivity within a group that was ethnically heterogeneous set the Mormon frontier apart from mining and other agricultural frontiers. So, too, did its demographic composition. Within a year of the original migration to Utah, there were approximately the same number of women as men. At about the same period in Oregon, only 42 percent of the rural population were women, while less than 31 percent of city dwellers were female. Utah's demographic distinctiveness persisted over the next few decades, even as more and more settlers arrived. Emigration from Europe was weighted in favor of women, a remarkable phenomenon in light of the male composition of European emigration as a whole. By 1870, 49.1 percent of Zion's residents were women, while only 41.5 percent of the settlers in Oregon were.

What accounted for the numbers of women flocking to Utah, and what was the attitude of the church toward them? What place did the church assign women in the new society, and what kind of a commitment did it require from them? Certainly the converts did not expect the slavery that New England novelists described so luridly; nor did they look forward to sexual liberation. Despite the institution of polygamy, the Mormon frontier did not offer women the sexual or familial liberation available in communities like New Harmony, Indiana, which

rejected marriage in favor of free love. Nor did the emphasis
on community usually mean communal living arrangements as
far-reaching as those in a settlement like Amana, which freed
women from much of the drudgery of housework.

Emigration for many of the women was, in fact, not explicitly
linked to liberation from traditional gender roles. Most came
with parents or husbands; missionaries carefully concealed or
minimized polygamy. Conversion was frequently a family affair,
triggered by the promise of heavenly salvation. But economic
rewards paralleled religious ones, for Zion's kingdom began not
in heaven but on earth. New settlers were smoothly integrated
into the frontier economy; the opportunities routinely provided
seemed especially dazzling when contrasted to the humble
background of most converts. Early land policy, for example,
provided all settlers with free land, and those with special skills
could always be assured of a livelihood. Ann Bringhurst's satisfaction with Zion was materialistic, and not surprisingly so.
"We have everything arround us we could asks," she wrote to
Olivia Wollerton in 1850. "We have the best plase in the world
to make money." Then, too, the church made emigration relatively easy. For two decades, a significant proportion of church
resources went to financing emigration through the Perpetual
Emigrating Fund. The fund loaned travel money to converts,
while missionaries made the arrangements. Rather than face the
trip alone like other emigrants, Mormon converts traveled as a
group with leaders. All knew that a livelihood awaited them at
the journey's end.

A minority of the women came without families. The recollections of one young Englishwoman show the pattern of conversion and emigration. The woman made initial contact with
missionaries in a most unlikely way when she hired a man and
his son to paint and paper her house. Hearing that the pair had
some "strange religiousness," she inquired about their peculiar
beliefs. The Mormon missionaries quickly took advantage of her
curiosity and soon provided her with books. As she remembered

much later, "I found myself believing! What should I do?" Other women's chance or purposeful encounters with missionaries raised the same question. Because of the group nature of emigration, single women and a surprising number of widows could easily be incorporated into the "gathering," and emigration followed conversion.

But if the going was instigated by faith and facilitated by travel arrangements, other motives encouraged solitary women to make the trip. General hostility to Mormonism spurred female and male converts to leave their homes. More positive factors fostering female emigration included recognition of women's individual spiritual gifts, like speaking in tongues and experiencing visions, and the sheer adventure of being able to participate in creating God's kingdom on earth. Finally, single converts faced a more promising material future in Utah than they often did at home, where their economic options were limited. Many were in domestic service, probably the most unpleasant of all female employments. Emigration broke the bonds of servitude, and at the journey's end, food, shelter, employment, perhaps even marriage awaited. In return for these benefits, women would have duties and obligations to perform on the frontier.

An evolving theology partly determined the official attitude of the church toward women. The *Book of Mormon*, which Joseph Smith revealed to the world in 1830, had almost nothing to say about women. Its virtual neglect of females was rooted in Smith's theology. He believed that Christ's Priesthood had been reinstated in Zion with all believing white males as potential members. Even though hierarchy existed (there were two ranks, the Aaronic, or lesser, priesthood and the Melchizedek), every man had religious duties ranging from conducting worship and instructing others in the faith to healing the sick. Religious duties and privileges bolstered male status. Mormon society was patriarchal, sanctioned by religious doctrine.

Women's spiritual fate depended entirely on their relationship with men. Only by becoming the wife of a man endowed with the priesthood could a woman hope for salvation. For the unmarried woman, the prospect was grim: spiritual annihilation.

Other aspects of Smith's theology partially compensated for women's spiritual inferiority. If a woman married, she and her husband both might acquire salvation, but only a woman could fulfill a crucial part of God's plan for the world. Mormons believed that the universe was filled with souls hungering for human bodies, without which salvation was impossible. As Brigham Young pointed out, "It is the duty of every righteous man and every woman to prepare tabernacles for all the spirits they can." Female reproduction was, therefore, the means of releasing souls from a limbolike existence. Ultimately childbearing brought heavenly rewards to both parents, for their position in heaven depended on the number of their offspring. (Polygamous families had a distinct advantage here.) Since women were so essential to God and men, the church assured them of participation in temple ceremonies.

The Mormon church's determination to build a self-contained Zion in Utah also affected the church's understanding of women's role and served as a counterweight to some of the more problematic aspects of theology. In the harsh desert landscape, Mormons dreamed of creating a self-sufficient kingdom, a retreat for the faithful and the basis for a new social order. To realize this vision, men and women both would have to contribute their labor. Especially during the early period of settlement (1847–1867), women were encouraged to work; laziness was condemned as a major sin. "We do not believe in having any drones in the hive," Mrs. Ezra Benson explained. "All are engaged in some useful occupation." Women were full economic partners, performing vital jobs, even those traditionally defined as male. So, Mrs. Benson pointed out, "some spin, others weave cloth . . . Some make up the clothing . . . others again make the butter and cheese, and attend to the cows, pigs and poultry." Still others might "plough and harrow the ground, plant the seed, and hoe up the weeds when the time comes.

They may also be seen irrigating the crops with water." Women not only had quilting bees but bees to build houses, dig canals, and erect fences. During the settlement period, in fact, women may have been more than economic partners. With husbands often away on church business, for years at a time if they were missionaries, women supported themselves and sometimes helped to support their husbands, all with the church's encouragement. Women had to be independent and self-reliant, Brigham Young pointed out, and mothers should make sure that they taught these qualities to their daughters: "Mothers in Israel, you . . . are called upon to bring up your daughters to pursue some useful avocation for a sustenance, that when they shall become the wives of the elders of Israel, who are frequently called upon missions, or to devote their time and attention to the things of the kingdom, they may be able to sustain themselves and their offspring."

The situation of Mormon women was, thus, paradoxical. Despite the emphasis on patriarchy and male spiritual superiority, gender roles overlapped. The goals of self-sufficiency and productivity led the church to encourage and praise those women who became producers, even though they might thereby become less dependent on male support. As one female traveler observed, "They close no career on a woman in Utah by which she can earn a living." In his colorful fashion, Young encouraged women long after the early years of settlement. "I want young women to learn business," he said. "I want them to be our telegraphers and clerks. Why, go into a store now for a yard of ribbon, and a great lazy, lubberly fellow comes rolling up like a hogshead of molasses . . . and cuts off the ribbon for you. Now that fellow we want out in the fields, up in the cañon, at work, and we want his and his fellows' places supplied by the young women."

Economic goals undermined conventional notions of female gentility. Partly because an interest in appearance and fashion made women consumers of goods from the outside and partly because Mormonism had a puritanical streak, church leaders emphasized some parts of the female image while playing down others. So Brigham Young warned against an interest in fashion and recommended that women wear "wooden-bottom shoes" and "use our old pantaloons and make caps out of them." Heber C. Kimball, one of Young's apostles, reminded Mormon women that corsets and petticoats harmed the female body and its reproductive organs. Mormon women were to be mothers, wives, and workers not well-dressed ladies of fashion.

With the emphasis on female productivity and on working toward goals collectively, it was not at all surprising that the church also encouraged female organizations and gave them important responsibilities. Joseph Smith had presided over the creation of a Female Relief Society in the 1840s, but it had disbanded during the years of persecution, migration, and early settlement in Utah. By the mid-1860s, Young was urging women to organize "against purchasing goods at the stores." He hoped that women would begin a home-manufacturing program, and a number of women's groups sprang up in response to his suggestions. Two years later, Young was more emphatic. "If the ladies would get up societies by which they could promote the home labor of their sex, they would do what was pleasing in the sight of heaven." Eliza Snow, wife of Joseph Smith and then of Brigham Young, responded to the call for action and began organizing branches of the Female Relief Society in every Mormon community.

With the church's backing, the Female Relief Society became a permanent fixture of Mormon women's lives, giving them an experience that differed from that of other pioneer women, whose organizations often had short and sporadic lives. Although the priesthood selected the female president, the society was not initially a male-dominated institution. Rather than using church funds, the society raised its own money and spent it; it even owned property. Early relief activities not only reflected Young's priorities but also focused on matters of special interest to women. Meetings were set aside for encouraging women's spiritual life with Bible readings, prayers, lectures, and discussions. It was this facet of the society's activities that led to the claim that women actually shared a kind of priesthood. Other meetings focused on charitable endeavors.

Women sewed, heard reports of their female home visitors who brought goods to the needy and evaluated their situations, and devised ways to help the poor help themselves. "To those who have strength to labor, it is far more charitable to give employment and so direct their energies that they can earn what they need," Young had suggested. The society was, in fact, in the business of running programs to train the poor.

After a period of hostilities with the Ute, the society was also in the business of ministering to the Indians. Young encouraged such activities by setting out the goals of civilizing, teaching, and improving the condition of the Ute "by your utmost faith and diligence." In 1854, Matilda Dudley and other women in her community established a society "for the purpose of making clothing for Indian women and children." Other women followed suit, ministering not only to Native Americans but to the needy in their own midst.

Within a few years after the Female Relief Society was reestablished in Utah, the Mormon hierarchy gave it new tasks judged essential for the community's survival. As the railroad approached Utah in the late 1860s, church leaders fearfully contemplated the possibilities of economic disruption as Gentile goods flowed into the territory. Women were essential actors in the campaign against the anticipated economic onslaught. Leaders urged the Relief Society to fight the demand for imports, especially among the young. Women responded by forming Retrenchment Societies to teach young women the useful skills of knitting, piecing quilts, and gleaning wheat, while encouraging their cultural aspirations. Later, women became involved in establishing and controlling cooperative stores that sold home manufactures and, then, in the 1870s, with developing home industries like silk manufacturing. In 1876, when Young wished to initiate a system of storing grain against future famine or disaster, he once more turned to women. "I have called upon and urged the brethren to lay up grain against a day of want," he explained, but "they do not follow my advice; they excuse themselves by saying their wives and daughters want the proceeds of the grain to buy hats and bonnets." Young's skepticism was evident in the description Emmeline Wells, later president of the Relief Society, provided. "He gave me quite a dissertation on the excuses made by the brethren," she recalled, "and then explained that if the sisters were told to save grain they would not sell it."

The importance of Relief Society operations gave women a power base and a channel of influence with the male power structure. Most of the influence was probably exercised gently behind the scenes; most often the organization cooperated with church directives. Mormon society did not encourage much freedom of thought, and women in the organization generally sympathized with church goals. But occasionally, Relief activities led to conflict. As women began their grain operations, for example, the question arose of who was to manage the wheat. When some of the bishops pressed for control, women disagreed and pointed to the terms of their original mission. Young backed them up and instructed bishops to leave the women alone. Women were to raise the wheat, glean it, and lend it to bishops when they needed it for the poor. But the bishops would have to ask. Certainly Young's support strengthened the organization's power, but even before his decision, women showed their determination to control their own operations. This sense of collective power also translated into individual autonomy. When the silk mission began, for example, local bishops once more were critical. One said he did not "like to see the sisters go out into the fields and around and carry bundles of mulberry boughs on their back." Husbands found silkworms in their parlors and unpleasant smells at home. Yet many women disregarded these complaints and pursued their new activity.

The Relief Society was far more important than this brief description of its spiritual and economic activities suggests. Since the society was an ongoing institution with significant tasks to perform, it provided an opportunity for Mormon women to develop a strong and positive sense of themselves. It was a means, too, of allowing most to pursue socially important tasks outside their own households and of encouraging some to learn organizational and business techniques. Aided by the Relief Society, a few women became teachers, social workers, and businesswomen. Susanna Cardon of Logan, for example, was an expert silk reeler, who left six children, including a year-old baby at home, to train other women to reel silk. The society also instructed women in health care and supported the first women doctors in Utah. In 1872, society president Eliza Snow asked, "Are there here, now, any sisters who have ambition enough, and who realize the necessity of it, for Zion's sake, to take up this study. There are some who are naturally inclined to be nurses; and such ones would do well to study medicine . . . If they cannot meet their own expenses, we have the means of doing so." Two married women responded and left their families while they attended the Women's Medical College in Philadelphia; they eventually became the first women doctors in Utah.

The position of women on the Mormon frontier was clearly far more complex than the common analogy to slavery would suggest. Mormon women had the support for a responsible and expanded social role that women on other frontiers did not. But when critics of Mormon society spoke of slavery, they did not take into account these facets of female experience. They were speaking of polygamy, which Mormons called the system of plural marriage. Although it is not clear whether most Mormon women were plural wives, the institution colored the experience of all women on the Mormon frontier and was central to their identification of themselves as Mormons. Did plural marriage, in fact, enslave women, as critics insisted, or purify them, as supporters argued?

Polygamy had no place in early Mormon theology, and as

commentators never tired of pointing out, the *Book of Mormon* condemned the practice in no uncertain terms. Yet Smith may well have begun thinking about polygamy by 1831, and by the early 1840s, he and other leaders privately began taking plural wives. To Smith, polygamy was a means of removing the evils of instability and individualism that were destroying American society. By linking individuals and families through marriage, he believed, polygamy would strengthen social, familial, and religious ties. The identification that Mormons made between themselves and the Jewish patriarchs provided scriptural precedents for the practice.

As Smith worked out the theoretical and ritualistic implications of polygamy, he revealed a new and compelling relationship between God and man. Smith came to believe two kinds of marriage existed. One was marriage for time, the other for eternity. The first was a marriage limited to earthly existence, while the second, performed in the temple with special rites, was a marriage for eternity. Those married for time could enter only into the lowest order of heaven, but those who chose a marriage for eternity were celestially mobile, eligible for heavenly glory; ultimately they might even become godlike. As a form of celestial marriage, polygamy contributed to heavenly status, for Smith believed that the more celestial wives a man had, and the more children they bore, the more honor he and his wives would enjoy in heaven: "We shall not marry . . . or be given in marriage [in heaven] hence it is necessary for us to marry here, and to marry as much as we can, for then in heaven a man will take the wives whom he married on earth, or who have been sealed to him by proxy; they will be his queens, and their children will be his subjects . . . hence we shall ourselves be gods!" Polygamy was a means of social purification and heavenly sanctification, not a means of sexual liberation.

Although members of the Mormon hierarchy practiced polygamy secretly before the migration to Utah, the doctrine and its theological justification were only announced publicly in 1852.

Polygamy was practiced openly for the next forty years in Utah and clandestinely for years after the Mormon leadership rejected it. While the acceptance of polygamy was obviously related to the elaborate theological framework, other factors were also important. Functionally, polygamy played a major role in committing Mormons to their society, as Smith had thought it would. Asked to give up the marriage form society at large sanctioned for the sake of their faith, Mormons in plural marriages were at odds with the outside world. Few polygamists apostatized. Furthermore, polygamy helped to reinforce group loyalties. In polygamy, familial and personal ties extended outward toward the group as a whole rather than inward toward the monogamous family. (It was this dissatisfaction with the privatism of monogamy and the role of women in marriage that led other nineteenth-century utopias like Oneida and New Harmony also to experiment with marital relationships.) Finally, polygamy provided a way to absorb single converts into the social order. When single or widowed women arrived in Utah, the church placed them in various households and hoped for marriage. Since many of these women were somewhat older than the average marriage age (they were usually between twenty-five and thirty-five), they would have been at a disadvantage in a monogamous culture. But polygamy meant that, no matter what their age, they might have husbands and families.

An open rejection of polygamy was equivalent to a rejection of Zion, for criticism from the outside made the doctrine the cutting point of loyalty to the religion and to the place. Over a forty-year period, the hierarchy urged the steadfast to prove their faith in Smith's revelations by adopting polygamy. Yet not all responded. The actual numbers of those practicing polygamy are unknown, since plural marriages were not recorded in public records. Estimates of those involved in plural marriage differ. Several studies have suggested that at the peak, moments of intense religious enthusiasm or periods of serious threats from the outside world, 15 to 20 percent of Mormon families were polygamous. At other times, these studies argue, the figure was probably closer to 10 percent. A very thorough examination of the community of St. George, in southern Utah, however, has found about a third of the married men were polygamists with nearly two-thirds of the women involved in plural marriages. In the small town of Alpine, in 1860, however, only one of the fifteen households was polygamous, but one historian suggests that as many as five of the other heads of households may have eventually taken a second wife. If these calculations are correct, then a majority of Alpine wives, like those in St. George, were in polygamous unions. Until scholars examine more Mormon settlements, it will not be possible to know for sure whether St. George was unusual, but there is a possibility that polygamy involved a minority of Mormon men but a majority of Mormon women.

Few of the unions, however, resembled those that New England novelists so vividly described. Of a sample of 1,784 polygamous marriages, 66.3 percent involved a husband and only two wives; 21.2 percent of the men took a third wife, but only 6.7 percent took a fourth. Less than 6 percent of the group had more than four wives. The statistical picture makes it clear that the typical polygamous marriage involved a husband and two wives.

Obviously economics was a factor. Few poor Mormons could take on the burden of a large family. Most of the big plural families, in fact, belonged to successful church leaders, who indicated their loyalty to church doctrine by marrying more than once. Then, too, there were controls. Only those Mormons "worthy of participation in the special blessings of the House of the Lord" were eligible for celestial marriage, a decision Brigham Young made himself. Adequate financial resources weighed heavily with Young, and many would-be polygamists were rejected for having insufficient means. Then, too, in communities where polygamy was common, married men had to compete with single men to secure the attentions of unmarried women.

Statistical profiles raise the possibility that, while many Mormon men gave verbal support to the institution and defended it against outside attacks, they rejected it for themselves. Even those who justified it most actively spoke of its heavy burdens and the need for personal sacrifice. As one woman in a monogamous marriage candidly admitted, "When I was told about plural marriage . . . before it was taught publicly, I went into a private room and prayed I might have power given to me that I should never speak against that principle. I knew by the Spirit of God that it was true . . . But have always been afraid of my own weakness and selfishness, but my children know that I have taught them to do right in it." A plural wife said, "Polygamy was hard to live by, both for the man and the woman."

No matter how common polygamous marriages were, they involved more women than men. Moreover, the institution affected all women. Each woman, whether married or not, had to confront the possibility of a plural marriage at some time in the future. Most observed the principle practiced by their neighbors. Almost all defended it when the outside world condemned it as evidence of Mormon corruption.

Statistical studies suggest that the average polygamous husband married first at twenty-three. His wife was three years his junior, and they lived together as a couple for thirteen years. At that point, the husband, now thirty-six, married a woman eleven years younger than his first wife. Chances were two to one that there would be no additional wives entering the family. But if the husband did marry again, his first wife would be thirty-seven, the second twenty-six, and the third only twenty-two.

All Mormon wives, whether in monogamous or polygamous unions, took Brigham Young's message to heart that God required them, "young and old . . . [to] be mothers in Israel." Unlike women on other frontiers, Mormon women apparently used no birth control. There were different fertility patterns among Mormon women, however. Both monogamous and plural wives were prolific. A study of one group of Mormon women revealed, for example, that the monogamous wife had an average of 7.83 children, while polygamous wives had 7.45. But the figures suggest that within polygamous marriages a more complicated situation existed than the averages indicate. The most common polygamous marriage was one with two wives, and in such a union, the fertility of the two women was more than twice that of the average monogamous wife, with the first wife being the most prolific. If a third wife entered the family, the family's total fertility increased by only 25 percent. The first wife, then, bore more children than the other wives and more children than the average monogamous wife. For all plural wives, the spacing between children, after their first, was less than the spacing between births of monogamous women. Whether these figures mean that women in plural marriages had more sex with their husbands than other married women is not clear. What is clear, however, is that polygamy did not lessen the cares of motherhood by decreasing fertility.

Statistics, perhaps, tell a dry story, but story there is. The age and fertility differences between polygamous wives make it clear that the first wife's experience in plural marriage differed in many respects from that of later wives. The most significant aspect of the first wife's marital situation was that she was the only wife for over a decade. Then, perhaps without much preparation, she had to confront the entry of a younger woman into the family and learn to share her husband with the newcomer. "It is the duty of a first wife to regard her husband not with a selfish devotion that would claim the whole of his society, time, and attention, but rather as owing attention to other women also, which they have a right to expect," explained one woman. Although the first wife might have a certain precedence or authority deriving from her longer relationship with her husband and had the only legal marriage, the arrival of a younger woman and of new children to rival her own was a difficult experience. In 1880, Mrs. H. D. Richards, first wife of a Mormon elder, confessed (in the words of her interviewer), "It was crushing at first but . . . as he was an elder . . . if it was necessary to . . . salvation . . . [to] let another share her pleasures, she would do so." The problem of children was more difficult, for Mrs. Richards admitted "that she should feel like wringing the neck of any other child than hers that should call him papa." Later, as the children arrived, she found that she could take an interest in them, but the interviewer added: "It is not at all the same feeling she has for her own flesh and blood. If his child and hers were drowning and but one could be saved, she should save her own."

The first wife had to accept polygamy, but additional wives chose it. Although the choice was theirs, it was not easy to join a relationship of long standing. Some women felt guilty about the disruption they caused. Annie Tanner, a second wife, reflected: "There is something so sacred about the relationship of husband and wife that a third party in the family is sure to disturb the confidence and security that formerly existed. So far as Aunt Jennie [the first wife] was concerned, I felt like an intruder." Tanner's own mother had been a second wife and had faced another common difficulty. Her husband's first wife enjoyed a preferred status; the first wife's home was the husband's headquarters, and she had charge of handing out household supplies. Tanner's mother's inferior position and dependency on the first wife was, at times, humiliating. Nor was a second wife's youth always an advantage, for it could make it more difficult to relate to the older woman. Some ended their isolation by becoming close to the first wife's children, but not all had this option. Finally, a second and later marriage had no legal standing.

Women's experience in polygamy also differed according to the period in which they married. The first polygamous wives coming out of a monogamous culture faced the painful task of rejecting strong cultural taboos. "When the principle of polygamy was first taught," Phoebe Woodruff recalled, "I thought it the most wicked thing I ever heard of; consequently I opposed it to the best of my ability, until I became sick and wretched." Prayer and the belief in Joseph Smith's prophetic powers eventually helped many women accept their husbands' desire to take additional wives. Some eased their anxieties by convincing themselves, as did Mrs. Richards, that "his love was not lustful; he married simply because his religion demanded it." The belief in a husband's pure motives was a common way of coping with the situation. Whatever the psychological burdens were, early plural wives also faced trying and primitive conditions; poverty, as most Mormons agreed, increased the tensions inherent to polygamy. Later, material conditions were far better, and it was possible to work out more elaborate living arrangements than during early pioneer days. By that time, society had had time to adapt to polygamy. But even as support for polygamy solidified, the persecution of polygamous families by federal authorities increased. Many second and third wives lived an underground existence, even delivering their own babies.

There is much evidence to suggest that Mormons found plural marriage difficult at all times. The song favored at local festivals indicated that it was a "trial." Memoirs and journals echoed the same belief. Why, then, did women choose to enter into such marriages? Certainly not for romantic love. This Martha Cox acknowledged: "It was not a marriage of love . . . [my family] claimed and in saying so they struck me a blow for I could not say that I had really loved the man as lovers love."

Some women, of course, never chose. Although husbands were supposed to consult their wives before marrying again, they did not always do so. Some, in fact, took additional wives over the vigorous protests of the first wife. So Mary Ann Hafen described the conditions of her marriage, noting, "Susette was opposed to his marrying again, but the authorities advised him to do so anyway, saying that she would be reconciled. I did not like to marry him under those circumstances, but being urged on by him and my parents, I consented." (It is hardly surprising that Mary Ann cried all the way to her wedding.)

Most women who recorded their thoughts about their marriages emphasized how seriously they took religious imperatives. "I knew the principle . . . to be correct," Martha Cox explained, for it was "the highest, holiest order of marriage." Eternal happiness depended on a husband's wives and their children. While this belief motivated most women, it had great impact on infertile wives. Annie Tanner was told by her future husband's first wife that, although she had an aversion to polygamy, she had failed to conceive after five years of marriage. So she concluded, "I can't deprive Marion of a family, and of all the girls I know, you are my choice." A study of polygamous families revealing that 31.2 percent of the marriages included at least two sisters suggests another motive. Women used plural marriages as a means of incorporating female relatives into their own families.

Younger wives were also drawn to polygamy because the attentions of an older man flattered them, while the practice seemed to offer social and economic status and perhaps emotional security. The latter attracted Martha Cox, who lived with a polygamous family as an unmarried woman and discovered that "perfect order prevailed . . . and did much to soften the prejudice I had formed in my mind against the principle of plural marriage. I learned here to pay respects to ordinances of the gospel which before I had treated lightly." Jane Woolsey, on the other hand, proposed to a fifty-five-year-old man while in her teens, saying, "A home is what I want & a kind Friend to protect me. You are the man of my choice & can furnish me with the home I want." Yet older women also had pragmatic reasons for accepting new wives in their homes. "I thank the Lord every day that now I am infirm," one woman explained, "Brother Samuel has her at his side to watch over him, and see that his health and comfort are attended to as he is growing old." The emphasis on the household help younger women might provide is supported by the number of women who entered a household as servants and ended as wives.

To generalize about how Mormon women felt about their own

polygamous situations is difficult, for their reactions differed. Some, for example, believing polygamy to be a religious obligation or at least likely, urged husbands to take wives. In promoting matches, they may have been trying to screen the candidates. Some found they could live harmoniously with new wives, but others could not. Especially when women still thought of the marriage as an exclusive relationship, polygamy, all too often, resulted in rivalry, jealousy, and competition.

Part of the women's problem with polygamy resulted from the institution's place in Mormon culture. Although theologically polygamy had firm roots and was defended warmly against outside attacks, the statistics suggest that the new social patterns were never thoroughly embedded in the culture. Monogamy remained the preference of the majority of men. In addition, there were never clearly defined standards or norms to guide those heeding the church's injunctions. Husbands, for example, were urged to be evenhanded with their money and time, but general principles never resulted in specific guidelines. Nor was the status of different wives ever formalized. Even the crucial procedures and rules for selecting a new wife were uncertain. Although men were supposed to discuss marriage plans with their wives, church leaders themselves, as Mary Ann Hafen's case indicates, complicated the process by taking sides. As one scholar has pointed out, polygamous societies normally develop distinctive housing patterns, for living arrangements are fundamental to the ultimate success of the institution. In Utah, however, housing for plural families varied widely, according to the individuals involved, their ideas, and resources. Some husbands chose to live with all their wives in a common house, although the women had their own rooms. Others established wives in separate houses, sometimes in the same community, sometimes in widely scattered locations. Some men rotated between houses, others used one house as a headquarters. Much evidence suggests that polygamy worked best in Utah when wives had their own homes and their husbands visited them, yet such an arrangement was never standardized. The uncertain place polygamy occupied in the culture and the variety of arrangements make generalization difficult.

Most sources, however, point to the painful adjustments polygamy demanded. Even Joseph Smith had trouble at home, since his first wife, Emma, opposed the principle. She was never to know how many women he actually married. Brigham Young urged polygamous families to try harder and so revealed the troubles polygamy brought. "It is frequently happening," he said, "that women say they are unhappy. Men will say, 'My wife, though a most excellent woman, has not seen a happy day since I took my second wife'; 'No, not a happy day for a year,' says one; and another has not seen a happy day for five years. It is said that women are tied down and abused: that they are misused and have not the liberty they ought to have; that many of them are wading through a perfect flood of tears because of the conduct of some men, together with their own folly." Young challenged the women to leave Zion or to adjust: "In their hearts that they will embrace the Gospel—the whole of it." In fact, there was another alternative beyond Young's take-it-or-leave-it approach, divorce. Although the church disapproved of it, the tensions of plural marriage made divorce necessary. Significantly, it was easier for wives than for husbands to obtain divorces.

The divorce system suggests that marriage was most difficult for polygamous wives, who had to share their husband's affection, time, and resources with other women and their children. Because the society lacked a commonly accepted way of allocating any of these, women were forced to depend on their husband's sense of fair play and generosity. Some women solved their financial dependency by learning to support themselves. If polygamy was as widespread as some studies suggest, women in poorer polygamous families had to become adept managers. Others tried to win their husbands by proficient housekeeping. Good housekeeping became a favored means of strengthening

marital affection and achieving stability, because polygamous
wives could adopt more forthright tactics only at some risk.
Nagging, for example, could easily backfire by driving a husband to another wife. "The wife whom he leaves behind is, of
course, broken-hearted," a Mormon plural wife explained. "She
would frequently blame herself and resolve never to have that
experience repeated."

Burdens of child rearing and decision making fell heavily on
polygamous wives. For "in polygamy, the man's interests are
scattered," one woman explained. "He may be influenced by
members of his other family, or families. He would need to be
almost a superhuman man to help each wife *equally* with the
problems of rearing a family, and to resist the biased influence
of other family members." Nor could these women necessarily
look forward to assistance or security in their later years. Since
the law only recognized the first marriage, plural wives were
not assured of sharing their husband's estate, nor were their
"illegitimate" children. Only if husbands gave wives (and/or
children) property before their death or specifically mentioned
their plural families in their wills would later wives and their
children be provided for.

The strain was not solely on the women, however. The economic burdens were real, and so were the emotional ones. As
one father told his daughter, who was contemplating becoming
a second wife, it was easy to win the affections of a girl, "but
it is not, in polygamy, an easy task to keep her affections." It
was, of course, more difficult to develop good relationships with
several wives than with one, and it was necessary to try, at least,
to appear impartial and fair with them all. Above all, men had
to avoid giving cause for jealousy, for jealousy was the bane of
polygamy and could make the marriage miserable for everyone.
Thus, courtships were brief and to the point. Once married, the
wise avoided showing any special affection to one wife over
another. The strains on both men and women in plural marriage
and the need to avoid giving cause for envy, in fact, led to a

minimization of romantic love before and after marriage. Young's insistence that Mormon women dress simply and unfashionably had more than an economic rationale behind it as his comment that he was "ashamed to see the tight clothes— to see the shape of the ladies" suggests. Physical attractions and romantic passions were antithetical to the smooth workings of the marriage system, and each sex was wise to keep a certain emotional distance from the other. Describing the ideal marital relationship, one wife said that she should be as "pleased to see [her husband] . . . when he came in as she was pleased to see any friend." Women counseled one another to take such a detached view. Thus, an older friend encouraged Mrs. Richards "to make herself happy whether her husband was here or not; not to think about it; where he was or who he was with, and that She would outgrow all the troubles she met at the outset."

If there were stresses and strains, however, there were also high stakes to make plural marriages work. How could men who failed to manage their earthly families expect heaven's highest honors? Women, too, focused on religious rewards. "I want to be assured of *my position in God's estimation,*" one plural wife revealed. "If polygamy is the Lord's order, we must carry it out." Such determination could make plural marriage succeed. One admittedly small study of polygamous families found more than half of the marriages very successful or reasonably successful. About a quarter of them reported some difficulty but were considered moderately successful nonetheless, while the other quarter reported serious problems.

It is inconceivable that so many of those involved would see their marriages as reasonably successful, however, if the only rewards were heavenly ones. Clearly, women would not defend the institution so heatedly unless, at least occasionally, they derived some earthly benefits from it. Women in polygamous marriages represented an ideal and gained prestige thereby. Their religious status often also signified high social and economic position, since church leaders and potential leaders were

more likely to be polygamous than the population at large.
Moreover, the glorification of motherhood helped to compensate
for some of the difficulties of being a plural wife. "Are you
tormenting yourselves by thinking that your husbands do not
love you?" Brigham Young asked Mormon wives. "I would not
care whether they loved you a particle or not; but I would cry
out, like one of the old, in the joy of my heart, 'I have got a
man from the Lord!' 'Halleluya! I am a mother—I have borne
an image of God!' " The ideological support for motherhood
(rather than wifehood) was matched on another level by the
rewards of motherhood. Because fathers could not supervise the
children of their various wives as closely as they could in monogamous marriages, wives often took charge of the children.
Though the responsibility could be, at times, a strain, many
women enjoyed rearing their children and identified with them
rather than with their husbands. Certainly they felt great pride
in their children. "My children, their life and health, was an
attainment," one wife reported, which no one "could take from
me."

Occasionally, polygamous wives also formed close and satisfying ties with one another. Sometimes ties of affection or
blood drew women into a plural household in the first place.
Whatever the original bonds, female friendships could become
more intimate and affectionate than relationships between
friends or relatives separated by circumstance. "We three . . .
loved each other more than sisters," one wife movingly testified,
and will "go hand in hand together down till eternity." The very
real practical advantages that polygamy could provide for
women equaled the emotional satisfactions. When polygamous
wives got along, they often divided the labor so as to free each
from some female chores. Mary Ann Bentley sketched the division of labor in her family. One wife, without children of her
own, became the family business head and general manager,
while the second wife spent most of her time weaving. The third
wife took responsibility for cleaning, cooking, and dish washing.
The family operation worked smoothly and amicably.

As polygamy could result in a certain freedom from domestic chores and responsibilities, so, too, could it lead to an independence from men themselves. Despite the church's emphasis on patriarchy, plural wives were more likely than monogamous wives to be household heads, and this status suggested the possibility for autonomy. Since both polygamy and the church made great demands on men's time, many plural wives learned to make decisions and handle routine details of management. They were also likely to share certain powers with their husbands. One study of polygamous marriages revealed that the men and women involved more often shared financial responsibilities than husbands and wives in monogamous marriages, where men wielded more power than women. When husbands were away on missionary trips or located their families in remote communities, women learned how to fend for themselves and to take pride in their ability to face life alone. "I had the attitude of many Mormon women in polygamy," one wife pointed out. "I felt the responsibility of my family; and I developed an independence that women in monogamy never know . . . [for the plural wife] becomes conscious of her own power to make decisions. She learns that it takes more than the authority of the leader in a patriarchal marriage to make a successful home." In the end, many women achieved a psychic independence, an "individual character as separate from . . . their husband['s]." Certainly, their activities belied the conventional stereotype of nineteenth-century woman as passive and economically dependent on her husband.

When all the pluses and minuses of polygamy are balanced, one must remember that although it was the approved standard many Mormon settlers quietly rejected it for themselves. Most of those in polygamous marriages accepted its trials and rewards. The home that non-Mormon women opened in Salt Lake City to receive women "escaping" from polygamy had only a few residents. But there was passive resistance, perhaps centralized in certain localities. Reminiscences highlight patterns. Martha Cox, for example, grew up in a monogamous family and openly admitted to prejudice against polygamy. When she changed her mind and decided to enter a plural household, her family vigorously opposed her. Her friends criticized her decision and pointed to the poverty of the family she had chosen to join. Female friends argued that she was demeaning herself by accepting a married man's proposal. Martha's only strong support came from "the good kind women whom I had chosen to share the burdens of life."

If there was opposition to polygamy within Mormon society, however, few in the outside world knew of it. Because the attack on polygamy was so clearly an attack on Mormon society as a whole, Mormons rose to defend it. Women were particularly vocal defenders, and over the years, their arguments strengthened their sense of collective identity just as much as they served to answer outside criticism. The *Woman's Exponent*, a publication established in 1872 and run largely by women for women, helped to create a sense of who Mormon women were. Certainly, they were not enslaved, nor were they unfit to carry out their moral and domestic obligations. Indeed, Mormon women took these responsibilities just as earnestly as American women did everywhere. Far from being degraded by their religion, the writers insisted, Mormon women were made stronger, more useful, and content.

The issue of polygamy and the efforts of the United States government to wipe it out furthered the sense of female collective identity by drawing women into organized protest. Mass meetings involving many women in monogamous marriages as well as those who practiced polygamy, petitions and resolutions against national antipolygamy legislation all testified to women's growing political awareness and to the evolution of an image of Mormon women as persecuted but justified in their beliefs. Female vindications of polygamy resembled those developed by their society as a whole, but women claimed that polygamy was a pragmatic institution benefiting women. Polygamy, women argued, created a more acceptable life for women than the one available to their counterparts in the outside world, for polygamy controlled men and their appetites. In Gentile society, lustful men exploited female prostitutes, and innocent wives suffered. In Mormon society, however, the option of polygamy eliminated the drive that led to prostitution and infidelity. Every woman could enjoy marriage, home, family, and a security ensured by the elimination of infidelity and the double standard. Furthermore, the institution provided plural wives with more time for themselves and offered more opportunities for independence than monogamy could.

Through their defense of polygamy, then, Mormon women were politicized, learned to evaluate their role in settling Utah, and gained a perspective on themselves as women rather than merely as isolated individuals on the frontier. The utopian nature of the frontier experience and the organization of frontier life had also contributed to a heightened female self-consciousness. Mormon leaders, planning for Utah's self-sufficiency, urged women to work toward collective goals, supported them in their departures from conventional roles, and praised them for their social and religious contributions. Female organizations brought women together to work for a variety of objectives and reinforced their sense of usefulness. For a few women, participation in the Mormon experiment also meant unexpected support for radically new social roles. The first women doctors in Utah were such women.

Of course, if the Mormon frontier experience did, in some ways, contribute to women's consciousness and helped to create a strong collective identity, there were costs and limitations. There was little place in Mormon society for the woman who could not accept the utopian vision or who openly challenged the goals and directives of the priesthood. Social experiments like polygamy created stress and demanded sacrifices from many of the individuals involved. The recollections of one of the first women doctors gives some sense of the personal suffering departure from conventional social roles might entail.

Responding to the call church leaders put out, Romania Bunnell Pratt decided to study medicine in Philadelphia. Romania convinced her husband she had made the right decision, sold her house and her piano to help finance her studies, and left five of her seven children with her mother. When she returned, she found her home "still, quiet and empty, but hearing voices in the orchard I wandered back and found my dear faithful mother and two youngest children gathering fruit. My heart was pierced with sorrow when my little ones opened wide their eyes in wonder and with no token of recognition of their mother. I wept bitterly that I had been forgotten by my babes." Because of the Mormon emphasis on the family, the acceptance of new roles could produce conflict and unhappiness. Romania ended by divorcing her husband of twenty years.

In the 1890s, when persecution by the federal government finally led the leadership to abandon polygamy, Utah gave up its attempt to maintain self-sufficiency and separation from the outside world and began its long process of integrating into American society. Even before that time, there were signs that the pattern of female experience on the Mormon frontier might ultimately resemble that of pioneer women elsewhere. Usefulness did not necessarily mean the rejection of domesticity. Indeed, Brigham Young's exhortations to Mormon women to be productive members of society suggested that women were already fully immersed in domesticity and needed to be reminded that important tasks existed outside their homes. And his attempts to persuade women to dress plainly in homemade garments testified to their interest in the female world of gentility and fashion. Bolts of cloth from the East topped the list of imports to Utah and were transformed into clothes that differed little from eastern fashions.

There are many indications, in fact, that Mormon women, like women on other parts of the frontier, wished to re-create a female sphere. During the earliest years, the need to survive conflicted with this goal, as it did on most frontiers. But as soon as they could, Mormon women shaped their female world. Census collectors in 1870 and 1880 noted that most women were "keeping house" rather than teaching, practicing medicine, or working in stores, despite the church's encouragement. Women's organizations, though teaching members new skills and providing them with socially valued work, did not usually mean the neglect of home and family. Even individual and collective identities worked out in opposition to criticism during the first decades of settlement could not be so sharp and clear once outside criticism ceased. And with the church's accommodation to the Gentile world, the leadership no longer had the same requests to make of Mormon women and no longer furnished the same support for expanded female roles. In fact, during the early twentieth century, Mormon women lost, rather than acquired, respect and power. Even their organizations ceased to play the independent role they once had. By the mid-twentieth century, indeed, Mormon women had become the bulwarks of social conservatism and staunch defenders of traditional gender norms.

What the Mormon frontier experiment did show, more clearly than other frontiers, was the power of domestic ideology. Despite frontier conditions and unique religious and social conditions, once again women found that domesticity gave their lives meaning. Since the lower-class background of Mormon emigrants is well established, the Mormon frontier gives plain evidence that ideology about woman's place affected the lower ranks of society as well as the middle levels. As Eliza Dilworth wrote to her brother in 1856, "Virtue is my motto and all my children are honnorabel." She was a true woman of her times.

"Will She Not Overstep
the Bounds of Propriety
If She Ventures
into the Arena of Action?"

Phoebe Judson's reminiscences, titled *A Pioneer's Search for an Ideal Home*, were shaped by her conviction that her life's meaning came from her quest for a perfect home. Her narrative catalogued all her temporary stopping places on the frontier, until finally she described the family's comfortable homestead, "remote from the world, surrounded by the beauties and bounties of nature." This lovely spot was the right location for the home she had so long desired. As time passed, however, the place became less remote, and the beauties and bounties of nature began to fade. In short, her narrative shows a community growing up around her home, a forest despoiled, all in the name of progress. Yet the changes, far from marring her home, only improved it, Phoebe thought. When a church with a bell was erected, Phoebe recalled she had "realized that my 'ideal home' was one more step nearer completion."

Phoebe Judson's comments highlight the pioneer determination to turn "wilderness" into civilization and to accept the costs involved in the transformation. Men and women like the Judsons believed in the necessity of progress, which they defined as re-creating communities and institutions in the West. But though the goal was widely accepted, the process of community building itself was not smooth; along with cooperation came dissension. Indeed, the transiency of frontier society, the different regional, cultural, religious, ethnic, and political loyalties found in a new community, the economic uncertainties of early frontier life, all suggest unavoidable clashes as communities were established and grew. Although early community histories rarely acknowledged the struggles, recently historians have looked behind the boosterism of local chronicles to discover the economic, political, and social battles for power that accompanied growth and modernization.

The new awareness of conflict, however, tends to focus on dissension in the male world, with only passing attention to the gender struggles implicit in community building. Yet Phoebe Judson's reminiscences are filled with clues about gender and class encounters. There was, she pointed out, initially no gambling den, no saloon, no drugstore "to cast its debasing gloom over . . . [the] captivating landscape" of the young town. Eventually, "a dark cloud" appeared in the form of two strangers who applied for a saloon license. "With hearts all aflame with love for husbands, sons and fathers," she recalled, the women "rallied to the rescue," only to find that rescue was not desired. "We visited by ones and twos, and in companies, the different members of the city council, and pleaded for the safety of our loved ones; but all in vain—our pleadings, prayers and entreaties—greed of gold carried the day."

Although the incident Phoebe described gave little indication of the women's anger and frustration at their defeat, it typified the kinds of encounters that routinely occurred with growth. Middle-class white men and women often held different visions of community. Men sought a community marked by outward order, but one providing individuals with the freedom to pursue their fortunes and pleasures. The vision could allow compromises with strict morality, as the frontier habit of doing business on the Sabbath and condoning prostitution testified. Indeed, nineteenth-century norms, in a sense, legitimated such compromises, for men were not really responsible for the moral order; women were. Many middle-class women saw the ideal community in a different light; it was to be a place of real, rather than apparent, order, a place without disruptive threats to family unity and purity. It was to be a place where men and women of all classes honored middle-class values and behavior.

If domestic ideology encouraged women to visualize the community in these terms, ironically it could involve them in organizational activities that contributed to the very social disorganization they deplored. Like Phoebe Judson and her friends, numerous western women would cause trouble by assaulting the male world and its standards and attacking the entrepreneurial ethic, that "greed of gold" Phoebe identified as the root of all evil. A few would even go on to wish for the vote rather than, as Phoebe put it, "bear the disgrace, poverty and heartrending sorrow in silent tears, without protest" when they saw the land "we have so dearly purchased and help to make blossom like the rose" sullied.

An examination of some of western women's activities shows how their organizations could move from community building to a disrupting reformism and assault on the male sphere. It also reveals, however, that, while frontier conditions may have sharpened gender conflict, these conditions did not lead to unique forms of organizational activity. The issues arousing women's groups in the West and the rationale used to justify their actions, their strategies, and their goals paralleled the course of eastern reform. In both places, organizational activities gained strength from and tended to reinforce the division of society along traditional gender lines. Far from providing a setting in which women liberated themselves from conventional views of gender relations, the frontier environment called for a reaffirmation of woman's nature. Even suffrage and coeducation, supposedly two badges of frontier freedom, suggest that the new society failed to reinterpret woman's place.

Of all their organized activities on the frontier, female charitable work seems, on the surface, to have had little potential for social disruption. As mothers, women were responsible for caring for the weak, the sick, the disabled. It was a short step from these domestic cares to charitable work, and for many a western woman the Civil War provided the incentive for such a step. Numerous Sanitary Aid Societies and Ladies Aid Societies were formed nationwide to help with the war effort. Society projects appeared both harmless and helpful, but even on the frontier the propriety of public charitable efforts had to be discussed. Elizabeth Thurston brought up the question before the Oregon Sanitary Aid Society in 1863. "What can woman do? Will she not overstep the bounds of propriety if she ventures into the arena of action?" she asked. The answer was, in her opinion, negative: "Thanks to the Sanitary Commission . . . all honor to the noble minds who projected it." Not all agreed, however, as the McMinnville Ladies Sanitary Aid Society in Oregon discovered. So careful were the ladies not to give unnecessary offense that their discussion of a July 4 celebration in 1865 led to the conclusion "that it was not best for us as a Society to do any thing about it, but to use our influence to induce the gentlemen of our village to get up a celebration." Despite their caution, their pious project of buying pocket Bibles for soldiers, and their decorous meetings ("always . . . opened by reading the Scriptures and prayer and generally characterized by unity of feeling and harmony of deliberation"), some accused the women of being disruptive. As one woman reflected, "Discouragements were not lacking, and many were the criticisms of those who 'went not with us.' "

Buying Bibles, supporting soldiers' families, raising money seemed harmless enough, even though some might object to these activities as unseemly. Certainly the charitable endeavors held little criticism of the male world, unless it was that men were so busy fighting the war they did not have time to care for its casualties. But other equally benevolent efforts suggested a far less flattering assessment of the male world, even if it was only implicit. The San Francisco Ladies' Protection and Relief Society, established in 1853, was one such organization. Its inspiration came from Mrs. A. B. Eaton, who opened her cottage door one day to find a young woman asking for assistance. Her brother, the woman said, had planned to meet her at the steamer but had never arrived, leaving her with nowhere to stay and no one to turn to for help. Realizing the economic and moral vulnerability of such a woman, Mrs. Eaton called together her friends to form a society to "render protection and assistance to strangers, to sick and dependent women and children." Within a year, the group had decided to open a home for "all respectable women in want of protection, employment in families or as needlewomen." The emphasis on respectability clarified the middle-class standards to which potential clients would be held while the occupational opportunities provided for them implied their working-class origins.

A bitter debate accompanied the decision to open the home, and some officers resigned. Although the reason for the disagreement is not clear, the implication that men were sexual predators may have offended some of the women. But shocking or not, many female charitable organizations that cared for destitute and homeless women and children were based on unflattering assessments of men. Certainly, many women felt it their duty to protect women and children who were at risk from men who could not be trusted.

At times, seemingly innocent charitable activities resulted in open criticism of the male order. The activities of the Wichita Ladies Aid Society show women moving to an explicit condemnation of the male community. During the 1870s, the agricultural frontier of Kansas experienced a series of natural calamities. Locusts and drought ravaged crops. As winter came

on, the women of Wichita organized to cope with what promised
to be widespread rural destitution. The women, however, faced
opposition from town boosters and property owners who rejected
the "whining" cries for aid. Fearing either to acknowledge the
extent of the disaster or to accept out-of-state aid, men minimized the situation because, as the newspaper concluded, the
truth "will retard immigration . . . They do not want the true
condition of the 'Great Arkansas Valley' known, for they say
that 'this valley has been advertised to the world as one of the
best agricultural countries in existence, and if we go east to
solicit aid to keep body and soul together, how can we ask
people to immigrate here?' " As winter wore on, the situation
of farming families became increasingly desperate. Women
struggled to relieve suffering and finally attacked townsmen in
an open letter in the newspaper. "It is *absolutely true*," they
wrote, "that there are families in the country whose only safety
from starvation lies in the charity of the people . . . that women
and children have no shoes and stockings . . . that many cabins
have no floors, and their inmates at this inclement season place
their beds upon the ground. To those who, like doubting Thomas
will not believe, we propose to furnish transportation into the
country and let them see for themselves . . . As far as the injury
to the country is concerned by the circulating of the truth, will
it hurt the country as much to help these people in their need,
as to let one man or woman die of cold or starvation?" The
doubting Thomases were, of course, men. The impassioned letter proved persuasive, and the women obtained supplies of food,
clothing, and cash to distribute to destitute families. When it
phased out operations late in the spring, the society had some
pithy comments for the male community, which had for so long
allowed its entrepreneurial and speculative vision to hinder relief efforts: "We have pursued our way, in regard to 'aid,' for
the last eight months, not without any hindrances and much
criticism."

As other chapters have suggested, early campaigns against

gambling, prostitution, and drinking more explicitly pitted women and their allies against the male world and the working-class women who were part of it than did their charitable endeavors. In the 1870s and subsequent decades, middle-class women in several major western cities developed ambitious strategies to assert their authority and to highlight the moral failings of men. Rather than focusing on the sexual sins of fallen women, organizations like the Chinese Mission House in San Francisco opened their doors to women in disgrace. As the names of many of these organizations make clear, white middle-class women were to rescue other women, in this case Chinese prostitutes, from lustful male predators, in this case Chinese men. The Chinese Mission House not only condemned male sexual desire but also upset the city's racial arrangements. When the white neighborhood heard of the plans to convert a building to a rescue home for Chinese women, it was "in an uproar" and "a mob threaten[ed] to tear down the building." Prominent men who harbored political ambitions that depended on male support wanted nothing to do with the effort to aid the victims of male viciousness and even prevented their wives and daughters from working for the mission. Even worse, Presbyterian ministers, apparently distressed at the independent course the women were charting, looked at the project with "distant reserve" or "openly opposed it."

Rescue homes expressed the female determination to eliminate vice and the double standard. They also testified to a powerful faith that a Christian middle-class home, presided over by a virtuous woman, had the power to redeem its inhabitants as well as society. The domestic ideal determined the character of the institutions. Matrons played the role of mother supervising the behavior and morals of the women who lived in the home. The young women had domestic chores that prepared them for either marriage or domestic service in a good family.

While rescue homes drew their sustenance from a female-centered vision of the community, their results pointed to the limits of female power. Providing a temporary home for Chinese prostitutes or rescuing prostitutes from brothels did not end prostitution or the determination of men to see it continue. Nor did Chinese residents follow the path reformers had laid out for them. The majority of Chinese women resisted attempts to transform them into middle-class Christian women. They had their own hopes and expectations. Many had come to the refuge to facilitate their marriage with Chinese suitors who were unable to pay off their contracts with brothel owners. They were drawn by the possibility of getting help, not by white cultural standards or Protestantism.

Refuge homes represented one aspect of women's reformism in the West but were far less significant than organizational efforts to control drinkers and end the power of liquor interests. Efforts to bring prohibition to the frontier epitomized their struggle with barbarism in the new society and with male tolerance of vice, which was motivated by its profit, its pleasure, or both.

In general, western prohibition campaigns paralleled eastern ones. As an organized movement, prohibition was a nineteenth-century response to a nineteenth-century problem. Alcoholic overindulgence was, of course, not new, but in the seventeenth and eighteenth centuries traditional customs and restraints had surrounded drinking. These were, however, breaking down as America changed from an agricultural society to a commercial, urbanized, industrialized society and as continual migration west undercut the force of tradition. At the same time, because of new distilling techniques and the reduction or elimination of government taxes on spirits, hard liquor was increasingly available. Beer and ale drinking declined in the first decades of the nineteenth century, while the consumption of hard liquor increased. Possibly, new cultural distinctions between the male and the female spheres also encouraged male drinking, either as an affirmation of masculinity or as a means of relieving tensions concerning it. In any case, by the early nineteenth century, drunkenness was endemic, and some began to see it as a dangerous social problem and a threat to family stability. This perception led to new efforts to control the consumption of liquor.

In the West, drinking seemed especially troublesome. The weakness of institutionalized restraints and the drudgery of so much of frontier life may well have fostered excessive private drinking. Certainly, the frontier saloons and whiskey tents encouraged public drunkenness with free lunches, the custom of allowing drinkers to fill their own glasses (the price being the same whether or not the glass was filled to the brim), and the encouragement of treating. Frontier accounts give ample evidence of long drinking bouts, especially in those communities on mining, cattle, or urban frontiers, where there were large transient male populations. As these communities matured, the signs of other male vices faded; gambling disappeared, and prostitution became discreet. But drinking did not. The number of saloons, in fact, increased with growth, and so, too, did their trade. California was the leader in this respect; by 1888, it was estimated that the state had a saloon for every sixteen voters. San Francisco boasted thirty-one times as many saloons as churches and had more than twice as many saloons in relation to its population as New York or Chicago and nine times as many as Boston or Philadelphia. Other western communities had less depressing statistics, but the problem was the same. Drinking was a threat to social stability and social values.

Since drinking was primarily a male phenomenon, early nineteenth-century temperance groups had been restricted to men. The roots of drunkenness, it was supposed, lay in the moral weakness of the individual drinker. By persuading drinkers (and nondrinkers) to take the pledge of abstinence, and then providing them with fellowship, it was hoped that they would abandon the evil habit. Early western temperance activities followed this pattern of moral persuasion. In the first year of the gold rush, for example, a San Francisco temperance meeting resulted in eighteen pledges and the prompt formation of the Washingtonian Society of San Francisco. Women, though not members of the society, lent their support to its efforts. Other early activities on the frontier resulted from the fear of liquor-crazed Indians. Oregon's 1844 legislation forbidding the introduction or sale of liquor in the territory was probably passed by the assembly with the Indian in mind.

With the passage of the "Maine law" at mid-century, the direction of national and western temperance activity changed. The law, which prohibited the production and distribution of drink, was aimed less at the moral reform of the individual drinker than at the legal restriction of liquor producers and distributors. Copied in a number of states, including Iowa and Nebraska, the legislation was significant because it brought the liquor question directly into politics. Although the legislation was eventually declared unconstitutional in most of the states where it had passed, the new approach seemed promising if unlikely to produce immediate results, since the Civil War consumed Americans' attention. A more serious drawback was prohibition's unpopularity with the men who would determine the outcome of any legal approach to the liquor problem.

When women entered the prohibition movement after the Civil War to become its main support, the strength of their male opposition was evident. An attempt to establish the right of local option failed to win even 30 percent of an 1887 vote in Washington Territory, for example. Though often defeated, the tactics women used in their prohibition campaigns in the West reveal the sharp edge, as well as the limitations, of their criticism of the male world.

Tactics used first in the Middle West in the 1870s inspired western prohibition activities. After a Christmas Eve church service in 1873, seventy irate women placed themselves in front of a local saloon in Hillsboro, Ohio, to sing and pray that the saloon stop serving and the drinkers stop drinking. This was not just a Christmas Eve stand; the women returned for months to harass the owners and drinkers. News of this extraordinary female behavior spread and inspired a women's crusade against saloons in both the East and the West.

Although visitations of the Ohio sort occurred in California, the women's crusade there adopted different techniques. California women had a special opportunity because the legislature had passed a local-option law. The law stated that if a quarter of the voters in a township or incorporated city or town petitioned the proper authorities, an election could be held to decide whether to close down saloons (in effect) by forbidding the sale of liquor in quantities of under five gallons. Women's Temperance Alliances were formed all over the state to get the liquor question to the voters. Strengthened by daily prayer meetings, the women sought signatures for the petitions needed for local-option elections and then canvassed the voters themselves. Although early campaigns were quiet, they became, with time, more aggressive and openly hostile to men, as women individually and collectively challenged men with explosive results. Efforts in San Jose revealed the rising tempers of both sexes. While some of the town's clergy criticized their efforts, and hecklers caused trouble, the women resolutely set up a temperance tent for their daily meetings. Election day approached, and tension grew. Determined to bring out as many helpers as they could, the activist women appealed to their stay-at-home sisters through a letter to the newspaper, which was marked by militant vocabulary. "Young ladies, throw away all timidity," they urged, "and come out to help us fight the hard battle on Saturday . . . If you are too bashful to talk, go with those that can, thus lending aid by merely your presence . . . Think not what people will say, but come boldly to the front and God will reward you." The letter encouraged women to adopt aggressive tactics, necessary in the struggle with evil.

On election day, women, sure of their righteousness, walked the streets in groups, giving speeches, arguing, and persuading men to support their cause. Fifty children were taken around to the different polling places to sing, "Father, dear father, come home with me now." Female tactics, despite some sweet smiles and the presence of little children, were correctly perceived as a challenge, and the mood became bitter. During the afternoon, one of the women, Sallie Hart, was heckled and booed so vociferously that the police were forced to hurry her away. The crowds became drunk and disorderly. When the votes were counted, the drinkers had won, 1,430 to 918. The next week in Alameda, the women's cause fared no better; a drunken mob chased the women into their temperance tent and further amused itself by holding a mock funeral for the intrepid but hated Sallie Hart. Despite the law, beer flowed freely during the election and certainly contributed to the day's violent and ugly tone, but the women themselves had triggered the disorder by approaching men to urge them to forsake the pleasures and profits of drink and to conform to the female vision of the ideal community.

In Portland, Oregon, women borrowed the tactics of their Ohio counterparts. Like California temperance advocates, they challenged masculine habits and fomented disorder. Female activities got off to a slow start as news of Ohio events reached Oregon in the winter of 1874. Though there was no defined plan of action, some Portland women, interested in the liquor problem, began to meet together. In March, their enthusiasm and involvement grew, as did their numbers, when they began to "exchange experiences" of their confrontations with drunken husbands, fathers, and sons. An energetic new organization, the Women's Temperance Prayer League, which met twice a day, grew out of their emotional exchanges. Soon the league was involved in a campaign to collect abstinence pledges and, as if this were not enough, openly exhorted saloonkeepers to close down their businesses. Even these activities did not satisfy most of the women. Although a few league members refused to adopt more militant tactics, most agreed to attack the saloons directly. First, the women haunted the saloons, soliciting pledges. Drinking men disliked being disturbed at the bar, but they didn't like it much more when the women began to pray and sing in front of the Webfoot Saloon, which became the symbol of THE SA-LOON. The situation became increasingly explosive as women appeared day after day with their prayers and songs. Some days saw only curious crowds and hoopla, others antagonistic mobs. The women were in and out of jail, but they always came back. They supported temperance candidates and petitioned city councils.

However, their campaign, like the efforts of their California counterparts, fizzled out. A scurrilous little broadside, purportedly the work of the league but actually the work of league opponents, caused an uproar and damaged the women's reputation as moral arbiters. Support, already damaged by female militance, evaporated. The weakhearted returned home, leaving the saloon safe for the time being in Portland.

The western prohibition campaigns of the 1870s, like earlier efforts in the West, came to nothing. The state supreme court declared California's local-option law unconstitutional, and temperance work flagged there, as it did in Oregon. The Women's Christian Temperance Union (WCTU), established in 1879 in California and in 1881 in Oregon, had a slow beginning in both places. The importance of female reform was not, therefore, that it succeeded, for it most obviously did not. Its importance was that it illustrated the role gender played in promoting different views of community and the lengths to which some women would go to realize their own. But reform also demonstrated the limits of female power. Men clearly perceived the threat female reform posed and often reacted fiercely, only to make women more certain than ever that theirs was a righteous if not victorious cause.

From one perspective, reformism radicalized women at least temporarily as they took to the streets, made speeches, and went to jail. But it is significant that western women, in the end, retired to their homes. Since their reform activities were rooted not in a new self-conception but in an expansive vision of themselves as community moral arbiters, most in the long run were reluctant to move far beyond this vision. The hint of sexual impropriety in the Portland broadside sent them swiftly home. Later workers in the WCTU avoided confrontational tactics and utilized a less threatening version of domesticity. Running a coffeehouse or sponsoring writing contests in schools was not difficult for women, or even for many men, to accept. In the long run, the WCTU raised female consciousness but brought about no thoroughgoing reformulation of the female role.

The western prohibition movement did not make most western women radicals. Western conditions, unique as they sometimes were, rarely led women to discard prevailing concepts of gender relations. A few outstanding women like Abigail Scott Duniway did believe that frontier life encouraged challenges to woman's place: "To bear two children in two and a half years from my marriage day, to make thousands of pounds of butter every year for market . . . to sew and cook, and wash and iron; to bake and clean and stew and fry; to be in short a general pioneer drudge . . . was not a pleasant business." But Duniway's rejection of conventional female life on the frontier seems the exception not the rule.

Duniway's final point suggests the need to evaluate carefully the claim that the frontier liberated women from conventional gender roles and made them nearly equal to men. Such an argument often emphasizes the fact that women gained suffrage in Wyoming and Utah shortly after the Civil War and that ten of the eleven western states gave women the vote by 1914, whereas only one eastern state had enfranchised women. The popularity of coeducation in western colleges and universities seems to buttress the idea that the West freed women from old constraints. Yet on closer examination, the evidence is less than conclusive.

The idea that political enfranchisement of women leads to social and sexual emancipation is one that historians have questioned. Although the implications of suffrage were radical, victory in the twentieth century did not bring about a revolution in society's attitudes toward women or in women's understanding of themselves. Nor did suffrage for white women lead them to press for its extension to nonwhite women. Certainly an investigation of western suffrage "triumphs" suggests that enfranchisement was not related to a radical reformulation of women's roles. A study of the two territories granting suffrage to women in 1869 and 1870 reveals that the vote was offered to white women not because they thought to ask for it but because it suited a minority of men to give it and that the arguments made in favor of granting women suffrage were conservative. Women were to vote not because they were the same as or equal to men but because they were different from men. The domestic conception of women provided the basis for the suffrage defense.

In Utah, granting suffrage to women was part of the attempt to maintain Mormon society and plural marriage. The suffrage issue came to the surface the very year that the transcontinental railroad pulled Utah into closer contact with the rest of the country and the very year that broad antipolygamy legislation was introduced in Congress. Mobilizing Mormon women as voters would serve several purposes. It would balance and perhaps neutralize the potential political power of Gentiles, who could now so easily come to Utah. More importantly, granting women the vote would prove to the rest of the country that Mormon women were not, in fact, slaves or prostitutes but highly regarded members of their community. The move would have the added benefit of gaining the support of eastern suffrage activists and organizations in the struggle to defeat antipolygamy legislation in Congress. There was little interest, however, in making any argument that women were to be men's equals. It was expected that they would keep their place and vote as they were told. The San Francisco *Chronicle* quoted a Mormon bishop as saying, "Our vote is solid and will always remain so. It will be thrown where the most good will be accomplished for the church. The women of Utah vote, and they never desert the colors of the church; they vote for the tried friends of the church. You can imagine the results which wisdom may bring about, with the assistance of a church organization like ours." Whether or not the paper's report was true, election statistics lent support to the claim. Mormon women voted solidly with their men.

The reasons for granting women the vote in Wyoming differed in details, but the same conservative impulse existed. In 1869 and 1870, the territory had only a small permanent population and all too many transient, lawless elements connected with building the railroad. By granting women suffrage, legislators hoped that they might attract stable and responsible settlers to the territory. They wanted not a new society but a tamed society. Recollections of the debate in the legislature stressed this point: *"The favorite argument . . . and by far the most effective was this:* it would prove a great advertisement, would make a great deal of talk, and attract attention to the legislature, and the territory, more effectually than anything else." These hopes were vain, but, once granted the vote, Wyoming women did introduce a small measure of propriety into Wyoming frontier life. At election time, they seem to have been treated courteously because men saw them as symbols of civilization and home. But women's attempts to wield powers connected with their status as voters showed just how little Wyoming men thought to grant full political, let alone social, equality. It is true that one woman was appointed justice of the peace, while a few others served on petit and grand juries once granted voting rights. But the female justice of the peace, after judging thirty or forty cases, was not nominated to run for regular election as a judge. And when a grand jury composed of six women and nine men in Laramie indicted all the saloons for not observing Sunday closings, many assumed that female influence was at work. The days of women on juries were limited. In 1870, the practice was ended on the grounds that jury duty had no connection with suffrage. It was 1950 before women served on Wyoming juries again.

These early western triumphs for woman suffrage were exceptional. After 1867, seventeen referenda on the issue of granting women the vote were held in eleven states. Of the eleven, eight were, it is true, west of the Mississippi—but of those eight, only two granted the vote to women. Perhaps there was more sympathy for voting on the question in the West, but there was also more interest in turning it down. In Oregon, for example, the question came to the vote six times after 1859, and despite all the energy and time devoted to the campaign, suffrage did not pass until 1911. A letter printed in the *Iowa State Weekly Register* in 1871 reflected the sentiments of much of the male community in the West when it came to the suffrage issue. If "all the principles that suffragists are promulgating to take firm root in society, become the law of our land," the writer pointed out, "our choicest treasures, the dear little daughters of to-day, will before the close of the next decade become a prey to the licentious libertine."

In other western states and territories, the question came up before the legislature, always an easier route than putting it before the male electorate. But results were the same. Whatever freedoms the West gave to women, it had not changed the thinking of men enough to make the majority of legislators favor granting full political rights to women. In the territory of Washington, for example, a legislator originally from Maine introduced a female suffrage bill in the first session of 1854. It was defeated, and the body ignored the issue until 1869, when a supporter once more introduced a suffrage bill. The debate was bitter and the measure attracted only five favorable votes. Two years later, the legislature rejected yet another bill, and since a few ardent women had insisted on trying to vote on the grounds that the 1866 election code defined voters as "*all* white citizens," it went on to respond to the women clearly. The act they devised warned all settlers that "hereafter no female shall have the right of ballot or vote at any poll or election precinct in this Territory, until the Congress of the United States of America shall, by direct legislation upon the same, declare the same to be the supreme law of the land." Ultimately, the Washington legislature was converted and granted suffrage. But when women began to exercise their political rights with some of the same moral fervor of the early Wyoming women, the state's supreme court voided the act. Another suffrage bill met the same fate. Finally, difficulties involved with suffrage led the constitutional convention to decide not to include female emancipation in the proposed 1889 state constitution but to allow voters to decide on that issue and prohibition separately; 40,152 men voted for the constitution, 19,546 for prohibition, but only 16,527 favored emancipation. It would be another twenty-one years before Washington women voted, and those few who had worked for the cause lost heart and gave up the fight.

While men were reluctant to offer women political rights, only a small number of women challenged them. The leaders of the campaign to bring suffrage to the western states were few, and they openly acknowledged that their support from other women was limited. Although a few states in the 1870s and 1880s allowed women some voting privileges on the local level, there was little pressure from women to expand those rights. Some of the suffrage leaders reasoned that, far from fostering interest in political equality, frontier conditions explained female apathy. Women were scattered in the country and therefore hard to reach and slow to develop bonds with other women. There was some truth in this analysis, but the underlying factor was women's lack of interest in political rights. Despite the inconvenience of frontier conditions, women organized for religious and charitable purposes, and they joined temperance organizations far more readily than they supported suffrage. Indeed, some women even organized against the woman suffrage movement. And in a similar fashion, when a registry board in Clarinda, Iowa, decided in 1871 that women might vote, the newspaper observed, "Several gentlemen got on their ear about it and erased their wives names. Several ladies got their precious backs up also, and erased their own names. None but the sons of Adam, however, offered to vote, and Clarinda is now as peaceable as Mary's little lamb."

Those women who pressed for political rights were atypical. Some of them, like Abigail Scott Duniway, came into suffrage work partly because of their experiences on the frontier. Without sufficient biographical information on early leaders, it is impossible to know how crucial the western environment was in bringing them into the struggle. A profile of the leaders of the California suffrage movement between 1897 and 1911 does exist, and, while the leadership of an earlier period may have been quite different, the profile offers some interesting suggestions. Of the 1,911 leaders covered, 65 percent were born before 1861, during the early settlement period. But the majority of the women came from New England or the Midwest, not from California. They were well educated, prosperous, Protestant, and married. Some of the women were obviously seeking independence and harbored angry feelings toward men, but others still saw themselves as true women, selfless and sacrificing. Their reasons for participating in the suffrage movement varied. The older women (born before the Civil War) tended to see the suffrage issue in humanitarian terms, while younger women were influenced by the new arguments that the vote offered a means of attacking social problems. There was little typically frontier about the group or its motivations.

The arguments such women developed to attract support from timid sisters and to disarm male opposition resembled those used elsewhere. Rarely did they urge their listeners or readers to think about developing themselves as individuals or to re-examine conventional gender norms. Nor did they mention job discrimination. Rather they argued that women should vote because their moral perspective and domestic responsibilities prepared them to ameliorate the problems of an increasingly complex world. The later victories of suffrage in the West stemmed from these conservative arguments reinforced by western experience with the vote. Those few states that had emancipated women early found little sign that female suffrage unleashed a revolution in social, gender, or race relations.

Superficially, the evidence connecting coeducation to the "freedom" of the West is convincing. In 1872, there were ninety-seven major private and public coeducational institutions in the country, and the majority of them, sixty-seven, were located in the West. Many assume that the popularity of coeducation in the West indicates that westerners believed in the equality of women's and men's intellectual capacities and the right of women to an equal education. More relevant, but rarely considered, is the question of whether the coeducational experience affected the way women viewed themselves.

Certain regional conditions and attitudes explain the popularity of coeducation in the West. The founding of new colleges and universities was part of the frontier experience. Fears that the new society would sink into barbarism stimulated missionaries to establish colleges as an "important part in Christian strategy," while bustling new communities intent on realizing boasts of a dazzling future contributed to the proliferation of colleges. Indeed, communities often vied for proposed institutions by donating sites and cash to the would-be founders. With the passage of the Morrill Act in 1862, which provided federal lands to initiate a system of public higher education, community competition for educational institutions increased.

The enthusiasm for founding colleges and universities was premature. Since most western states had few public secondary schools, there were not enough qualified students of either sex to give substance to the college title. Most early colleges were in fact high schools. The year after the University of Kansas was so ambitiously started, though "somewhat embryonic" in form, there were only two students in the college course, but sixty-eight pupils in the preparatory department. The number of institutions and the limited pool of students led colleges to compete for students both to justify their existence and to gain operating funds. Most private colleges were financially shaky, established long before their communities or religious denominations were able to support them on a regular basis. Nor did the land grants that provided the impetus to public education offer a steady revenue; state legislators were usually niggardly in helping out fledgling public institutions. These factors meant that any and all students were welcome on any and all levels. Both of the college students at the University of Kansas were women.

The instability of early institutions fostered coeducation, even if separation of the sexes was the initial goal. The 1864 charter for the University of Kansas called for male and female branches, with the women's branch separate and taught by women. Lack of funds prevented realizing such a plan, however. Coeducation was a financial necessity and one whose wisdom was highlighted during the Civil War. During those years, as men left school for the war, only the presence of women students allowed many schools to stay open. And, as time passed, private colleges faced increasing competition from state schools. Coeducation offered a means of survival for many private institutions.

Certainly, much of the education provided for women in these early days reflected conventional cultural assumptions about women. The status of women in the land-grant schools, devoted to teaching the agricultural and mechanical arts, is a case in point. Though some of the impetus behind the schools was the belief in equal education, the objective was seldom realized. The work requirement predictably put women in the most traditional places, the laundry, the dining room, and, of course, the kitchen. Eventually, experience with the work requirement led some of the schools to develop courses in "domestic economy," which further differentiated the women students from the men. At Iowa Agricultural College, for example, the president's wife was responsible for lecturing on cooking to the women working in the college kitchen. Her teaching inspired her to develop a department of "cookery and the household arts" for the women students, and, by 1875, she had established the first experimental kitchen in the United States. By 1890, similar departments existed in Kansas, Oregon, and South Dakota. This preparation was aimed not at training women for a career but at preparing them for marriage. Land-grant colleges primarily instructed women to be teachers first and wives later.

The land-grant colleges often had special "ladies' courses" for the female student body. Nor was the practice confined to these schools. When the University of Washington was established in the 1860s, newspaper ads announced female courses on the college and preparatory level. Readers were informed that "MISS. MAY W. THAYER, formerly a Teacher in the University, has been engaged as assistant, and in addition to the branches usually taught, will give particular instruction in Etiquette, Conversation, Needlework, &c." As time passed, two separate college tracks appeared: the classical one for men and another, often only three years in length, for women, who substituted music, painting, drawing, and modern languages for the more difficult classics and higher mathematics. Not until the end of the century did women in many western colleges study the male curriculum. Similar reservations about women in higher education were revealed in the treatment of female faculty. When the University of Oregon first opened, for example, professional women taught in the prep department, but they were soon replaced by male college graduates who wanted a few terms in the classroom before beginning another profession.

Although coeducation became an accepted practice in the West, women were not seen as intellectually equal to men nor were they treated the same. Stereotypes of women as weak in body and intellect were still current despite the experience of the frontier. Special facilities protected "frail" women in some schools; at the University of Washington, the women lived in the president's house under the watchful eye of his wife rather than in the dormitory. Women were excluded from certain campus activities. College campuses, in fact, provided many symbolic statements of women's true status, and few women missed the message. At Grinnell, for example, the female literary society invited a prominent woman to speak at commencement in 1869 and caused a controversy on the campus. The faculty was up in arms and pressed the trustees to write a letter to the speaker's husband informing him that "the Faculty and Trustees of the College are not yet prepared to allow a woman to occupy the college platform at commencement." It is hardly surprising that little thought was given to the coeds, for it was clear that the future of educated women was perhaps a teaching job but probably marriage.

Nor, of course, was a college education of any kind the typical experience for women in the West or elsewhere. The earliest comprehensive statistics collected by the U.S. Commissioner of Education revealed that only a quarter as many women as men received any postsecondary education and that most of them attended either normal schools or seminaries and academies that did not offer a college degree. Furthermore, coeducation was not an early frontier commitment. In 1870, most of the women students in colleges and universities still were found in women's colleges rather than in coeducational institutions. This would shift in the following ten years, but to look at the western educational system as a badge of woman's freedom in the West seems inappropriate.

Women like Abigail Scott Duniway, who spent most of her life working unsuccessfully for woman suffrage, perpetuated the myth that frontier women had a more egalitarian status in the new society. "Nowhere else, upon this planet, are the inalienable rights of women as much appreciated as on the newly settled borders of these United States," she announced. "Men have had opportunities, in our remote countries, to see the worth of the civilized women, who came with them, or among them, to new settlements after the Indian woman's day." Duniway's image making was, no doubt, an attempt to push men on the issue of female rights, but it neither described the reality of western female experience nor did it achieve her tactical goals. Certainly, frontier social and sometimes political arrangements stood in contrast to those in the East. But this was hardly because men appreciated the "inalienable rights of women." Women valued themselves and were valued for their traditional qualities. When women collided with the male world, it was often precisely because they believed in their traditional role and sought to live up to it. The collisions could be bitter, for the realities of frontier life and male priorities often made them so. But few responded by casting off convention. The behavior of a suffrage group in Walla Walla, Washington, in the 1880s is instructive. After seeing the men of their territory defeat the suffrage question, the women quietly retired, never bothering to meet together again, either to make future plans or even to preside over their organization's demise.

Epilogue

In the last decades of the nineteenth century and the opening years of the twentieth, many western women must have reflected on the dramatic changes they had witnessed during their lifetimes. The significance women drew from the past differed dramatically according to their circumstances and their social, economic, and racial position in western society. Mrs. Van Court, who, with her husband, had experienced one disappointment after another in California—ranching, farming, and dairying ventures all failed—finally achieved success in Oakland. There she ran a boardinghouse while her husband worked in a mill. At eighty-two, she was a contented woman. Despite all the disappointments, now she was "living a very comfortable . . . peaceful life, happy with the love of my children . . . and . . . friends."

Perhaps Buffalo Bird Woman, a member of the Hidatsa tribe, was also comfortable "in a house with chimneys" and happy to be near her son and his wife. But she was filled with a sense of loss. Sometimes she rose early and went out to the cornfields, where, as she hoed, she sang "as we did when I was young. [But] No one cares for our corn songs now." Her son was very much part of the new world. He had received his education at the white man's school, farmed, and raised cattle. His wife cooked meals on her own stove.

Buffalo Bird Woman's son thought the changes were good, and he played a leading role in encouraging other Hidatsa to adopt the ways of white civilization. But Buffalo Bird Woman did not share his perspective. "Sometimes at evening I sit, looking out on the big Missouri," she explained. "In the shadows I seem again to see our Indian village, with smoke curling upward from the earth lodges; and in the river's roar, I hear the yells of the warriors, the laughter of little children as of old. It is but an old woman's dream . . . Our Indian life, I know, is gone forever."

When Buffalo Bird Woman contemplated the past, she wept for herself and for her people. For the women who traveled the overland route in the middle decades of the century, the tears had come as they left family homes in the East and sometimes as they confronted the difficulties of frontier life. Mrs. Van Court, who gave birth to a son with only the assistance of a Spanish-speaking midwife and who was "in mortal fear of the Digger Indians," "cried and cried till I was hysterical" when her female friend arrived at the ranch to help her care for the baby. But those crises had passed, and women saw what emigrant guidebooks had promised—"all the enjoyments and luxuries of civilized life."

Later in life, some of the white women of the pioneer generation returned east by train to visit old homes and family. As they headed back to the West, they sped over the plains and prairies and thought of the months spent in lurching, jolting wagons many years before. "It seems very strange now that we ever had the patience to travel so slowly," one woman mused. She, like other women, reflected on those early years and the transformations she had witnessed. If only to answer the never-ending questions—"Did I come around the Horn, cross the Isthmus, or come across the plains? Was I not afraid of the Indians and much more?"—white women began to write down their life stories. Pioneer reunions, with parades, dinners, and visits, also featured addresses that attempted to set the frontier experience in some perspective. If not all agreed on what the frontier had meant, all were convinced that they had made history. Looking back over long lives, men and women compressed their life stories in order to elaborate on their pioneer experience. That time was, for some of them, "more real than the present."

None could overlook the contrast between the moment of writing and the past about which they wrote. For some, the present suffered in the comparison. Because of the relationship between emigration and age, the pioneer experience had coincided for most of them with young adulthood, when bodies were strong and dreams still possible. Nostalgia for lost youth colored their recollections, and the pioneer period became a golden age marked by youthful simplicity, virtue, and happiness. As writers contemplated the present, they noted subtle signs of decline. First of all, their ranks were thinning. Every pioneer reunion mourned the passing of some of their number, while those who remained felt increasingly the burdens of old age. Although all acknowledged the material advances that had transformed the frontier, they also pointed to the social complexity and the loss of character that seemed to have accompanied progress. Pioneer women noted the pretentiousness of the present and the lamentable spinelessness and artificiality of youth, always carefully excluding their own children from such generalizations.

As women thought about early frontier experiences, they contrasted their behavior with that of the new generation. If they did not know it before, these women realized now how strong and successful they had been in meeting the challenges of frontier life. Of course, many had had little choice but to do so.

But that did not diminish their heroism. Describing an emigrant giving birth on the Overland Trail, one woman typically concluded, "Think of the women now who have a doctor, a trained nurse and a girl in the kitchen and then do not do as well."

Even if the past seemed golden, it was impossible to reject the present altogether. For had not women helped to create it? Those who refused to romanticize the past looked back with surprise at their life so many years before. "It all seems like a far away dream to me now," one wrote. "I don't know how I stood it and how I was satisfied. I suppose it was because I was young and we lived almost altogether in the future. It never came home to me till afterward how poor and desolate our home was." These recollections emphasized the hardships and privations of frontier life. Had they known what lay in store, some admitted, they would not have set out so lightheartedly. Although they remembered the pioneer period with distaste, these women also described themselves as courageous and brave. They had been not weak but strong; they had been not passive but active. They had triumphed over frontier conditions heroically. "The true pioneer combines every element of the hero," announced a speaker at an Iowa Pioneer Reunion in 1885. His listeners agreed. Whether the past had been the best time of all or the worst, women knew that they had been at their best.

Although some of the women felt ambivalent about the nature of the society they had worked to create and the social changes they saw around them, the blame, they felt, was not theirs but that of those who followed them. None questioned their civilizing mission. Their recollections highlighted efforts to establish orderly family life in the wilderness and expanded on female contributions to early community life. Women, an address to the Iowa pioneers pointed out, had "helped to make the settlement a success. They brought the bible with them and organized the Sunday school. They were superintendent and teacher, and with their women's work assisted in building the school houses and the churches, and in laying the foundations of civilized society. And they laid the foundations of society better than they knew."

Few women had the inclination to reflect on what the creation of society meant for the other women who inhabited the West. Had they done so, they would have wondered about the success of their civilizing mission, perhaps even its justice.

In places as far apart as Los Angeles and northern New Mexico, Hispanic women adapted to new economic and cultural realities brought about by white settlement, but not in the way that would-be civilizers had imagined. As husbands, fathers, and brothers abandoned traditional pursuits for seasonal wage work, Hispanic women learned to fend for themselves. More and more women found themselves managing households and families for at least part of the year. Their new situation accorded with neither traditional Hispanic norms nor Anglo domestic ideals. Although many proved eager to acquire new conveniences like stoves, and some New Mexican women even attended Protestant missionary schools, few adopted the way of life white pioneer women had worked so hard to establish. Their behavior suggested that middle-class white women's civilizing mission had not enjoyed complete success in the West.

The experiences of Indian women made it clear that the civilizing process was not benign. Although the situation of Native American women differed from group to group, civilization represented hardship and often decline. A Paiute woman, Sarah Winnemucca Hopkins, revealed the corruption of Indian agents who cheated native peoples on reservations out of supplies: "Our poor children are crying to us for food, and we are powerless to help the little ones." On the Sioux reservation of Devils Lake in North Dakota, native women lost status. Officials negotiated only with men and encouraged them to become farmers. Since women had traditionally carried on horticulture, white policy undermined women's importance. Sioux women adjusted to new realities, continuing their gathering activities and using new domestic skills like quilting and lace making to earn extra cash, but new gender arrangements were not to their benefit. Xwelas, a S'klallam woman, did not live on a reservation, but her attempts to get along in the new world were problematic. Encouraged by her tribe and hoping that an alliance with white men would work to her advantage, Xwelas married three white men. Two of them abandoned her, and the third was a drunkard who violently mistreated her. The experiences of these women played no part in white women's evaluations of the pioneer era.

Because white women's recollections and reminiscences were so narrowly focused on the world they had helped to create, they could look back with satisfaction. Even if the present was less heroic than the past, there was much about which they could be proud. Despite the references to decadence, recollections often end by describing a thriving and changing community and the progress of husband, children, and grandchildren. If proof were needed of pioneer women's accomplishments, it was available. Phoebe Judson's reminiscences made the point that so many others echo: "After all the trials and hardships that have been our lot while journeying through the wilderness, I would not exchange my 'buried' life, as it has been called, for the 'wear and tear' of the fashionable society woman who must fulfill her social obligations, with no fruit to show as the result of her hard labor."

Bibliography

A good deal of the time spent researching this book was devoted to studying pioneer women's documents. Many of their journals, reminiscences, and letters are still unpublished; some were printed in limited quantities and are now rare items. It is, therefore, especially difficult to do without footnotes. Since this book is intended for the general reader rather than the scholar, however, I will merely enumerate the most important published works that I consulted and cite the locations of the collections that proved most helpful in my work. Those who are interested in exploring women's experience on the frontier will be able to start with the published works mentioned here and will find a wealth of material in the following repositories.

The western collection at the Bancroft Library, University of California at Berkeley, is justifiably famous. There are large numbers of Overland Trail diaries deposited there and interesting transcriptions of interviews with pioneer women done late in the nineteenth century. The Henry E. Huntington Library collections in Pasadena, California, were useful, although at the time I used them, they were poorly catalogued for anyone interested in women's history. Manuscript and rare-book holdings at the Beinecke Library, Yale University; the Schlesinger Library, Radcliffe College; the Milton Eisenhower Library, Johns Hopkins University; Stanford University; and at the Library of

Congress proved valuable, as did the western collections at the Newberry Library in Chicago. The archives at the University of Oregon in Eugene were particularly rich, and the archivist, Martin Schmitt, unfailingly courteous. The University of Washington's manuscript collection, while hardly as extensive as that at the University of Oregon, yielded additional information about the pioneer period in the Pacific Northwest. I also consulted records at the Society of California Pioneers, which proved disappointingly skimpy on women pioneers. The California Historical Society, the Oregon Historical Society, and the State Historical Society of Iowa yielded a wealth of information. The Iowa state archivist has done a superb job of cataloguing women's manuscripts, and it was a pleasure to work there. I also went to the Connecticut Historical Society to read the records of the Board of National Popular Education.

Clyde A. Milner II, Carol A. O'Connor, and Martha A. Sandweiss have edited a valuable collection of essays on many aspects of western history in *The Oxford History of the American West* (New York: Oxford University Press, 1994). Geoffrey C. Ward's book *The West: An Illustrated History* (Boston: Little Brown & Co., 1996), a companion piece for Stephen Ives's and Ken Burns's television series on the West, has a strong narrative, scholarly essays, and excellent illustrations. Treatments that focus specifically on women include Lillian Schlissel, Vicki L. Ruiz, and Janice Monk's edited volume, *Western Women: Their Land, Their Lives* (Albuquerque: University of New Mexico Press, 1988); Virginia Scharff, "Gender and Western History: Is Anybody Home on the Range?" *Montana: The Magazine of Western History* 41 (spring 1991), pp. 62–65; and Susan Armitage and Elizabeth Jameson, eds., *The Women's West* (Norman: University of Oklahoma Press, 1987).

Examples of the "new western history" include Patricia Nelson Limerick's *The Legacy of Conquest: The Unbroken Past of the American West* (New York: W. W. Norton & Co., 1987); Patricia Nelson Limerick, Clyde A. Milner II, and Charles E. Rankin, eds., *Trails: Toward a New Western History* (Lawrence: University Press of Kansas, 1991); William Cronon, George Miles, and Jay Gitlin, eds., *Under an Open Sky: Rethinking America's Western Past* (New York: W. W. Norton & Co., 1993); and John R. Wunder, "What's Old About the New Western History: Race and Gender," *Pacific Northwest Quarterly* 85 (April 1994), pp. 50–58.

Ronald Takaki suggests the importance of race and ethnicity in *A Different Mirror: A History of Multicultural America* (Boston: Little Brown & Co., 1993). See also Gilbert G. González and Raúl Fernández, "Chicano History: Transcending Cultural Models," *Pacific Historical Review* 63 (November 1994), pp. 469–97; Antonia I. Castañeda, "Women of Color and the Rewriting of Western History: The Discourse, Politics, and Decolonization of History," *Pacific Historical Review* 61 (November 1992), pp. 501–33; and Lawrence B.

de Graaf, "Race, Sex, and Region: Black Women in the American West, 1850–1920," *Pacific Historical Review* 49 (May 1980), pp. 285–313.

1

Good introductions to women's history include Mary P. Ryan, *Womanhood in America from Colonial Times to the Present* (New York: New Viewpoints, 1975); Mary P. Ryan, *Cradle of the Middle Class: The Family in Oneida County, New York, 1790–1863* (New York: Cambridge University Press, 1981); and Carl Degler, *At Odds: Women and the Family in America from the Revolution to the Present* (New York: Oxford University Press, 1980). See also John Demos's "The American Family in Past Time," *American Scholar* 43 (summer 1974), pp. 422–46. Studies of the status of women in the early nineteenth century include Nancy F. Cott's excellent book *The Bonds of Womanhood: "Woman's Sphere" in New England, 1780–1835* (New Haven: Yale University Press, 1977) and Caroll Smith-Rosenberg's article on the close emotional relationships women routinely formed with one another, "The Female World of Love and Ritual: Relations Between Women in 19th-Century America," *Signs* 1 (fall 1975), pp. 1–29. Anne Firor Scott in *The Southern Lady: From Pedestal to Politics, 1830–1930* (Chicago: University of Chicago Press, 1970) illustrates the power of domestic ideology in the South. Other stimulating work on women in the first half of the nineteenth century includes Ronald W. Hogeland, " 'The Female Appendage': Feminine Life-Styles in America, 1820–1861," *Civil War History* 17 (June 1971), pp. 101–14; Barbara Welter, "Anti-Intellectualism and the American Woman: 1800–1860," *Mid-America* 48 (October 1966), pp. 258–70; John C. Ruoff, "Frivolity to Consumption: Or Southern Women in Antebellum Literature," *Civil War History* 18 (September 1972), pp. 213–29; Glenda Gates Riley, "The Subtle Subversion: Changes in the Traditionalist Image of the American Woman," *Historian* 32 (February 1970), pp. 210–27; and Charles E. Rosenberg, "Sexuality, Class and Role in 19th-Century America," *American Quarterly* 25 (May 1973), pp. 131–53. On benevolent work, see Lori D. Ginzberg, *Women and the Work of Benevolence: Morality, Politics, and Class in the Nineteenth-Century United States* (New Haven: Yale University Press, 1990). Kathryn Kish Sklar's fine biography *Catharine Beecher: A Study in American Domesticity* (New Haven: Yale University Press, 1973) is essential not only for an understanding of this remarkable woman but also for an understanding of the ideology about woman's place that emerged in the first half of the nineteenth century. Joan N. Burstyn's "Catharine Beecher and the Education of American Women," *New England Quarterly* 47 (September 1974), pp. 386–403, supplements Sklar's work. Ruth Miller Elson's *Guardians of Tradition: American Schoolbooks of the 19th Century* (Lincoln: University of Nebraska Press, 1964) suggests how widespread views of woman's place were while B. M. Stearns, "Early Western Magazines for Ladies," *Mississippi Valley Historical Review* 18 (December 1931), pp. 319–30, and David Donald and Frederick A. Palmer, "Towards a Western Literature, 1820–1860," *Mississippi Valley Historical Review* 35 (December 1948), pp. 413–28, show how quickly the publishing industry followed the move west.

Richard Slotkin's *Regeneration Through Violence: The Mythology of the American Frontier, 1600–1860* (Middletown: Wesleyan University Press, 1973) treats the Boone legend in detail. Helen B. Kroll's "The Books That Enlightened the Emigrants," *Oregon Historical Quarterly* 45 (June 1944), pp. 103–23, describes emigrant guidebooks. Some of these, like Lansford Hastings, *The Emigrants' Guide to Oregon and California* (New York: Da Capo Press, 1969), and Joseph E. Ware, *The Emigrants' Guide to California* (Princeton: Princeton University Press, 1932), have been reprinted and are available in many libraries. Roy Harvey Pearce, "The Signs of the Captivity Narrative," *American Literature* 19 (March 1947), pp. 1–20; David T. Haberly, "Women and the Indians: *The Last of the Mohicans* and the Captivity Tradition," *American Quarterly* 28 (fall 1976), pp. 431–43; Annette Kolodny, *The Land Before Her: Fantasy and Experience of the American Frontiers, 1630–1860* (Chapel Hill: University of North Carolina Press, 1984); and June Namias, *White Captives: Gender and Ethnicity on the American Frontier* (Chapel Hill: University of North Carolina Press, 1995) explore the captivity tales. Stories written by and for women about western life are sprinkled through the pages of *Godey's Lady's Book*. Caroline M. Kirkland's accounts of western life, including *A New Home—Who'll Follow? Or Glimpses of Western Life* (New York: L. S. Frarars, 1830) and Lydia H. Sigourney's *The Western Home and Other Poems* (Philadelphia: Parry & McMillan, 1854), are also good primary sources. Secondary sources include Randal V. Mills's "Emerson Bennett's Two Oregon Novels," *Oregon Historical Quarterly* 41 (December 1940), pp. 367–81, and Mary Kelley's "The Unconscious Rebel: Studies in Feminine Fiction, 1820–1880" (Ph.D. diss., University of Iowa, 1974).

2

Studies of women emigrants include John Mack Faragher and Christine Stansell, "Women and Their Families on the Overland Trail to California and Oregon, 1842–1867," *Feminist Studies* 2 (1975), pp. 150–60; John Mack Faragher, *Women and Men on the Overland Trail* (New Haven: Yale University Press, 1979); and Lillian Schlissel, *Women's Diaries of the Westward Journey* (New York: Schocken Books, 1982). Also useful are Lucy Jane Bledsoe, "Adventuresome Women on the Oregon Trail: 1840–1867," *Frontiers* 7 (1984), pp. 22–28; Robert L. Munkres, "Wives, Mothers, Daughters: Women's Life on the Road West," *Annals of Wyoming* 42 (October 1970), pp. 191–224; Ruth Barnes Moynihan, "Children and Young People on the Overland Trail," *Western Historical Quarterly* 6 (July 1975), pp. 279–94; Georgia Willis Read, "Women and Children on the Oregon-Trail in the Gold-Rush Years," *Missouri Historical Review* 39 (October 1944), pp. 1–23; Michael B. Husband's "To Oregon in 1843: The Backgrounds and Organization of the 'Great Migration' " (Ph.D. diss., University of New Mexico, 1970); John D. Unruh, Jr., *The Plains Across: The Overland Emigrants and the Trans-Mississippi West, 1840–1880* (Urbana: University of Illinois Press, 1979); and Thomas A. Rumer, *The Wagon Trains of '44: A Comparative View of the Individual Caravans in the Emigration of 1844 to Oregon* (Spokane: The Arthur H. Clark Co., 1990).

Kenneth L. Holmes has collected a wonderful selection of overland accounts by women, most of them never before published, in *Covered Wagon Women: Diaries & Letters from the Western Trails, 1840–1890* (Spokane: The Arthur H. Clark Co., 1983–1989). Other trail diaries and reminiscences in print include Lavinia Honeyman Porter, *By Ox Team to California: A Narrative of Crossing the Plains in 1860* (Oakland: Oakland Enquirer Publishing Co., 1910); Mary Jane Hayden, *Pioneer Days* (San Jose: Murgotten's Press, 1915); Lodisa Frizzell, *Across the Plains to California in 1852* (New York: New York Public Library, 1915); Margaret M. Hecox, *California Caravan: The 1845 Overland Trail Memoir of Margaret M. Hecox* (San Jose: Harlan-Young Press, 1966); Agnes Ruth Sengstacken, *Destination: West!* (Portland: Binsfords & Mort, Pubs., 1942); Phoebe Goodell Judson, *A Pioneer's Search for an Ideal Home* (Tacoma: Washington State Historical Society, 1966); Mary Ringo, *The Journal of Mrs. Mary Ringo* (Santa Ana: privately printed, 1956); Harriet Scott Palmer, *Crossing Over the Great Plains by Ox-Wagons* (no place, no publisher, no date); Miriam Davis Colt, *A Heroine of the Frontier* (Cedar Rapids: privately printed, 1941); Lucy Rutledge Cooke, *Crossing the Plains in 1852* (Modesto: privately printed, 1923); Julia Archibald Holmes, *A Bloomer Girl on Pike's Peak* (Denver: Denver Public Library, 1949); Sarah J. Cummins, *Autobiography and Reminiscences* (La Grande: La Grande Printing Co., 1914); Elizabeth Lord, *Reminiscences of Eastern Oregon* (Portland: Irwin-Hudson Co., 1903); Luzena Stanley Wilson, *Luzena Stanley Wilson: '49er* (Mills College: Eucalyptus Press, 1937); Emma Shepard Hill, *A Dangerous Crossing and What Happened on the Other Side* (Denver: Smith-Brooks, 1914); and Mary E. Ackley, *Crossing the Plains and Early Days in California's Golden Age* (San Francisco: privately printed, 1928). Still other primary sources can be found in journals: "Diary of Mrs. Elizabeth Dixon Smith Geer,"

Oregon Pioneer Association Transactions 35 (1907), pp. 153–79; "Diary of Mrs. Amelia Stewart Knight, an Oregon Pioneer of 1853," *Oregon Pioneer Association Transactions* 56 (1928), pp. 38–53; "Diary of Asahel Munger and Wife," *Oregon Historical Quarterly* 8 (December 1907), pp. 387–405; "Diary of a Trip Across the Plains in 1863," *Oregon Pioneer Association Transactions* 47 (1919), pp. 178–226; "Diary of Maria Parsons Belshaw, 1853," *Oregon Historical Quarterly* 33 (December 1932), pp. 318–33; "Diary of Celina E. Hines," *Oregon Pioneer Association Transactions* 46 (1918), pp. 69–125; "Overland by Ox-train in 1870: The Diary of Maria Hargrave Shrode," *Quarterly of Historical Society of Southern California* 26 (March 1944), pp. 9–37; "Diary of Mrs. Cornelia A. Sharp: Crossing the Plains from Missouri to Oregon in 1852," *Oregon Pioneer Association Transactions* 30 (1902), pp. 171–88; "From Ithaca to Clatsop Plains: Miss. Ketcham's Journal of Travel," *Oregon Historical Quarterly* 62 (September, December 1961), pp. 237–87, 337–402; "Iowa to California in 1862; The Journal of Jane Holbrook Gould," *Annals of Iowa* 37, 38 (fall 1964 and winter, spring, and summer 1965), pp. 460–76, 544–59, 623–40, 68–75; "Crossing the Plains in 1852, Mrs. Cecilia Emily McMillen Adams," *Oregon Pioneer Association Transactions* 32 (1904), pp. 288–329.

Those interested in emigration songs might look at John Anthony Scott, *The Ballads of America: The History of the United States in Song and Story* (New York: Bantam Books, 1966); Harold W. Thompson, *A Pioneer Songster: Texts from the Stevens-Douglass Manuscript of Western New York, 1841–1856* (Ithaca: Cornell University Press, 1958); and John A. Stone et al., *The Pacific Song Book: Containing All the Songs of the Pacific Coast and California* (San Francisco: D. E. Appleton, 1861).

Kathryn Kish Sklar's *Catharine Beecher*, cited earlier, gives an account of Beecher's efforts to send young teachers to the West.

Materials on western missionaries include my *Converting the West: A Biography of Narcissa Whitman* (Norman: University of Oklahoma Press, 1991) and my articles "Empty Harvest at Waiilatpu," *Columbia: The Magazine of Northwest History* 6 (fall 1992), pp. 22–31, and "Narcissa Whitman: The Significance of a Missionary's Life," *Montana: The Magazine of Western History* 41 (spring 1991), pp. 2–15. Also helpful are the entire issue of *Idaho Yesterdays* 31 (spring/summer 1987) and Deborah Lynn Dawson, " 'Laboring in My Savior's Vineyard': The Mission of Eliza Hart Spalding" (Ph.D. diss., Bowling Green State University, 1988). For background, consult Colin Brummitt Goodykoontz's *Home Missions on the American Frontier with Particular Reference to the American Home Mission Society* (Caldwell: The Caxton Printers, Ltd., 1939). R. Pierce Beaver's *All Loves Excelling* (Grand Rapids: William B. Eerdmans Pub. Co., 1968) focuses on women going to foreign missions, but the motivation of home missionaries was similar. Worth looking at is Janice Cessna Clarke's "Women of the Oregon Missions" (unpublished seminar paper, Reed College, 1963).

3

Early life on the agricultural frontier is comprehensively treated in Gilbert C. Fite's *The Farmers' Frontier, 1865–1900* (New York: Holt, Rinehart & Winston, 1966). Dean L. May has written a provocative study suggesting the need to escape the notion of one agricultural frontier. His *Three Frontiers: Family, Land, and Society in the American West, 1850–1900* (New York: Cambridge University Press, 1994) illustrates the cultural differences between agricultural frontiers. Peter G. Boag details the process of settlement in *Environment and Experience: Settlement Culture in Nineteenth-Century Oregon* (Berkeley: University of California Press, 1992). Useful demographic profiles of frontier areas include George M. Blackburn and Sherman L. Richards, "A Demographic History of the West: Nueces County, Texas, 1850," *Prologue* 4 (spring 1972), pp. 3–20; William Bowen, "The Oregon Frontiersman: A Demographic View," in Thomas Vaughan, ed., *The Western Shore: Oregon Country Essays Honoring the American Revolution* (Portland: Durham & Downey, 1975), pp. 181–97; David J. Wishart, "Age and Sex Composition of the Population of the Nebraska Frontier, 1860–1880," *Nebraska History* 54 (spring 1973), pp. 106–19; and Mary Anne Norman Smallwood, "Childhood on the Southern Plains Frontier, 1870–1910" (Ph.D. diss., Texas Tech., 1975). Rapid settlement patterns are discussed by David J. Wishart in "The Changing Position and Nature of the Frontier of Settlement on the Eastern Margins of the Central and Northern Great Plains, 1854–1920" (Ph.D. diss., University of Nebraska, Lincoln, 1968) and by Milton E. Holtz in "Early Settlement in Eastern Nebraska: A Case Study of Cass County" (master's thesis, University of Nebraska, Lincoln, 1964).

Wilson H. Grabill, Clyde V. Kiser, and Pascal K. Whelpton give an introduction to family size in *The Fertility of American Women* (New York: John Wiley & Sons, 1958). Linda Gordon's book, *Woman's Body, Woman's Right: A Social History of Birth Control in America* (New York: Grossman Publishers, 1976), is a must. Fertility patterns on the Midwestern frontier are the subject of John Modell's "Family Fertility on the Indiana Frontier, 1820," *American Quarterly* 23 (December 1971), pp. 615–34, and James Edward Davis's *Frontier America, 1800–1840: A Comparative Demographic Analysis of the Settlement Process* (Glendale, California: Arthur H. Clark Co., 1977). For case studies of the trans-Mississippi West, refer to Mildred Throne, "A Population Study of an Iowa County in 1850," *Iowa Journal of History* 45 (October 1959), pp. 305–30; Seymour V. Connor, "A Statistical Review of the Settlement of the Peters Colony, 1841–1848," *Southwest Historical Quarterly* 57 (July 1953), pp. 38–64; Blaine T. Williams, "The Frontier Family: Demographic Fact and Historical Myth," in Harold M. Hollingsworth and Sandra L. Myres, eds., *Essays on the American West* (Arlington: University of Texas Press, 1969), pp. 40–65. Also important are Maris A. Vinovskis's "Socioeconomic Determinants of Interstate Fertility Differentials in the United States in 1850 and 1860," *Journal of Interdisciplinary History* 6 (winter 1976), pp. 375–96; and Richard A. Easterlin, "Factors in the Decline of Farm Family Fertility in the United States: Some Preliminary Research Results," *Journal of American History* 63 (December 1964), pp. 600–14.

Earl Pomeroy discusses the different regional backgrounds of emigrants in *The Pacific Slope: A History of California, Oregon, Washington, Idaho, Utah, and Nevada* (New York: Alfred A. Knopf, 1965). Raymond D. Gastil's "The Pacific Northwest as a Cultural Region," *Pacific Northwest Quarterly* 64 (October 1974), pp. 147–56, is also helpful.

Work on women includes Karen J. Blair, ed., *Women in Pacific Northwest History:* An Anthology (Seattle: University of Washington Press, 1988); Lillian Schlissel, Byrd Gibbens, and Elizabeth Hampsten, *Far from Home: Families of the Westward Journey* (New York: Schocken Books, 1989); Elliott West, *The Way West: Essays on the Central Plains* (Albuquerque: University of New Mexico Press, 1995); Michael Fellman, "Julia Louisa Lovejoy Goes West," *Western Humanities Review* 39 (summer 1977), pp. 227–42; Harriette Andreadis, "True Womanhood Revisited: Women's Private Writing in Nineteenth-Century Texas," *Journal of the Southwest* 31 (summer 1989), pp. 179–204; Christine Stansell, "Women on the Great Plains, 1865–1890," *Women's Studies* 4 (1976), pp. 87–98; Glenda Riley, "Women's Responses to the Challenges of Plains Living," *Great Plains Quarterly* 9 (summer 1989), pp. 174–84; her book, *Frontierswomen: The Iowa Experience* (Ames: Iowa State University Press, 1981); and Una M. Brooks "The Influence of the Pioneer Women Toward a Settled Social Life in the Llano Estacado" (master's thesis, West Texas State Teachers College, 1942). Collections of primary sources include P. Richard Metcalf, ed., *The American People on the Western Frontier* (West Haven: Pendulum Press, 1973); Christiane Fischer, *Let Them Speak for Themselves: Women in the American West, 1849–1900* (Hamden, Conn.: The Shoestring Press, 1977); and C. Richard King, ed., *Victorian Lady on the Texas Frontier: The Journal of Ann Raney Coleman* (Norman: University of Oklahoma Press, 1971). Individual women's accounts of the early settlement period include Lois Barton, ed., *One Woman's West: Recollections of the Oregon Trail and Settling of the Northwest Country by Martha Gay Masterson, 1838–1916* (Eugene, Oregon: Spencer Butte Press, 1986); the volumes by

Sengstacken and Judson already cited; Mollie Sanford's lively journal, *Mollie: The Journal of Mollie Dorsey Sanford in Nebraska and Colorado Territories, 1857–1866* (Lincoln: University of Nebraska, 1959); Mary Bennett Ritter, *More Than Gold in California, 1899–1933* (Berkeley: The Professional Press, 1933); Polly Jane Purcell, *Autobiography and Reminiscences of a Pioneer* (no place, no publisher, no date); Sarah Brewer-Bonebright, *Reminiscences of Newcastle, Iowa, 1848: A History of the Founding of Webster City, Iowa* (Des Moines: Historical Dept. of Iowa, 1921); and Elise Dubrich Isley, *Sunbonnet Days* (Caldwell: Caxton Printers Ltd., 1935). The two-volume collection of letters of Ephraim Adams and his wife, Elisabeth, provides material on many phases of Iowa frontier life, *A Collection of Letters* (Berkeley: Copy Centers of Berkeley, 1973, 1974).

The following primary sources have been published in various journals and are worth consulting: Maria Cable Cutting, "After Thoughts," *Oregon Historical Quarterly* 63 (June–September 1962), pp. 237–41; "A Nebraska Homesteading Story—1872," *Nebraska History* 12 (October–December 1929), pp. 377–98; "The Letters of Charles and Helen Wooster: The Problems of Settlement," *Nebraska History* 46 (June 1965), pp. 121–37; "Mrs. Butler's 1853 Diary of Rogue River Valley," *Oregon Historical Quarterly* 41 (December 1940), pp. 337–66; "Letters of John and Sarah Everett, 1854–1864; Miami County Pioneers," *Kansas Historical Quarterly* 8 (February, May, August, November 1939), pp. 3–34, 143–74, 279–310, 350–83; "Diary of Col. and Mrs. I. N. Ebey," *Washington Historical Quarterly* 7, 8 (July, October 1916, January 1917), pp. 239–46, 307–21, 40–62; "An Autobiography and a Reminiscence," *Annals of Iowa* 37 (spring 1964), pp. 241–60; "Pioneer Life in Palo Alto County, Memoirs of E. May Lacey Crowder," *Iowa Journal of History and Politics* 46 (April 1948), pp. 156–98; "Private Journal of Mary Ann Owen Sims," *Arkansas Historical Quarterly* 35 (summer and fall 1976), pp. 142–87, 261–91; "Two Letters by a Pioneer from Arkansas," *Oregon Historical Quarterly* 45 (September 1944), pp. 228–37; "The Letters of Roselle Putnam," *Oregon Historical Quarterly* 29 (September 1928), pp. 242–62; "The Reminiscences of Mrs. Dilue Harris," *Quarterly of the Texas State Historical Association* 4, 7 (October and January 1901, January 1904), pp. 85–127, 155–89, 214–22. "The Letters of Ed Donnell, Nebraska Pioneer," *Nebraska History* 41 (June 1960), pp. 123–52, give his candid views of marriage and married life, while Rufus Rittenhouse tells of childhood in *Boyhood Life in Iowa Fifty Years Ago* (Dubuque: Charles B. Door, 1880). A midwife's experience is covered in "19th Century Midwife, Some Recollections," *Oregon Historical Quarterly* 70 (March 1969), pp. 39–49.

An idea of the experience of Native American and other non-Anglo women can be found in Patricia Albers and Beatrice Medicine, eds., *The Hidden*

Half: Studies of Plains Indian Women (Washington, D.C.: University Press of America, 1983); Steven J. Crum, *The Road on Which We Came: A History of the Western Shoshone* (Salt Lake City: University of Utah Press, 1994); Gretchen M. Bataille and Kathleen Mullen Sands, *American Indian Women Telling Their Lives* (Lincoln: University of Nebraska Press, 1984); Laura F. Klein and Lillian A. Ackerman, eds., *Women and Power in Native North America* (Norman: University of Oklahoma Press, 1995); Janet LeCompte, "The Indian Women of Hispanic New Mexico, 1821–1846," *Western Historical Quarterly* 12 (January 1981), pp. 17–35; Peter Nabokov, ed., *Native American Testimony: An Anthology of Indian and White Relations, First Encounter to Dispossession* (New York: Thomas Y. Crowell, 1978); Glenda Riley, *Women and Indians on the Frontier, 1825–1915* (Albuquerque: University of New Mexico Press, 1984); Coll-Peter Thrush and Robert H. Keller, Jr., " 'I See What I Have Done': The Life and Murder Trial of Xwelas, A S'klallam Woman," *Western Historical Quarterly* 26 (summer 1995), pp. 168–83; John J. Killoren, *"Come, Blackrobe": De Smet and the Indian Tragedy* (Norman: University of Oklahoma Press, 1994); Sarah Winnemucca Hopkins, *Life Among the Piutes: Their Wrongs and Claims* (New York: G. P. Putnam's, 1883); Richard Griswold del Castillo, *La Familia: Chicano Families in the Urban Southwest, 1848 to the Present* (South Bend: University of Notre Dame Press, 1984); and Cheryl J. Foote, *Women of the New Mexico Frontier, 1846–1912* (Niwot: University Press of Colorado, 1990). See also *New Mexico Historical Review* 57 (October 1982).

4

In addition to works dealing with frontier settlements cited in the section on chapter 3, the reader might refer to Frederick A. Shannon's *The Farmers' Frontier, 1865–1900* (New York: Holt, Rinehart & Winston, 1966). The pathbreaking book on the urban frontier is Richard Wade's *The Urban Frontier: The Rise of Western Cities, 1790–1830* (Cambridge: Harvard University Press, 1959). Gunther Barth deals with the rapid pace of urbanization on the frontier in *Instant Cities: Urbanization and the Rise of San Francisco and Denver* (New York: Oxford University Press, 1975). Studies of individual cities include Kenneth W. Wheeler's *To Wear a City's Crown: The Beginnings of Urban Growth in Texas, 1836–1865* (Cambridge: Harvard University Press, 1968) and A. Theodore Brown's *Frontier Community: Kansas City to 1870* (Columbia: University of Missouri Press, 1963). An overview is provided by Lawrence H. Larsen, *The Urban West at the End of the Frontier* (Lawrence: Regents Press of Kansas, 1978).

Rural mobility patterns are discussed in Throne's work and others mentioned in the bibliography for chapter 3 and in William L. Bowers's "Crawford Township, 1850–1870: A Population Study of a Pioneer Community," *Iowa Journal of History* 58 (January 1960), pp. 1–30. Social and economic inequalities are the subjects of Paul W. Gates's "Frontier Estate Builders and Farm Laborers," in Walker D. Wyman and Clifton B. Kroeber, eds., *The Frontier in Perspective* (Madison: University of Wisconsin Press, 1957), pp. 143–63. Herbert T. Hoover gives a graphic picture of the poorer pioneers and selections of letters in "John Milton Leeper: Pioneer Farmer," *Nebraska History* 52 (spring 1971), pp. 32–44.

Urban inequality and transiency are the subjects of William Grover Robbins's "The Far Western Frontier: Economic Opportunity and Social Democracy in Early Roseburg, Oregon" (Ph.D. diss., University of Oregon, 1969) and the theme of two articles, "Community Conflict in Roseburg, Oregon, 1870–1885," *Journal of the West* 12 (October 1973), pp. 618–32, and "Opportunity and Persistence in the Pacific Northwest: A Quantitative Study of Early Roseburg, Oregon," *Pacific Historical Review* 39 (August 1970), pp. 279–96. Susan Jackson has treated Houston in "Movin' On: Mobility Through Houston in the 1850's," *Southwestern Historical Quarterly* 81 (January 1978), pp. 251–82. For comparisons with the East, see Stephan Thernstrom, *The Other Bostonians: Poverty and Progress in the American Metropolis, 1880–1970* (Cambridge: Harvard University Press, 1973). Mary C. Wright provides valuable information on women in Portland in "The World of Women: Portland, Oregon, 1860–1880" (master's thesis, Portland State University, 1973).

The part women played in establishing and staffing community institutions can be discovered in their reminiscences, letters, and journals. In addition, Wallace D. Farnham provides suggestive information on women's cultural role in "Religion as an Influence in Life and Thought: Jackson County, Oregon, 1860–1890" (Ph.D. diss., University of Oregon, 1955). Richard M. Bernard and Maris A. Vinovskis examine eastern teachers and establish the proportion of Massachusetts women who taught in "The Female School Teacher in Ante-Bellum Massachusetts," *Journal of Social History* 10 (March 1977), pp. 332–45. It may be that the proportion of western women teaching was similar to that in the East. Ruth A. Gallaher gives information on frontier wage discrimination in *The Legal and Political Status of Women in Iowa: An Historical Account of the Rights of Women in Iowa from 1838–1918* (Iowa City: State Historical Society of Iowa, 1918). See also Keith E. Melder, "Woman's High Calling: The Teaching Profession in America, 1830–1860," *American Studies* 13 (fall 1972), pp. 19–32; Wayne E. Fuller, "Country Schoolteaching on the Sod-House Frontier," *Arizona and the West* 17 (summer 1975), pp. 121–40; David Tyack, "The Tribe and the Common School: The District School in Ashland, Oregon, in the 1860s," *Call Number* (spring 1966), pp. 13–23; Barbara J. Finkelstein, "The Moral Dimensions of Pedagogy: Teaching Behavior in Popular Primary Schools in Nineteenth-Century America," *American Studies* 15 (fall 1974), pp. 79–89; and Joseph F. Kett, *Rites of Passage: Adolescence in America 1790 to the Present* (New York: Basic Books, 1977).

The subject of children and the frontier has a small literature. See Sylvia D. Hoffert, "Childbearing on the Trans-Mississippi Frontier, 1830–1900," *Western Historical Quarterly* 22 (August 1991), pp. 273–88; Elliott West, *Growing Up with the Country: Childhood on the Far Western Frontier* (Albuquerque: University of New Mexico Press, 1989); and Elliott West and Paula Petrik, eds., *Small Worlds: Children & Adolescents in America, 1850–1950* (Lawrence: University Press of Kansas, 1992).

New work on religion in the West includes Carl Guarneri and David Alvarez, eds., *Religion and Society in the American West: Historical Essays* (Lanham, Md., University Press of America, 1987); Ferenc M. Szasz, ed., *Religion in the West* (Manhattan: University of Kansas Press, 1984); and his book *The Protestant Clergy in the Great Plains and Mountain West, 1865–1915* (Albuquerque: University of New Mexico Press, 1988). Women's importance to religious life is apparent in Barbara Welter's essay "The Feminization of American Religion, 1800–1860," and in her book *The Feminization of American Culture* (New York: Knopf, 1977), in William L. O'Neill, ed., *Insights and Parallels; Problems and Issues of American Social History* (Minneapolis: Burgess Publishing Co., 1973). Several works deal with the importance of ministers' and missionaries' wives, including Lois A. Boyd and R. Douglas Brackenridge, *Presbyterian Women in America: Two Centuries of a Quest for Status* (Westport, Conn.: Greenwood Press, 1983), and Hilah F. Thomas and Rosemary Skinner Keller, eds., *Women in New Worlds: Historical Perspectives on the Wesleyan Tradition* (Nashville: Abingdon Press, 1981).

Among primary sources written by women are "Ketturah Belknap's Chronicle of the Bellfountain Settlement," *Oregon Historical Quarterly* 38 (September 1937), pp. 265–99; Mary W. Gaylord, *Life and Labors of Rev. Reuben Gaylord* (Omaha: Rees Printing Co., 1889); Mary M. Boardman, *Life and Labours of the Rev. W. E. Boardman* (New York: D. Appleton & Co., 1887); Lois L. Murray, *Incidents of Frontier Life* (Goshen, Ind.: Evangelical Methodist United Mennonite Publishing House, 1880); A. J. Marshall, *The Autobiography of Mrs. A. J. Marshall, Age 84 Years* (Pine Bluff, Ark.: Adams-Wilson Printing Co., 1897); Ruth McKee, ed., *Mary Richardson Walker; Her Book* (Caldwell: Caxton Printers, Ltd., 1945); and "A Missionary's Wife Looks at Missouri: Letters of Julia Barbard Strong," *Missouri Historical Review* 47 (July 1953), pp. 329–46. Ministers' letters and reminiscences also provide insights into women's work in the churches. See Ephraim Adams, *The Iowa Band* (Boston: Congregational Pub. Soc., 1870); John L. Dyer, *The Snow-Shoe Itin-*

erant: An Autobiography of the Rev. John L. Dyer (Cincinnati: Cranston &
Stowe, 1890); Myron Eells, *Father Eells or the Results of Fifty-five Years of
Missionary Labors in Washington and Oregon: A Biography of Rev. Cushing
Eells* (Boston: Congregational Sunday-School and Pub. Soc., 1894); "Estab-
lishing a Church on the Kansas Frontier: The Letters of Rev. O. I. Woodford
and His Sister Henrietta, 1857–1859," *Kansas Historical Review* 37 (summer
1971), pp. 153–91; "Diary of George H. Atkinson, DD.," *Oregon Historical
Quarterly* (March–December 1939, March–June 1940), pp. 52–63, 168–87,
265–82, 341–61, 416–33, 288–304; "Correspondence of the Rev. Ezra
Fisher," *Oregon Historical Quarterly* 16, 17 (March, December 1915; March,
December 1916), pp. 65–104, 277–310, 379–413, 55–76, 147–76, 267–339,
431–80; "American Home Missionary Society Letters from Iowa," *Annals of
Iowa* 37 (summer and fall 1963), pp. 45–76, 95–120. Unpublished letters
from missionaries to the American Home Missionary Society are available on
microfilm. A good analysis of the pattern of missionary careers is Peter
French's "The Home Missionary in Oregon: Individual Failure and Organizational Success" (bachelor's thesis, Reed College, 1968).

Church discipline is treated by Robert Norton Peters, "From Sect to
Church: A Study in the Permutation of Methodism on the Oregon Frontier"
(Ph.D. diss., University of Washington, 1973). For an example of church records, see "Minutes West Union Baptist Church," *Oregon Historical Quarterly*
36 (September, December 1935), pp. 247–62, 365–79.

Richard S. Alcorn points out the cultural influence of the small but permanent groups but in another location in his article "Leadership and Stability
in Mid-19th-Century America: A Case Study of an Illinois Town," *Journal of
American History* 61 (December 1974), pp. 685–702. As for like-minded later
settlers, see James C. Malin, "Kansas: Some Reflections on Culture Inheritance and Originality," *Midcontinental American Studies Journal* 2 (fall 1961),
pp. 3–19, and Dorothy O. Johansen, "A Working Hypothesis for the Study of
Migrations," *Pacific Historical Review* 36 (February 1967), pp. 1–12. Don
Harrison Doyle's "Social Theory and New Communities in 19th-Century
America," *Western Historical Quarterly* 8 (April 1977), pp. 151–65, emphasizes the tension between disintegrating and stabilizing factors in early communities, while his article "The Social Functions of Voluntary Associations
in a 19th-Century Town," *Social Science History* 1 (spring 1977), pp. 333–
55, shows how voluntary associations helped to tie communities together.

Beverly J. Stoeltje describes images of women on the frontier in " 'A Helpmate for Man Indeed,' The Image of the Frontier Woman," *Journal of American Folklore* 88 (January–March 1975), pp. 25–41.

5

The dramatic events of the gold rush and subsequent mining frontiers have produced a rich historical literature, and only a few of the works can be mentioned here. Among helpful general studies of the mining frontier and the life that flourished are Rodman Wilson Paul, *Mining Frontiers of the Far West* (New York: Holt, Rinehart & Winston, 1963); John Walton Caughey, *Gold Is the Cornerstone* (Berkeley and Los Angeles: University of California Press, 1948); W. Turrentine Jackson, *Treasure Hill: Portrait of a Silver Mining Camp* (Tucson: University of Arizona Press, 1963); Duane A. Smith, *Rocky Mountain Mining Camps: The Urban Frontier* (Bloomington: Indiana University Press, 1967); and Vardis Fisher and Opal Laurel Holmes, *Gold Rushes and Mining Camps of the Early American West* (Caldwell: Caxton Printers Ltd., 1968). Two broad studies that assess the impact of the gold rush on California's development are David Lavender, *California: Land of New Beginnings* (New York: Harper & Row, 1972), and Kevin Starr, *Americans and the California Dream, 1850–1915* (New York: Oxford University Press, 1973). Examinations of specific aspects of frontier life include Ralph Mann's *After the Gold Rush: Society in Grass Valley and Nevada City, California, 1849–1870* (Stanford: Stanford University Press, 1982), as well as his short article "The Decade After the Gold Rush: Social Structure in Grass Valley and Nevada City, California, 1850–1860," *Pacific Historical Review* 41 (November 1972), pp. 484–504; Lyle Allen Schwarz's "Theater on the Gold Frontier: A Cultural Study of Five Northwest Mining Towns, 1860–1870" (Ph.D. diss., Washington State University, 1975); Georges Sabagh's "A Critical Analysis of California Population Statistics with Special Reference to Census Data: 1850–1870" (master's thesis, University of California, Berkeley, 1941); William Francis Hanchett's "Religion and the Gold Rush, 1849–1854: The Christian Churches in the California Mines" (Ph.D. diss., University of California, 1952); his article, "The Question of Religion and the Taming of California, 1849–1854," *California Historical Quarterly* 32 (March, June 1953), pp. 49–56, 119–44; Alice Cowan Cochran's "Miners, Merchants, and Missionaries: The Role of Missionaries and Pioneer Churches in the Colorado Gold Rush and Its Aftermath, 1858–1870" (Ph.D. diss., Southern Methodist University, 1975); and Lynn I. Perrigo's "Law and Order in Early Colorado Mining Camps," *Journal of American History* 28 (June 1941), pp. 41–62. A very good study of San Francisco that considers early female residents is Roger W. Lotchin's *San Francisco 1846–1856: From Hamlet to City* (New York: Oxford University Press, 1974).

The meaning of the gold rush for nonwhite groups can be gleaned from Douglas Monroy's *Thrown Among Strangers: The Making of Mexican Culture in Frontier California* (Berkeley: University of California Press, 1990) and Albert L. Hurtado's fine but troubling study *Indian Survival on the California Frontier* (New Haven: Yale University Press, 1988).

Eliza W. Farnham raised the question of how women would fare in California in *California, In-Doors and Out; Or, How We Farm, Mine, and Live Generally in the Golden State* (New York: Dix, Edwards & Co., 1856). Elisabeth Margo answered Farnham's question and provided a useful analysis for this study in her *Taming the Forty-Niner* (New York: Rinehart & Co., 1955). More recent studies have been done by Jo Ann Levy, *They Saw the Elephant: Women in the California Gold Rush* (Norman: University of Oklahoma Press, 1992); Joan M. Jensen and Gloria Ricci Lothrop, *California Women: A History* (Parks, Nev.: Materials for Today's Learning, 1988); Ronald M. James, Richard D. Adkins, and Rachel J. Hartigan, "Competition and Coexistence in the Laundry: A View of the Comstock," *Western Historical Quarterly* 25 (summer 1994), pp. 165–84; George Blackburn and Sherman Ricords, "Unequal Opportunity on the Mining Frontier: The Role of Gender, Race and Birthplace," *Pacific Historical Review* 62 (February 1993), pp. 19–38; and Paula Petrik, *Women and Family on the Rocky Mountain Mining Frontier, Helena, Montana, 1865–1900* (Helena: Montana Historical Society, 1987). Primary sources for the mining frontier are rich. See Ruth B. Moynihan, Susan Armitage, and Christiane Fischer Dichamp, eds., *So Much to Be Done: Women Settlers on the Mining and Ranching Frontier* (Lincoln: University of Nebraska Press, 1990).

Luzena Wilson's recollections, cited earlier, give a vivid picture of her early life in California. Louise Amelia Knapp Clappe, *The Shirley Letters from the California Mines, 1851–1852* (New York: Alfred A. Knopf, 1949); Anna Lee Marston, ed., *Records of a California Family: Journals and Letters of Lewis C. Gunn and Elizabeth Le Breton Gunn* (San Diego: no publisher, 1928); Mary Jane Megquier, *Apron Full of Gold: The Letters of Mary Jane Megquier from San Francisco, 1849–1856* (San Marino: The Huntington Library, 1949); Mary M. Mathews, *Ten Years in Nevada: Or Life on the Pacific Coast* (Buffalo: Baker, Jones & Co., 1880); Sarah Royce, *A Frontier Lady: Recollections of the Gold Rush and Early California* (New Haven: Yale University Press, 1932) record the impressions of some women, mostly from New England, of mining life, as does "A Literate Woman in the Mines: The Diary of Rachel Haskell," *Journal of American History* 31 (June 1944), pp. 81–98. Other useful primary collections include Bianca Morse Frederico and Myrtle Brown, eds., *Gold Rush: The Letters of Joel and Ann Brown, 1852, 1854–1855* (no place, privately printed, 1972); Dale L. Morgan and James R. Scobie, eds., *Three Years in California: William Perkins' Journal of Life at Sonora, 1849–1852* (Berkeley and Los Angeles: University of California Press, 1964); *Gideon Lee Knapp and Augusta Murray Spring His Wife: Extracts from Letters and Journal* (New York: no publisher, 1909); Ledyard Frink, ed., *Journal of the Adventures of a Party of California Gold-seekers* (Oakland: no publisher, 1897); Joseph Schafer, ed., *California Letters of Lucius Fairchild* (Madison: State Historical Society of Wisconsin, 1931); Anthony and Allison Sirna, eds., *The Wanderings of Edward Ely: A Mid-Nineteenth Century Seafarer's Diary* (New York: Hastings House, 1954); and Walker D. Wyman, *California Emigrant Letters* (New York: Bookman Assoc., Pubs., 1952).

Ministers have left vivid pictures of their battles on the mining frontier. D. S. Tuttle, *Reminiscences of a Missionary Bishop* (New York: Thomas Whittaker, 1906); William Taylor, *Seven Years' Street Preaching in San Francisco, California: Embracing Incidents, Triumphant Death Scenes, etc.* (New York: Carlton & Porter, 1857); S. H. Willey, *Thirty Years in California: A Contribution to the History of the State, from 1849 to 1879* (San Francisco: A. L. Bancroft & Co., 1879); and "Selected Letters of Osgood Church Wheeler," *California Historical Quarterly* 27 (March, June, September, December 1948), pp. 9–18, 123–31, 229–36, 301–09, suggest that Protestant ministers, no matter what their denomination, viewed the mining frontier as a major challenge to morality and Christianity. See also Laurie Maffly-Kipp's study, *Religion and Society in Frontier California* (New Haven: Yale University Press, 1994).

Several studies of prostitution are helpful. See Marion S. Goldman, *Gold Diggers & Silver Miners: Prostitution and Social Life on the Comstock Lode* (Ann Arbor: University of Michigan Press, 1981); Jacqueline Baker Barnhart, *The Fair but Frail: Prostitution in San Francisco, 1849–1900* (Reno: University of Nevada Press, 1986); Anne M. Butler, *Daughters of Joy, Sisters of Misery: Prostitutes in the American West, 1865–1890* (Urbana: University of Illinois Press, 1985). Benson Tong analyzes the situation of Chinese prostitutes in *Unsubmissive Women: Chinese Prostitutes in Nineteenth-Century San Francisco* (Norman: University of Oklahoma Press, 1994). W. N. Davis, Jr., points to the rich material on prostitution (and other aspects of mining society) contained in court records in "Research Uses of County Court Records, 1850–1879: An Incidental of Intimate Glimpses of California Life and Society," *California Historical Quarterly* 52 (fall and winter 1973), pp. 241–66, 338–65.

The divorce question is treated by Nelson Manfred Blake, *The Road to Reno: A History of Divorce in the United States* (New York: Macmillan Co., 1962); J. P. Lichtenberger, *Divorce: A Social Interpretation* (New York: McGraw-Hill Book Co., 1931); William L. O'Neill, *Divorce in the Progressive Era* (New Haven: Yale University Press, 1967); and Walter Francis Willcox, "The Divorce Problem: A Study in Statistics," *Studies in History, Economics and Public Law* 1 (1891), pp. 9–89. Robert L. Griswold has examined divorce in California in *Family and Divorce in California, 1850–1890* (Albany: State University of New York Press, 1982), while Paula Petrik has looked at Montana in "If She Be Content: The Development of Montana Divorce Law, 1865–1907," *Western Historical Quarterly* 18 (July 1987), pp. 261–92.

6

The Mormon frontier is best understood in relation to other nineteenth-century utopian experiments. Rosabeth Moss Kanter's *Commitment and Community: Communes and Utopias in Sociological Perspective* (Cambridge: Harvard University Press, 1972) gives an excellent analysis of factors distinguishing successful attempts to establish a new and more perfect society. Raymond Lee Muncy's *Sex and Marriage in Utopian Communities: 19th Century America* (Bloomington: University of Indiana Press, 1973) provides little analysis but detailed descriptions of gender arrangements in a number of nineteenth-century utopian settlements. Mark Holloway gives another overview in *Heavens on Earth: Utopian Communities in America, 1680–1880* (New York: Dover Pubs., 1966), as does Robert V. Hine in *California's Utopian Colonies* (San Marino: The Huntington Library, 1953). William Lawrence Foster's study "Between Two Worlds: The Origins of Shaker Celibacy, Oneida Community Complex Marriage, and Mormon Polygamy" (Ph.D. diss., University of Chicago, 1976) suggests some of the linkages between the gender arrangements of three different communities and is a provocative work. Studies of other utopian components of Mormon life include Ephraim Edward Ericksen, *The Psychological and Ethical Aspects of Mormon Group Life* (Salt Lake City: University of Utah Press, 1975); Gustive O. Larson, *Prelude to the Kingdom: Mormon Desert Conquest, a Chapter in American Cooperative Experience* (Francestown, N.H.: Marshall Jones Co., 1947); William J. McNiff, *Heaven on Earth: A Planned Mormon Society* (Oxford: The Mississippi Valley Press, 1940); Edward J. Allen, *The Second United Order Among the Mormons* (New York: Columbia University Press, 1936); Leonard J. Arrington, "Orderville, Utah: A Pioneer Mormon Experiment in Economic Organization," *Utah State Agricultural College Monograph Series* 2 (March 1954), pp. 5–44; Hamilton Gardner, "Cooperation Among the Mormons," *Quarterly Journal of Economics* 32 (May 1917), pp. 461–99; his "Communism Among the Mormons," *Quarterly Journal of Economics* 37 (November 1933), pp. 134–74; and Joel Edward Ricks, "Forms and Methods of Early Mormon Settlement in Utah and the Surrounding Region, 1847–1877," *Utah State University Press Monograph Series* 11 (January 1964), pp. 2–141. Also useful are Mario S. De Pillis's "The Quest for Religious Authority and the Rise of Mormonism," *Dialogue* 1 (spring

1966), pp. 68–88, and L. H. Kirkpatrick, "When a Bishop Was a Shepherd of His Flock," *Western Humanities Review* 19 (fall 1956), pp. 386–88.

Thomas F. O'Dea's *The Mormons* (Chicago: University of Chicago Press, 1957) sets the Mormon experience in religious perspective. Robert Bruce Flanders discusses early Mormon history in *Nauvoo: Kingdom on the Mississippi* (Urbana: University of Illinois Press, 1965). The story is continued in Stanley P. Hirshson, *The Lion of the Lord: A Biography of Brigham Young* (New York: Alfred A. Knopf, 1969); Wallace Stegner, *The Gathering of Zion: The Story of the Mormon Trail* (New York: McGraw-Hill Book Co., 1964); William Mulder, *Homeward to Zion: The Mormon Migration from Scandinavia* (Minneapolis: University of Minnesota Press, 1957); Nels Anderson, *Desert Saints: The Mormon Frontier in Utah* (Chicago: University of Chicago Press, 1942); Norman F. Furniss, *The Mormon Conflict, 1850–1859* (New Haven: Yale University Press, 1960); F. Mark McKiernan, Alma R. Blair, and Paul M. Edwards, eds., *The Restoration Movement: Essays in Mormon History* (Lawrence: Coronado Press, 1973); and Gustive O. Larson, *The "Americanization" of Utah for Statehood* (San Marino: The Huntington Library, 1971).

The bad press Mormons routinely received in the nineteenth century is treated by Leonard J. Arrington and Jon Haupt, "Intolerable Zion: The Image of Mormons in Nineteenth Century American Literature," *Western Humanities Review* 22 (summer 1968), pp. 243–60; Charles A. Cannon, "The Awesome Power of Sex: The Polemical Campaign Against Mormon Polygamy," *Pacific Historical Review* 43 (February 1974), pp. 61–82; and Richard Olsen Cowan, "Mormonism in National Periodicals" (Ph.D. diss., Stanford University, 1961). A few firsthand views of the Mormons are "A Lady's View of Utah and the Mormons, 1858: A Letter from the Governor's Wife," *Western Humanities Review* 10 (winter 1955–56), pp. 27–35; Elizabeth Wood Kane, *Twelve Mormon Visits in Succession on a Journey Through Utah to Arizona* (Salt Lake City: University of Utah Library, 1974); and Richard F. Burton, *The City of the Saints and Across the Rocky Mountains to California* (New York: Alfred A. Knopf, 1963).

The part women played on the Mormon frontier and the ways in which their religion affected the experience there have received some study. Leonard J. Arrington gives a general introduction in "Women as a Force in the History of Utah," *Utah Historical Quarterly* 38 (winter 1970), pp. 3–6, and "The Economic Role of Pioneer Mormon Women," *Western Humanities Review* 9 (spring 1955), pp. 145–64. Helpful essays are included in Maureen Ursenbach Beecher and Lavina Fielding Anderson, eds., *Sisters in Spirit: Mormon Women in Historical and Cultural Perspective* (Urbana: University of Illinois Press, 1987); Vicky Burgess-Olson, ed., *Sister Saints* (Provo: Brigham Young University Press, 1978); and Claudia Bushman, ed., *Mormon Sisters: Women in Early Utah* (Cambridge: Emmeline Press Ltd., 1976). Studies of two important women reveal a good deal of information about the pioneer period: Juanita Brooks, *Emma Lee* (Logan: Utah State University Press, 1975) and Jill C. Mulvay, "The Liberal Shall Be Blessed: Sarah M. Kimball," *Utah Historical Quarterly* 44 (summer 1976), pp. 205–21. Lucile Johnson focuses on the Ladies Relief Society in "A Social Analysis of the L.D.S. Relief Society" (master's thesis, Utah State Agricultural College, 1950), while Keith Calvin Terry looks at medical women in "The Contribution of Medical Women During the First Fifty Years in Utah" (master's thesis, Brigham Young University, 1964).

Kimball Young's *Isn't One Wife Enough?* (New York: Henry Holt & Co., 1954) provides a lively introduction to polygamy and contains information collected from family and friends. The demographic impact of polygamy receives attention in James E. Smith and Phillip R. Kunz, "Polygyny and Fertility in Nineteenth-Century America," *Population Studies* 30 (November 1976), pp. 465–80; Stanley S. Ivins, "Notes on Mormon Polygamy," *Western Humanities Review* 10 (summer 1956), pp. 229–39; and Dean L. May, "People on the Mormon Frontier: Kanab's Families of 1874," *Journal of Family History* 1 (winter 1976), pp. 169–92. Larry M. Logue suggests that polygamy may have been widespread in *A Sermon in the Desert: Belief and Behavior in Early St. George, Utah* (Urbana: University of Illinois Press, 1988). See also Jessie L. Embry, "Effects of Polygamy on Mormon Women," *Frontiers* 7 (1984), pp. 56–61. An early tract on polygamy is the subject of Lawrence Foster's "A Little-Known Defense of Polygamy from the Mormon Press in 1842," *Dialogue* 9 (1974), pp. 21–34. Studies that give some sense of women's experience in polygamy include Herbert Ray Larsen, " 'Familism' in Mormon Social Structure" (Ph.D. diss., University of Utah, 1954); J. E. Hulett, Jr., "Social Role and Personal Security in Mormon Polygamy," *American Journal of Sociology* 45 (January 1940), pp. 542–53; Juanita Brooks, "A Close-Up of Polygamy," *Harpers Magazine*, February 1934, pp. 299–307; Mary Ann Hafen, *Recollections of a Handcart Pioneer of 1860* (Denver: privately printed, 1938); and Annie Clark Tanner, *A Mormon Mother: An Autobiography* (Salt Lake City: University of Utah Press, 1969). Gustive O. Larson points out that attempts to "liberate" Mormon women failed in "An Industrial Home for Polygamous Wives," *Utah Historical Quarterly* 38 (summer 1970), pp. 263–75.

The ways in which Mormonism contributed to women's self-awareness are apparent in Gail Farr Casterline's " 'In The Toils' or 'Onward for Zion': Images of the Mormon Woman, 1852–1890" (master's thesis, Utah State University, 1974) and Sherilyn Cox Bennion's "The *Woman's Exponent*: Forty-two Years of Speaking for Women," *Utah Historical Quarterly* (summer 1967), pp. 222–39. Kathleen Marquis assesses the impact of traditional ideas of woman's sphere in " 'Diamond Cut Diamond': Mormon Women and the Cult of Domesticity in the 19th Century," *University of Michigan Papers in Women's Studies* 2 (1974), pp. 105–23.

7

The struggles involved in community growth are suggested by Don Harrison Doyle's "Social Theory and New Communities in 19th-Century America," *Western Historical Quarterly* 8 (April 1977), pp. 151–65. Not much attention has been paid to women's charitable endeavors on the frontier, but Robert R. Dykstra's *The Cattle Towns* (New York: Alfred A. Knopf, 1968) is suggestive of the disruptive nature of some of these activities. Rowena Beams's *"Inasmuch . . . ": The One Hundred Year History of the San Francisco Ladies' Protection and Relief Society, 1853–1953* (San Francisco: James J. Gillick & Co., 1953) tells the story of one organization.

Women's efforts to shape the community are analyzed by Peggy Pascoe, *Relations of Rescue: The Search for Female Moral Authority in the American West, 1874–1939* (New York: Oxford University Press, 1990) and Susan M. Yohn, *A Contest of Faiths: Missionary Women and Pluralism in the American Southwest* (Ithaca: Cornell University Press, 1995). Women's work in the temperance movement has attracted more interest than their charitable efforts. Ronald G. Walters in *American Reformers, 1815–1860* (New York: Hill & Wang, 1978) devotes a chapter to the early nineteenth-century temperance movement, while Norman H. Clark in *Deliver Us from Evil: An Interpretation of American Prohibition* (New York: W. W. Norton & Co., 1976) gives a good overview of national efforts during the century. Studies of western temperance activities at the state level include Gilman M. Ostrander, *The Prohibition Movement in California, 1848–1933* (Berkeley and Los Angeles: University of California Press, 1957); Norman H. Clark, *The Dry Years: Prohibition and Social Change in Washington* (Seattle: University of Washington Press, 1965); John E. Caswell, "The Prohibition Movement in Oregon, 1836–1904," *Oregon Historical Quarterly* 39 (September 1938), pp. 235–61; and Malcolm H. Clark, Jr., "The War on Webfoot Saloon," *Oregon Historical Quarterly* 58 (March 1957), pp. 48–62. Ross Evans Paulson's *Women's Suffrage and Prohibition: A Comparative Study of Equality and Social Control* (Glenview: Scott, Foresman & Co., 1973) sets the prohibition and suffrage movements in a comparative framework.

Abigail Scott Duniway tells a vivid if incomplete story of her suffrage battles in *Path Breaking: An Autobiographical History of the Equal Suffrage Movement in Pacific Coast States* (New York: Schocken Books, 1971). Eleanor Flexner's *Century of Struggle: The Women's Rights Movement in the United*

States (Cambridge: Belknap Press, 1975) was one of the first studies of women's fight for the vote and is well worth reading. David Morgan gives a good overview of suffrage activities in *Suffragists and Democrats: The Politics of Woman Suffrage in America* (Michigan State University Press, 1972). Alan P. Grimes in *The Puritan Ethic and Woman Suffrage* (New York: Oxford University Press, 1967) emphasizes the conservatism of western suffrage victories as do the following studies: Beverly Beeton, *Women Vote in the West: The Woman Suffrage Movement, 1869–1896* (New York: Garland Press, 1986); Anne M. Benjamin, *A History of the Anti-Suffrage Movement in the United States from 1895 to 1920* (Lewiston, New York: Edwin Mellen Press, 1991); and Suzanne M. Marilley, *Woman Suffrage and the Origins of Liberal Feminism in the United States, 1820–1920* (Cambridge: Harvard University Press, 1996). Studies of state battles include Dennis Anthony Fus, "Persuasion on the Plains: The Woman Suffrage Movement in Nebraska" (Ph.D. diss., Indiana University, 1972); the following articles by T. A. Larson, "Dolls, Vassals, and Drudges—Pioneer Women in the West," *Western Historical Quarterly* 3 (January 1972), pp. 5–16; "Woman Suffrage in Wyoming," *Pacific Northwest Quarterly* 56 (April 1965), pp. 57–66; "The Woman's Rights Movement in Idaho," *Idaho Yesterdays* 16 (spring 1972), pp. 2–19; "The Woman Suffrage Movement in Washington," *Pacific Northwest Quarterly* 67 (April 1976), pp. 49–62; "Montana Women and the Battle for the Ballot," *Montana: The Magazine of Western History* 23 (January 1973), pp. 24–41; A. Elizabeth Taylor, "The Woman Suffrage Movement in Texas," *Journal of Southern History* 17 (May 1951), pp. 194–215; her "The Woman Suffrage Movement in Arkansas," *Arkansas Historical Quarterly* 15 (spring 1956), pp. 17–52; Gordon Morris Bakken, "Voting Patterns in the Wyoming Constitutional Convention of 1889," *Annals of Wyoming* 42 (October 1970), pp. 224–42; Billie Barnes Jensen, "Colorado Woman Suffrage Campaigns of the 1870's," *Journal of the West* 12 (April 1973), pp. 254–71; and Nelson A. Ault, "The Earnest Ladies: The Walla Walla Woman's Club and the Equal Suffrage League of 1886–1889," *Pacific Northwest Quarterly* 42 (April 1951), pp. 123–37. Ronald Schaffer gives an interesting profile of suffrage leaders in "The Problem of Consciousness in the Woman Suffrage Movement: A California Perspective," *Pacific Historical Review* 45 (November 1976), pp. 469–94.

What western educational opportunities meant for women has hardly been studied. Jill K. Conway raises some of the significant questions in "Perspectives in the History of Women's Education in the United States," *History of Education Quarterly* 14 (spring 1974), pp. 1–12. Ronald W. Hogeland points out that coeducation did not necessarily mean equal education in "Coeducation of the Sexes at Oberlin College," *Journal of Social History* 6 (1972–73), pp. 160–76. A detailed but unfocused account of women's educational opportunities is provided by Thomas Woody in *A History of Women's Education in the United States* (New York: The Science Press, 1929). More analytical and concise is Mabel Newcomer's *A Century of Higher Education for American Women* (New York: Harper & Bros. Pubs., 1959).

Daniel Boorstin describes the local boosterism that led to the proliferation of colleges in the West in *The Americans: The National Experience* (New York: Random House, 1966). The religious impulse is the subject of Donald G. Tewksbury's *The Founding of American Colleges and Universities Before the Civil War with Particular Reference to the Religious Influences Bearing upon the College Movement* (New York: Teachers College, 1932); Bernard J. Kohlbrenner, "Religion and Higher Education: An Historical Perspective," *History of Education Quarterly* 1 (June 1961), pp. 45–56; Natalie Naylor, "The Ante-Bellum College Movement: A Reappraisal of Tewksbury's Founding of American Colleges and Universities," *History of Education Quarterly* 13 (fall 1973), pp. 261–74; James Findlay, "The SPCTEW and Western Colleges: Religion and Higher Education in Mid-Nineteenth Century America," *History of Education Quarterly* 17 (spring 1977), pp. 31–62.

Other views of institutional growth and change are Frederick Rudolph, *The American College and University* (New York: Alfred A. Knopf, 1962); John S. Brubacher and Willis Rudy, *Higher Education in Transition: A History of American Colleges and Universities, 1630–1976* (New York: Harper & Row, 1976); Earle D. Ross, *Democracy's College: The Land-Grant Movement in the Formative State* (Ames: Iowa State College Press, 1942); and Edward Danforth Eddy, Jr., *Colleges for Our Land and Time: The Land-Grant Idea in American Education* (New York: Harper and Bros., 1956). Although few of the following studies focus on women, their experience in coeducational environments can be extracted from William Warren Ferrier, *Ninety Years of Education in California, 1846–1936: A Presentation of Educational Movements and Their Outcomes in Education Today* (Oakland: West Coast Printing Co., 1937); Roy W. Cloud, *Education in California: Leaders, Organizations, and Accomplishments of the First Hundred Years* (Stanford: Stanford University Press, 1952); Michael McGiffert, *The Higher Learning in Colorado: An Historical Study, 1860–1940* (Denver: Sage Books, 1964); John Scholte Nollen, *Grinnell College* (Iowa City: State Historical Society of Iowa, 1953); Robert E. Belding, "Iowa's Brave Model for Women's Education," *Annals of Iowa* 43 (summer 1976), pp. 342–48; Louise Molde Lex, "Mary Newbury Adams, Feminist Forerunner from Iowa," *Annals of Iowa* 43 (summer 1976), pp. 323–41; Clifford S. Griffen, *The University of Kansas: A History* (Lawrence: University Press of Kansas, 1974); Charles M. Gates, *The First Century at the University of Washington, 1861–1961* (Seattle: University of Washington Press, 1961); Edmond S. Meany, "Early Records of the University," *Washington Historical Quarterly* 8

(April 1917), pp. 114–23; James Rood Robertson, "Origin of Pacific University," *Oregon Historical Quarterly* 6 (June 1905), pp. 109–46; and Henry D. Sheldon, *History of University of Oregon* (Portland: Binfords & Mort, Pubs., 1940).

Epilogue

In addition to the sources already listed, the following works were helpful in assessing how women evaluated their pioneer years: *Reports of Annual Reunions of the Old Settlers of Johnson County, 1866–1897* (no place, no publisher, no date); *Reminiscences of Oregon Pioneers* (Pendleton: East Oregonian Pub. Co., 1937); Abner Sylvester Baker, "The Oregon Pioneer Tradition in the 19th Century: A Study of Recollection and Self-Definition" (Ph.D. diss., University of Oregon, 1968); and Valeda Katharine Wood, "The Life of the Pioneer Woman on the Kansas-Nebraska Frontier" (master's thesis, University of Nebraska, Lincoln, 1940).

Index